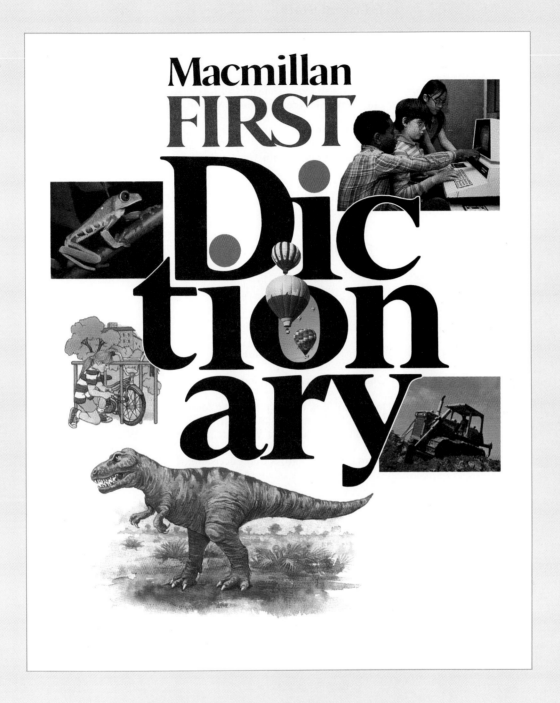

Macmillan FIRST Dictionary

Judith S. Levey/Editor in Chief

Macmillan Publishing Company
New York
Collier Macmillan Canada
Toronto
Maxwell Macmillan International Publishing Group
New York   Oxford   Singapore   Sydney

Editorial Staff

Editor in Chief	Judith S. Levey
Managing Editor	Helen Margaret Chumbley
Editors	Mary Louise Byrd, Deirdre Dempsey, Archie Hobson, Mary Ann Maderer, Susan R. Norton, Patricia Clements Shuldiner
Production Manager	Karen L. Tates
Proofreaders	Patricia Bonder, Phyllis Ger, Jerilynn Famighetti
Keyboarding/Production	Robert Gampert, John Mariano, Nick Scelsi, Margot A. Bonelli
Computer Consultants	Casey Lee, Robert Keefe

Art Staff

Design Director	Zelda Haber
Associate Design Director	Joan Gampert
Art Director	Murray Belsky
Design	Lee Goldstein, Anna Sabin. *Back matter*: MKR Design
Photo Research	Omni-Photo Communications, Inc.
Artists	John Gampert, Susan Jaekel, Jan Jones, Dora Leder, Susan Lexa, Diana Magnuson, Susan Magurn, Melodye Rosales, Judith Sutton, Susan Swan, Gonzalez Vincente. *Back matter:* Gwen Connally, R. R. Donnelley Cartographic Services, Betsy Feeney, Dennis Hockerman, Karen Loccisano, Robert Marinelli
Clerical Assistant	David Salinas

Pages 2–386, 388–401 of this dictionary are published in a text edition under the title
Macmillan/McGraw-Hill Primary Dictionary.

**Copyright © 1990 by Macmillan Publishing Company,
a division of Maxwell Macmillan International Publishing Group**

Macmillan Publishing Company, 866 Third Avenue, New York, NY 10022
Collier Macmillan Canada, Inc., 1200 Eglinton Avenue East, Suite 200, Don Mills, Ontario M3C 3N1

This book is a completely revised and expanded edition of the *Macmillan Very First Dictionary*.
Printed in the United States of America

10 9 8 7 6 5 4 3 2 1

Library of Congress Cataloging-in-Publication Data

Macmillan first dictionary / Judith S. Levey, editor in chief.
p.   cm.
Rev. and expanded edition of: Macmillan very first dictionary.

Summary: An alphabetical list of nearly 2200 common words with meanings, explanatory sentences, and illustrations for those words considered "conceptual."

ISBN 0-02-761731-9

1. English language—Dictionaries, Juvenile. [1. English language—Dictionaries.] I. Levey, Judith S., date.

PE1628.5.M3   1990
423—dc20   90-6062 CIP AC

Table of Contents

How To Help A Child Use This Book

The *Macmillan First Dictionary* is designed for children who have progressed beyond the *Macmillan Picture Wordbook* and are now ready to be introduced to a dictionary.

The *Macmillan First Dictionary* consists of an alphabetical list of nearly 2,200 of the most common words in the English language. These words, shown in **heavy boldface** type, are called main entries. Each main entry listed in this dictionary is followed by an explanation of the meaning of the word. These explanations are called definitions. Each definition is phrased as if a child were asking the question "What does _____ mean?" or "What's a _____?" For example, the definition for **bench** reads "A **bench** is a long seat." The definition is usually followed by one or more example sentences that show how the word is used in context. The example sentences reflect a child's experiences—they deal with parents, sisters and brothers, grandparents, friends, school, and the like. For **bench,** the example sentence is "Grandmother and I sat on a **bench** in the park and fed the birds."

Children will also learn that some words are spelled alike but have totally different meanings. These words, called homographs, come from different roots and have no relation to each other except for identical spelling. To show this distinction, each homograph is listed as a separate entry with its own superscript number (see **date¹** and **date²** on the Sample Page). The *Macmillan First Dictionary* will also help children understand words that sound alike but have different meanings and different spellings. These words are called homophones. The words **sea** and **see, flower** and **flour,** and **way** and **weigh** fall into this category.

Children who have begun to read will also discover that some words can develop from other words. These related words can be found as **boldface subentries** under the main entry word. For example, **magical** appears as a subentry under **magic**. In addition, children can learn that words change depending on how they are used. The different forms of a word are shown following a blue triangle (▲) and include the plurals of nouns and the various forms of adjectives and verbs. The Sample Page opposite this page shows some typical main entries from the *Macmillan First Dictionary.*

The more than 550 colorful photographs and illustrations in this book will also contribute to a child's understanding of words. Children will see what unfamiliar objects look like and will better comprehend a word that expresses a concept when they see it illustrated. Each illustration has a caption that explains the content of the picture or adds information to the entry. There are also whimsical illustrations introducing the letters of the alphabet that will add fun to the study of words.

Through the *Macmillan First Dictionary* children will learn new words to describe their expanding experiences. And as they use these new words, they will further develop their vocabulary and improve their reading and writing skills. We hope that you and the children you share this book with will have fun exploring the exciting world of words together.

Sample Page

dance   MAIN ENTRY

1. **Dance** means to move your body to music.   DEFINITION

At the party, we played music and **danced**. A person who **dances** is called a **dancer**.   SUBENTRY

▲ **danced, dancing.**   VERB FORMS

2. A **dance** is the way you move your body to music. My friend showed me a **dance** that she learned in another country. ▲ **dances.**   DEFINITION NUMBERS

danger

Danger means that something could happen to hurt you. The bird escaped **danger** by flying away from the cat. ▲ **dangers.**   EXAMPLE SENTENCE

   ILLUSTRATION

Jimmy and Tina saw the **DANGER** sign and knew they had to be careful.   CAPTION

date¹

A **date** is the day of the month or the year when something happens. Amy marked the **date** of her birthday on the calendar. ▲ **dates.**

date²   HOMOGRAPHS

A **date** is a dark, sweet fruit that grows on trees. ▲ **dates.**   PLURAL

deep

Deep means very far down. The dog dug a **deep** hole in the ground to hide its bone.

▲ **deeper, deepest.**   ADJECTIVE FORMS

How Words Came to Be

Many, many years ago, people did not know how to talk. These early people pointed their fingers or waved their arms to give messages. They probably made some sounds, like "mm" or "huh" or "ugh." But they did not have words.

Then, after thousands of years had passed, people began to use words. Perhaps one person said "water" when he or she was thirsty and other people began to say "water," too. No one knows for sure.

We don't know which words were used first or when they came into use. But a few of the words we use today can be traced to easy baby sounds. A baby says "ma ma ma" and "da da da." Who are the first people the baby knows? For most babies, they are Mama and Dada. And the words for those people in some languages are like these easy baby sounds.

Some other words are like sounds we hear around us. We say that bees *buzz* and dogs *bark.* Buzz is a word like the sound that bees make. Bark is a word like the sound a dog makes. We say a big bell goes *ding-dong.* These words are like the sounds themselves. Can you think of others?

When we are young, we learn words like *sleep, eat, no!* and *I love you* by hearing other people say them. Later we learn to read and write. We learn more words as we read them.

For a long time, early people did not know how to read or write. They learned all their words by hearing them. As the early people moved from place to place, they sometimes changed the sound of a word a little. So we say "mama" or "mother" in English. A German child says *"Mutter."* A Russian child says *"mati."* A child who speaks Spanish says *"madre."* Long ago these words all came from the same word. We say they come from the same *root* word. And they have the same meaning.

Many words in English are similar to words in some other languages because they come from the same root words. Words that share the same root usually sound and look something alike. *Milch* is the German word for milk and is similar to our word in English because both words come from the same root word, *meolc.*

But the words for milk in French, Spanish, and Italian are very different from the English word. That's because they come from the root word *lac*. So, in French, the word for milk is *lait*. It sounds like "lay." In Spanish, milk is *leche*. In Italian, it is *latte*.

Today people speak more than 3,000 different languages in different parts of the world. In some lands, people who live just a few miles from one another speak different languages. They use different words for the same things. They cannot understand one another. This makes it hard to be friends.

If someone said to you, *"Apportez-moi du lait, s'il vous plaît,"* would you understand? Not unless you knew the French language. Would you understand *"Traigame leche, por favor"*? Not unless you knew a little Spanish. Those sentences sound very different from "Bring me some milk, please," in English. But they mean the same thing.

Sometimes a word gets a new meaning in the same language. Take our word *car*. To us a car means an automobile. But the word car used to have another meaning. Long, long ago, people used a cart that they

called a *carrus*. As many years went by, the word *carrus* became *cart* or *car*. These carts or cars were very useful. They were made in many lands. Words for them—*car, carro, carre, kara*—came into many languages.

Later there were *railway cars* and *streetcars*. Then the automobile was invented. Many English-speaking people called it a *car*. So the old word came to stand for something new.

Not all languages use the same word for car. In French, the word is *voiture*. In Spanish, it is *coche* or *carro*. *Wagen* is the German word for car.

Sometimes a new word is needed. *Carpool* is a new word that was created to describe a new situation. One of the meanings of *pool* is to work together, or take turns, doing something. *Carpool* means to use a car to ride to work together or to take turns driving children to school in the same car.

That is the way new words come to be. When we need a word for something new, we often make the new word from old roots. Our language is growing with new words all the time.

How Writing

People learned how to talk long before they learned how to write. But without writing, they could not send messages very far. And they could not keep a record of things they sold or traded.

Then, about 5,000 years ago, people started to draw pictures to describe the world they lived in. That was the first way of writing, and it was called *picture writing*. In the beginning, people just drew pictures of things—a deer, a child, a boat, a house, a fire.

Later they drew pictures to show what they did or felt. They would draw pictures for words like *travel, give, pay, love.* Then they could send long messages. They could keep count of what they sold or traded. They did all this with small pictures and lines.

Came to Be

Beautiful picture writing was created thousands of years ago in ancient Egypt. Some of it was carved in stone and took a long time to make. We can still see some of this picture writing today.

As time passed, picture writing came to have more and more words. The people in Egypt could write longer and longer messages. They could write poems. They could even write books. They wrote their books on strips of paper called *papyrus* that they could unroll and roll up. They did not turn pages as we do today.

In China many years ago, people had a different picture for every word they wrote. It took them a long time to draw all these pictures. So they changed many of the pictures to a few lines and boxes that they could draw much faster. They called these simple pictures *characters*. (Writing with characters is still used in China today.)

Picture writing continued for many, many years. Then, finally, someone thought of having a simple mark stand for each sound in a word. We call the mark that was created for each sound a *letter*. All the letters we use make up the *alphabet*. Most languages today use some kind of alphabet, but not all languages use the same alphabet.

The letters in our English alphabet look quite different from the letters in some other alphabets. And some alphabets use more letters than we use in English. The Russian language has 33 letters in its alphabet. Some languages have even more. Do you know how many letters the English alphabet has? The right answer is 26.

We put our 26 letters together to make thousands and thousands of words. There are so many English words! You can learn a new word every day as long as you live. You will never know them all. But it is fun to know and use new words. You will find nearly 2,200 words in this book.

How to Use Your Dictionary

Rob's **nickname** is on the front of his shirt.

The *Macmillan First Dictionary* has been written just for you. It has been created to help you explore the wonderful world of words. You can learn about the words that you find in your reading and the words that you want to use in your writing. If you hear someone use a word and you want to know what it means, you can look it up in this dictionary. And if you need to know how a word is spelled, this book will give you the answer.

How do you look for these words? There's an easy way for you to find every single one of them. A dictionary is really just a long list of words that are in the same order as the letters of the alphabet. If you know the alphabet, you can find the words you are looking for. The words that begin with **A** come first, and they are followed by words that begin with **B,** and then come words that begin with **C.** The list keeps going until you reach the last letter of the alphabet, **Z.** The words under each letter are also in alphabetical order. To find the word **adventure,** you look in the **A** section. To find **alligator,** you keep going in the **A** section. To find **cloud,** look under the **C** words. **Zebra** can be found in the last section of the book with the other **Z** words. The words you are looking for are called main entries. The main entries are printed in **heavy black letters** and are on a line all by themselves.

Everything you need to know about each main entry comes right after the main entry word. First you will find what the entry word means. That part is called the definition. Next you will see sentences that show you how the word should be used. Those are called example sentences. Sometimes words are spelled the same but have very different meanings, like **date**[1] and **date**[2]. If you look on the Sample Page (page v), you will find **date**[1] and **date**[2] and their different meanings.

In the *Macmillan First Dictionary,* you will find different words that mean the same thing, like **cab** and **taxi.** You'll also learn that some words are short for longer words, like **bike** for **bicycle.** And you will discover that words change when they are used in different ways. For example, **story** becomes **stories** when we talk about more than one of them. And **open** becomes **opened** when we mean something that happened before and is not happening now. You can find these changes after the blue triangle (▲).

In the back of the dictionary, you will find even more words. These are words that have been put together in groups. You will see pages with Words That May Confuse You, Months of the Year and Days of the Week (see Calendar), Numbers, Weights and Measures, and Money. You will also find a map of the United States that shows the states and their capitals, and another map that shows the world with the continents and oceans.

There are many pictures in this dictionary. A picture sometimes makes it much easier to understand what a word means. Some of the pictures show what things are, and others show something being done. Each picture has a sentence that tells you about it. If you look at the pictures on these pages, you will see how pictures can give you a better idea of what words mean.

Now that you know all about the *Macmillan First Dictionary,* the next thing to do is to start having fun using it!

It's nice to sit **close** to someone you love.

Mr. Williams is helping us put on our **costumes** for the play.

An Amazing Ape

a
1. When you say **a**, you mean one. We have **a** computer in our classroom.
2. A also means each. The mail is brought to our house once **a** day.

able
When you are **able** to do something, you know how to do it or have the power to do it. Michael is **able** to count up to 10. Penguins are not **able** to fly. ▲ **abler, ablest.**

about
1. Andy has a book that shows pictures of dogs and tells how to take care of them. Andy's book is **about** dogs.
2. About also means almost. You use **about** when you are not really sure of something. There are **about** 20 children in the second grade.

above
Above means over or in a higher place than something. The birds flew **above** the tops of the trees. There is a light **above** my bed.

absent
When you are **absent**, you are away from a place. Mario is **absent** from school today because he is sick.

accident
An **accident** is something that happens and is not expected. **Accidents** can be good or bad. Terry found a quarter by **accident** when he bent down to tie his shoe. Emily had an **accident** and fell when her roller skate hit a rock.
▲ **accidents.**

accomplish

When you **accomplish** something, you finish it. It took us a long time to **accomplish** everything on our list, but we did it.
▲ **accomplished, accomplishing.**

ache

Ache means to hurt. Dad's back **aches** because he moved furniture all afternoon. Barbara's arm **ached** after she pitched in the baseball game. ▲ **ached, aching.**

acorn

An **acorn** is the nut that grows on an oak tree. The squirrel carried an **acorn** in its mouth. ▲ **acorns.**

acrobat

An **acrobat** is a person who can walk on a wire that is high above the ground or do other exciting things. We watched the **acrobats** do somersaults high in the air. ▲ **acrobats.**

across

Across means from one side to the other. Everyone ice-skated **across** the pond and then back again. Karen and Elsie live **across** the street from us.

act

1. Act means to do something. Firefighters have to **act** quickly to put out fires.
2. Act also means to be in a play or a movie. Everyone in our class is going to **act** in the school play. A person who **acts** in a play or a movie is called an **actor.** ▲ **acted, acting.**

activity

An **activity** is something that you do. My favorite **activity** is swimming. ▲ **activities.**

The strongest **acrobat** is at the bottom, and the smallest one is on top.

add

1. Add means to put numbers together to find out how many there are. If you **add** 3 and 4, you get 7. Jane **added** the prices of the books to see if she had enough money to buy them. When you **add** numbers, you are doing **addition**.

2. Add also means to put things together. Larry likes to **add** strawberries to his cereal. Our neighbors **added** a new room to their house. ▲ **added, adding.**

Mary and Tom have **added** 3 + 6. Who has the correct answer?

address

Your **address** is the place where you live. Carol's **address** is 34 James Street. The **address** of our school is 375 River Road. I keep the names and **addresses** of my friends in a special book. ▲ **addresses.**

Kim is writing the **address** of her friend Ann.

adopt

When you **adopt** a child, that child becomes part of your family. Mr. and Mrs. Bryant were very happy when they **adopted** the new baby. My best friend was **adopted** when he was 2 years old. ▲ **adopted, adopting.**

adult

An **adult** is a person who is a grown-up. Your parents are **adults**. ▲ **adults**.

adventure

An **adventure** is a special thing to do. **Adventures** are new and different and are maybe a little frightening. I like to read books about **adventures** in space. Sam's first trip in an airplane was an **adventure**. ▲ **adventures**.

The ride down the river was a great **adventure**.

advertisement

An **advertisement** tells you about something to buy or something to go to. It can be words or pictures. I see **advertisements** for cereal on television. A short word for **advertisement** is **ad**. ▲ **advertisements**.

afford

Afford means to have the money to pay for something. Lisa counted her money to see if she could **afford** the red sweater. ▲ **afforded, affording**.

afraid

When you are **afraid**, you have a feeling that something bad might happen. Our dog is **afraid** of thunder. Pat is **afraid** to swim in deep water.

after

1. After means at a later time than something else. Dan came to my house **after** school. Tuesday comes **after** Monday.
2. After also means chasing or looking for something. The big dog ran **after** the ball that Kara threw.

afternoon

Afternoon is the part of the day between noon and evening. Our school day ends at 3 o'clock in the **afternoon.** ▲ **afternoons.**

again

When you do something **again,** you do it one more time. Ralph liked the dinosaurs so much that he wanted to go to the museum **again.** We're going to stay at the lake **again** next summer.

If they had read the sign, they wouldn't have stood **against** the fence.

against

1. **Against** means not on the same side. Our school played a baseball game **against** another school. Only three people voted **against** Sharon for class president.
2. **Against** also means toward or touching something. Tom threw the ball **against** the wall. Rosa left her bicycle **against** the tree.

age

Age is how old a person or thing is. What **age** are you? My brother learned to play the piano when he was my **age.** ▲ **ages.**

ago

Ago means before now. Our kittens were born two days **ago.**

agree

When you **agree** with someone, you think or feel the same way that person does. We **agreed** to name our cat Tabby. ▲ **agreed, agreeing.**

ahead

Ahead means in front of something or someone. Meg was **ahead** of the others in the race. Four people were **ahead** of us in line.

There is one person **ahead** of Rae at the post office.

air

Air is what we breathe. **Air** is all around us, but usually we cannot see it or smell it. Sometimes there is pollution in the **air.**

air conditioner

An **air conditioner** is a machine that makes air cool and clean. **Air conditioners** are used in cars and in offices, homes, and other buildings. The **air conditioner** in our car has not been working very well. ▲ **air conditioners.**

This **airplane** makes long trips in a short time.

airplane

An **airplane** is a large machine that can fly. It has two wings and one or more engines to make it go. **Airplanes** carry people, packages, and other things from one place to another. **Plane** is a short word for **airplane.** ▲ **airplanes.**

7

airport

An **airport** is a place where airplanes take off and land. It has buildings where people can wait and where airplanes can be checked and fixed. The **airport** was really busy the night we waited for Sarah's plane to arrive. ▲ **airports.**

alarm

An **alarm** is a bell or some other thing that makes a loud noise. We use the **alarm** on our clock to wake us up in the morning. When the fire **alarm** rang, everyone left the building quickly. ▲ **alarms.**

Players on our baseball team dress **alike**.

alike

When things are **alike,** they are the same. All the puppies have brown fur and look **alike.** Loretta and her sister sometimes wear sweaters that are **alike.**

alive

When a person or thing is **alive,** it is living. You are **alive.** When there is no rain, we water the garden to keep the flowers **alive.**

all

All means every one or the whole amount. **All** of us are going to swim in the pool this afternoon. It snowed **all** night. **All** the milk is gone.

alligator

An **alligator** is an animal with a long body, a long tail, and short legs. It has a large mouth with many sharp teeth. **Alligators** live in rivers and swamps. They look like crocodiles, but have shorter heads.
▲ **alligators.**

This **alligator** is resting by the edge of the water.

allow

Allow means to let someone do something. Tod and Teri's parents sometimes **allow** them to stay up later on Saturday nights.
▲ **allowed, allowing.**

allowance

An **allowance** is an amount of money that is given to someone. Margaret gets an **allowance** once a week. George earns his **allowance** by setting the table and helping with the dishes. ▲ **allowances.**

all right

When something is **all right,** it is good enough. That picture looks **all right** over the piano. When you are **all right,** you feel fine. April fell off her bicycle, but she is **all right.**

Penny can **almost** reach the first elevator button.

almost

Almost means close to. Lewis is **almost** as tall as his father. It is **almost** 2 o'clock.

When Freddie is **alone,** he likes to work on his alphabet puzzle.

alone

If you are **alone,** you are not with anyone else. Are you going to the game **alone?** When I am **alone,** I enjoy reading and listening to music.

along

1. **Along** means from one end of something to the other. People stood all **along** the street watching the parade.
2. **Along** also means together with someone or something. Do you want to come **along** with me to the park? Tina always takes crayons and paper **along** when her family goes on car trips.

Brian reads a story **aloud** to his friends.

aloud

Aloud means loud enough so that others can hear you. The children took turns reading the story **aloud.**

alphabet

The **alphabet** is the set of letters we use to write words. There are 26 letters in the English **alphabet.** They are **A, B, C, D, E, F, G, H, I, J, K, L, M, N, O, P, Q, R, S, T, U, V, W, X, Y,** and **Z.** ▲ **alphabets.**

alphabetize

When you **alphabetize** things, you put them in order by the letters of the alphabet. The words **ant, baby, cat, door, drum, kite, machine, monkey,** and **paint** are **alphabetized.**
▲ **alphabetized, alphabetizing.**

already

Already means before now. We have to walk to school because the bus has **already** left.

also

Also is used when you mean more than just one person or thing. Jane likes to ride her bicycle, and she **also** likes to swim.

always

Always means all the time or every time. Leopards **always** have spots. Our dog **always** barks when she sees me.

am

Am comes from the word **be.** I **am** happy that you can come to visit. I **am** cooking some soup.

amaze

When something **amazes** you, it surprises you very much. It will **amaze** me if I win the race. The magician's tricks **amazed** us all. ▲ **amazed, amazing.**

ambulance

An **ambulance** is a special kind of car that is used to carry people who are sick or hurt to a hospital.
▲ **ambulances.**

Jay and Elise are seeing the inside of an **ambulance** for the first time.

American

1. A person who lives in the United States is called an **American.** A person who lives in North America or South America is also called an **American.** ▲ **Americans.**

2. If something is **American,** it comes from or is about the United States. There is an **American** flag in our classroom. **American** also means something that comes from or is about North America or South America.

among

1. Among means with or in the middle of things or people. Ted sat **among** his friends.

2. Among also means that there is some for each. Nan divided the paper and pencils **among** the children.

amount

An **amount** is how much of something you have. We brought a large **amount** of food to the picnic. ▲ **amounts.**

We like to **amuse** each other with hand puppets.

amuse

Amuse means to make someone smile or laugh. We **amused** the baby by making funny sounds. ▲ **amused, amusing.**

an

We use **an** instead of **a** before words that start with the letters **a, e, i, o,** and **u.** I drew a picture of **an** elephant under **an** umbrella.

and

1. And is used to mean also. Betsy has a dog **and** a cat.
2. And is used when we add numbers. When we add 2 **and** 2, we get 4. Another word for **and** is **plus.**

angry

When people are **angry,** they feel unhappy and are mad at someone or something. Mom was **angry** at the dog for chewing her slippers. ▲ **angrier, angriest.**

animal

An **animal** is anything that is alive that is not a plant. **Animals** can move from one place to another. A boy, a girl, a cow, a bird, a fish, and a snake are all **animals.**
▲ **animals.**

anniversary

An **anniversary** is the day of the year when something important happened in an earlier year. March 9th is my parents' wedding **anniversary.** ▲ **anniversaries.**

annoy

Annoy means to bother someone. Loud noises can **annoy** me. ▲ **annoyed, annoying.**

another

Another means one more. May I please have **another** sandwich? The first sweater was too small, so Tim tried on **another** size.

Today is the **anniversary** of the opening of the pizza store.

Rita's skates are loose, so she is putting on **another** pair of socks.

Patti likes to **answer** the phone for her mom.

This is how an **ant** looks under a magnifying glass.

answer

1. When someone speaks or writes to you, you **answer** the person by saying or doing something. We **answer** people when they ask us a question, or call us, or send us a letter. ▲ **answered, answering.**

2. When you **answer** someone, you give that person an **answer.** The teacher liked my **answer** to the question. Sally wrote me and is waiting for my **answer.** ▲ **answers.**

ant

An **ant** is a small insect that lives in the ground. **Ants** live together in large groups. We watched the **ants** on the ground carrying large pieces of leaves. ▲ **ants.**

any

1. **Any** means one, but it is not important which one. You may use **any** crayon in this box. Kate can swim faster than **any** of her friends.

2. **Any** also means some. The cat didn't leave **any** food in its bowl. Do you have **any** paper and pencils? I don't have **any** time to ride my new skateboard today.

3. **Any** can also mean every. **Any** child can play this game. **Any** person who lives in our town can swim in the swimming pool.

anyone

Anyone means one person, but it is not important which person. **Anyone** can play on the swings in the playground. Another word for **anyone** is **anybody.** Has **anybody** found my mittens?

anything

Anything means one thing, but it is not important which thing. Do you want **anything** to eat?

apart

1. Apart means away from one another. We planted the flowers 12 inches **apart** so they would have room to grow.
2. When you take something **apart**, you make it into pieces. Joe took the wagon **apart** to see why the wheels would not turn.

Kevin and his father know how to take things **apart** and fix them.

apartment

An **apartment** is a room or a group of rooms that people live in. There are 20 **apartments** in that building. ▲ **apartments.**

ape

An **ape** is a large animal that can walk and stand almost as straight as a person can. **Apes** are like monkeys, but they do not have a tail. ▲ **apes.**

apologize

Apologize means to say you are sorry for something you said or did. I **apologized** to my brother for breaking his truck.
▲ **apologized, apologizing.**

appear

Appear means to be seen. The sun is just beginning to **appear** over the mountains. A herd of deer **appeared** at the edge of the woods this morning. ▲ **appeared, appearing.**

appetite

When you have an **appetite,** you want to eat. Billy has a big **appetite** after he plays football. When our dog was sick, it had no **appetite.** ▲ **appetites.**

apple

An **apple** is a round fruit with red, yellow, or green skin. **Apples** grow on trees. ▲ **apples.**

aquarium

An **aquarium** is a container that is filled with water and holds fish and other animals. Some **aquariums** are small glass boxes. Others are huge and hold large animals like sharks and whales. Jessica has three fish in her **aquarium.** ▲ **aquariums.**

We saw a whale when we visited the **aquarium.**

are

Are comes from the word **be.** How **are** you? We **are** going to the circus today. There **are** two libraries in our town.

area

An **area** is a part of a larger place. There is an **area** in the park where we can have a picnic. Our cafeteria has an **area** where you can make your own salad. In our classroom, we have one **area** for reading, one **area** for music, and another **area** for studying science. ▲ **areas.**

We are studying plants, water, and magnets in our science **area.**

aren't

Aren't means "are not." We **aren't** ready to go yet. **Aren't** you coming with us to the park?

argue

Argue means to fight with words. When people **argue,** they sometimes talk in a loud, angry way. The children **argued** about who would pitch for their baseball team. ▲ **argued, arguing.**

arm

1. The **arm** is the part of your body between your shoulder and your wrist. Terry's **arms** are tired from carrying the heavy bags of groceries. Some animals have **arms** too. The baby monkey put its **arms** around its mother and went to sleep.
2. Machines and other things can also have **arms.** The **arm** of this chair is made of wood. The **arm** of the crane lifted a huge rock from the ground. ▲ **arms.**

Billy and Jane **argue** over which channel to watch.

Mr. Stevens is telling us about the **armor** that knights wore long ago.

Patrick can get his arms **around** his dog.

armor

Armor is a heavy suit that is made of metal. People wore **armor** long ago to protect themselves during battles. We saw many suits of **armor** at the museum.

army

An **army** is a large group of people who fight for their country in a war. After three days, the **armies** stopped fighting. ▲ **armies.**

around

1. **Around** means on all sides of a person or thing. Sue put her arms **around** her baby brother. There is a tall fence **around** the playground at school.
2. **Around** also means on the other side of something. The public library is **around** the corner.
3. **Around** can also mean in a circle. The wheels of the bicycle went **around** and **around.**
4. **Around** can also mean near or close to. My brother is playing somewhere **around** the house. I'll meet you at **around** six o'clock.

arrive

Arrive means to come to a place. Our dinner guests are going to **arrive** soon. The train **arrived** 10 minutes late. We will be **arriving** in town at 9 o'clock. ▲ **arrived, arriving.**

arrow

1. An **arrow** is a thin stick that has a point at one end and feathers at the other. **Arrows** are shot from bows.
2. An **arrow** is often shown on a sign to point the way to something. The **arrow** on the sign shows the way to the beach. ▲ **arrows.**

art

Art is something beautiful made by a person. Drawings, paintings, and statues are pieces of **art.**

artist

An **artist** is a person who makes drawings, paintings, and other beautiful things like statues. ▲ **artists.**

When these young **artists** finish painting, they will hang up their pictures.

as

Jan can swim **as** well **as** Betty can. Is it **as** cold today **as** it was yesterday? Arnold is in the same class **as** I am.

ash

Ash is a gray powder that is left after something has burned. There was a pile of **ashes** where we had burned the leaves.
▲ **ashes.**

ashamed

When you are **ashamed,** you feel unhappy about something wrong that you have done. Martha was **ashamed** that she had hurt her friend's feelings.

ask

1. You **ask** a question when you want to learn something. I'll **ask** Eric if he knows where my baseball is. Let's **ask** the police officer how to get to the park. We need to **ask** what time it is, too.
2. You also **ask** a question when you want to have something. Please **ask** if you want another sandwich. Marcia **asked** for help when she couldn't open the window.
▲ **asked, asking.**

asleep

When you are **asleep,** you are sleeping. Bryan had a funny dream while he was **asleep.**

All of the bats in the cave are **asleep.**

astronaut

An **astronaut** is a person who goes into space. **Astronauts** travel in spaceships. Some **astronauts** have walked on the moon. ▲ **astronauts.**

at

1. At is used to tell where something is. The bird was **at** the top of the tree. The bus stopped **at** the corner. The baby deer stood **at** its mother's side without moving.
2. At is also used to tell when something happens. Marta goes to bed **at** 8 o'clock. We agreed to meet in front of the school **at** 3 o'clock.

The **astronaut** is floating in outer space.

ate

Ate comes from the word **eat.** Rick **ate** two sandwiches for lunch yesterday.

attach

Attach means to join one thing to another. Jamie used tape to **attach** the sign to the wall. Rebecca **attached** a yellow straw basket to her bicycle. ▲ **attached, attaching.**

Terry is **attaching** a wire to the battery.

attention

When you pay **attention,** you watch and listen carefully. The children paid **attention** to what the teacher was saying.

attic

An **attic** is the space or room below the roof of a house. **Attics** are sometimes used as places to keep old clothes or furniture. ▲ **attics.**

Everyone in the **audience** enjoyed the concert.

audience

An **audience** is a group of people gathered to hear and see something. My family was in the **audience** for my school play. ▲ **audiences.**

aunt

Your **aunt** is your father's sister or your mother's sister. Your uncle's wife is also your **aunt.** ▲ **aunts.**

author

An **author** is a person who has written a book, story, play, or poem. Another word for **author** is **writer.** ▲ **authors.**

automobile

An **automobile** is something to ride in. **Automobiles** have four wheels and an engine to make them go. Another word for **automobile** is **car.** ▲ **automobiles.**

autumn

Autumn is a season of the year. **Autumn** comes after summer and before winter. During the **autumn,** in some places the leaves turn red, yellow, and orange before they fall from the trees. Another word for **autumn** is **fall.** ▲ **autumns.**

awake

When you are **awake,** you are not sleeping. We knew the dog was **awake** when it started to bark.

award

An **award** is something that is given to a person who has done something special. Patsy and Vernon got **awards** for writing the best stories. ▲ **awards.**

away

1. We use **away** to show that something or someone has gone from a place. The rabbit ran **away** when it saw us. I have to put my toys **away** before I go to bed. Our aunt stayed with us when Mom and Dad went **away.**
2. **Away** also means at a distance. My cousin lives 3 miles **away** from us.
3. We also use **away** to show that we no longer have something. I threw **away** my old dirty sneakers. We gave **away** one of the kittens to my friend.

awful

Awful means terrible or very bad. An **awful** fire caused that store to close. The medicine I had to take tasted **awful.**

These trees change colors in the early **autumn.**

Sandy's cow won three **awards** at the fair.

23

Bb

Beaver Busy Brushing

baby
A **baby** is a very young child. Children are called **babies** before they know how to walk or talk. Grandma took a picture of the new **baby.** ▲ **babies.**

baby-sitter
A **baby-sitter** is a person who takes care of children when their parents are not at home. Our **baby-sitter** reads stories to us. ▲ **baby-sitters.**

back
1. Your **back** is the part of your body that is behind your chest. Jenny floated on her **back** in the pool.
2. The **back** of something is the part that is farthest away from the front. My desk is at the **back** of the classroom. ▲ **backs.**
3. When you put something **back,** you return it to where it was. Please put the book **back** on the shelf.

backpack
A **backpack** is a soft bag that is worn on the back. It fits over the shoulders and is used to carry things. Students use **backpacks** to carry books and other small things. Campers use **backpacks** to carry food, clothes, and other things. ▲ **backpacks.**

backward
When something is going **backward,** it has its back first. The wagon rolled **backward** down the hill. Cara had her sweater on **backward.** This word is also spelled **backwards.** Jerry was walking **backwards** and fell. Can you spell your name **backwards?**

backyard

A **backyard** is the yard behind a house. Mario planted a vegetable garden in the **backyard.** June has a swing in her **backyard.** ▲ **backyards.**

bad

1. When people or animals are being **bad,** it means that they are doing something they should not be doing. The **bad** dog chewed up my best sweater.
2. When something is **bad,** it is not good. It is a **bad** idea to go out without an umbrella on a rainy day. Jana has a **bad** singing voice. Toni's singing voice is **worse** than Jana's.
3. When something is **bad,** it also means very strong. We had a **bad** storm last night. Carol and Richard both have **bad** colds.
▲ **worse, worst.**

bag

A **bag** is something to put things in. It is usually made of paper or plastic. I helped take the groceries out of the **bag.** Jessie bought two **bags** of peanuts and gave me one. ▲ **bags.**

bake

Bake means to cook food in an oven. We **baked** a birthday cake for Mom last night. ▲ **baked, baking.**

bakery

A **bakery** is a store that bakes and sells breads, cakes, and cookies. Our **bakery** sells carrot cake. ▲ **bakeries.**

Uncle John works in a **bakery**.

John has good **balance**.

balance

Balance means to keep something in a place so it does not fall off or roll away. The seal at the circus can **balance** a ball on its nose. ▲ **balanced, balancing.**

bald

When people are **bald,** they have little or no hair on their heads. Zack was **bald** when he was born. ▲ **balder, baldest.**

ball

A **ball** is something that is round. **Balls** are used in many kinds of games. A baseball, a football, and a tennis **ball** are different kinds of **balls.** ▲ **balls.**

ballet

A **ballet** is a kind of dance. People who dance in **ballets** must learn special steps and ways of holding their bodies as they move to the music. ▲ **ballets.**

The class is learning a new step in **ballet.**

balloon

A **balloon** is a bag that gets big when you blow air into it. **Balloons** come in many different colors and sizes. We blew up red and green **balloons** for the Christmas party. ▲ **balloons.**

banana

A **banana** is a long fruit with yellow or red skin. **Bananas** grow in bunches on big plants that look like trees. ▲ **bananas.**

band

A **band** is a group of people who play musical instruments together. The school **band** plays music that we march to. ▲ **bands.**

bandage

A **bandage** is a piece of cloth that is put over a cut to keep it clean and protect it. ▲ **bandages.**

bang

1. A **bang** is a loud, sudden noise. When it is windy, the door shuts with a **bang.** ▲ **bangs.**
2. **Bang** means to make a loud, sudden noise. Laura likes the sound of someone **banging** pots in the kitchen because it means she will be eating soon. ▲ **banged, banging.**

bank

A **bank** is a place to keep money. Sometimes people borrow money from **banks.** My aunt works in a **bank.** Jim put a nickel in his toy **bank.** ▲ **banks.**

The sky is full of **balloons.**

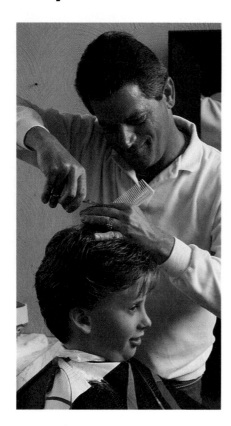

The **barber** is cutting Bobby's hair.

Patricia and Rosie like walking **barefoot** on the beach.

bar

A **bar** is something that is longer than it is wide. You can wash your hands with the **bar** of soap in the bathroom. The bird cage had metal **bars.** ▲ **bars.**

barbecue

When people **barbecue,** they cook food outdoors over a fire. Last night we **barbecued** chicken and corn.
▲ **barbecued, barbecuing.**

barber

A **barber** is a person who cuts hair. Mom took me to the **barber** because my hair was too long. ▲ **barbers.**

bare

Bare means without clothes or cover. In the winter, many trees lose their leaves and become **bare.** This floor looks very **bare** without a rug on it. ▲ **barer, barest.**

barefoot

When your feet are bare, we say you are **barefoot.** Peter likes to take off his shoes and socks and walk **barefoot** on the grass.

bargain

When something costs less than usual, it is called a **bargain.** This shirt is a **bargain** for 9 dollars. ▲ **bargains.**

barge

A **barge** is a boat with a flat bottom. **Barges** are used to carry things like logs and sand on rivers. ▲ **barges.**

bark[1]

Bark is the outside cover of a tree. The **bark** on most trees is thick and rough. ▲ **barks.**

bark²

Bark means to make the sound that a dog makes. Our dog **barks** when it is hungry or frightened.
▲ **barked, barking.**

barn

A **barn** is a building on a farm. Cows and horses are kept in the **barn.** We went to feed the horses in the **barn.** ▲ **barns.**

base

1. A **base** is the bottom part of something. It is the part that something stands on. The **base** of the statue is made of marble.
2. A **base** is also one of the four corners of a baseball field. I hit the ball so far I was able to run all the way to second **base.** ▲ **bases.**

The farmer stores hay in the **barn** for the animals.

baseball

1. Baseball is a game that is played with a ball and a bat by two teams. The players try to hit the ball with the bat and run around the bases.
2. Baseball is also the name of the ball that is used in the game of **baseball.**
▲ **baseballs.**

basement

The **basement** is the bottom floor of a building. **Basements** are usually below the ground. Dad made a room in the **basement** where we can play games and have parties.
▲ **basements.**

29

These **baskets** hold a lot of cherries.

Will Carla get the **basketball** in the net?

basket

A **basket** is something used to hold things. **Baskets** can be made of straw, pieces of wood, wire, or other things. Cary put his books in his bicycle **basket**. We put all the food for the picnic into a big **basket**. ▲ **baskets**.

basketball

1. **Basketball** is a game that is played with a large ball by two teams. The players try to throw the ball through a ring with a net hanging from it.
2. **Basketball** is also the name of the ball used in this game. ▲ **basketballs**.

bat¹

A **bat** is a strong stick that is made of wood. It is used in playing baseball and other games. ▲ **bats**.

bat²

A **bat** is also a small animal that looks like a mouse with wings. **Bats** sleep during the day and fly around at night. ▲ **bats**.

bath

When you take a **bath**, you wash yourself with soap and water. Mom gave the baby a **bath**. ▲ **baths**.

bathing suit

A **bathing suit** is something you wear when you swim. After Sean and Lauren went swimming, they hung their **bathing suits** outside to dry. ▲ **bathing suits**.

bathrobe

A **bathrobe** is a loose coat you wear before and after you take a bath or when you relax. ▲ **bathrobes**.

bathroom

A **bathroom** is a room with a sink, a toilet, and often a bathtub or a shower. Mike brushes his teeth in the **bathroom.**
▲ **bathrooms.**

bathtub

A **bathtub** is a very big container that you fill with water and sit in to take a bath.
▲ **bathtubs.**

The car won't start until the **battery** is fixed.

battery

A **battery** is something that makes electricity. Flashlights, smoke alarms, and some radios run on **batteries.** ▲ **batteries.**

battle

A **battle** is a fight between two persons or groups. Weapons are often used in a **battle.** The two armies fought a **battle.** ▲ **battles.**

bay

A **bay** is a part of an ocean or lake that stretches out into the land. ▲ **bays.**

be

I will **be** at the library all afternoon. Barbara wants to **be** a doctor when she grows up. Have you **been** to the circus yet?
▲ **been, being.**

beach

A **beach** is land that is close to a lake or an ocean. Most **beaches** are covered with sand.
▲ **beaches.**

What a good day to be at the **beach.**

bead

A **bead** is a small, round piece of plastic, glass, or wood with a hole in it. We made necklaces with **beads.** ▲ **beads.**

beak

A **beak** is the hard part of a bird's mouth. Some birds have long, sharp **beaks.** ▲ **beaks.**

bean

A **bean** is a seed that is eaten as a vegetable. There were green **beans** and yellow **beans** in the salad. ▲ **beans.**

bear

A **bear** is a large animal with thick brown, black, or white fur. ▲ **bears.**

beard

A **beard** is the hair that grows on a man's face. My grandfather has a short, white **beard.** ▲ **beards.**

beast

A **beast** is any animal with four legs. Lions, tigers, and dogs are all **beasts.** ▲ **beasts.**

beat

1. **Beat** means to hit something again and again. The rain **beat** against the window.
2. **Beat** also means that a person does something better than someone else. Nancy **beat** Lynn in the race. ▲ **beaten, beating.**

Lisa likes to **beat** her drum.

beautiful

When something is **beautiful,** it is very pretty to look at or listen to. Herb drew a **beautiful** picture of a horse. The chorus sang a **beautiful** song. The sunset last night was **beautiful.**

beaver

A **beaver** is an animal with a large, flat tail and strong teeth. It uses its teeth to chew through wood. **Beavers** live in or near rivers. They use sticks and mud to build dams to protect their homes. ▲ **beavers.**

The **beavers** are hard at work building a dam.

became

Became comes from the word **become**. The baby soon **became** tired of playing and went to sleep.

because

We use **because** to tell why something is happening. I am closing the door **because** it is cold in here. The players are happy **because** they won the game.

become

Become means to grow to be something different. The seed I planted will **become** a flower. ▲ **became, becoming.**

bed

A **bed** is a place to sleep. She was in **bed** by 8 o'clock. The dog's **bed** is in my room. ▲ **beds.**

bedroom

A **bedroom** is a room that people use for sleeping. Our apartment has two **bedrooms**. When I woke up this morning, the sun was coming in through my **bedroom** window. ▲ **bedrooms.**

bee

A **bee** is a black and yellow insect with four wings. Some **bees** make honey. ▲ **bees.**

been

Been comes from the word **be.** Mona and Josh have **been** playing in the yard. I have never **been** to a rodeo.

beetle

A **beetle** is an insect with hard wings in the front that can fold and cover the thin wings in the back. ▲ **beetles.**

The **bee** has come to the flower for food.

before

Before means ahead of in time or place. The number 4 comes **before** 5. We will be home **before** lunch. We got to the store **before** it opened. I've never met that girl **before**.

beg

Beg means to ask for money or other help. The poor woman **begged** for food. ▲ **begged, begging.**

begin

Begin means to do the first part of something. The carpenters will **begin** to build the house next month. Have you **begun** your homework yet? A **beginner** is a person who is starting to do something for the first time. ▲ **began, begun.**

beginning

Beginning means the first part or the time something **begins**. The **beginning** of the story was better than the end. Tomorrow is the **beginning** of spring vacation. ▲ **beginnings.**

behave

1. **Behave** means to act in a good way. Our teacher told us to **behave** in the classroom.
2. **Behave** also means to act in any one way. How did the baby **behave** at the doctor's office? ▲ **behaved, behaving.**

behind

Behind means at the back of. Carl sits **behind** Patty in school. The baby ducks walked **behind** their mother. Jack hid **behind** the tree.

Christopher's dog is **begging** for a treat.

The baby is riding **behind** his mother in a backpack.

The Liberty **Bell** cracked the first time it was rung.

being

1. **Being** comes from the word **be**. The children were having a good time **being** silly.
2. A **being** is a person or animal. People are human **beings**. ▲ **beings**.

believe

When you **believe** something, it means that you think it is true or real. Aunt Kate could not **believe** that she won a thousand dollars. ▲ **believed, believing**.

bell

When it is struck, a **bell** makes a sound that rings. The sheep all wore little **bells** around their necks. We heard the school **bell** ring and knew we were late. ▲ **bells**.

belong

1. When something **belongs** to you, it means that you own it. Does this ball **belong** to Ann?
2. If something **belongs** in a place, it means that is where it should be. This dictionary **belongs** on the second shelf. ▲ **belonged, belonging**.

below

Below means in a lower place. Mario hung the picture he drew **below** mine.

belt

A **belt** is something you wear to keep your pants or skirt up. I need to wear a **belt** with these pants because they are too big for me. ▲ **belts**.

bench

A **bench** is a long seat. Grandmother and I sat on a **bench** in the park and fed the birds. ▲ **benches**.

Davy and Jamie are peeking out of the tent, one **below** the other.

bend

Bend means to move something so that it is not straight. Margaret's older brother is so strong that he can **bend** a metal bar. Francis **bent** down to help pick up the books that Pedro had dropped. The trees are **bending** in the wind.
▲ **bent, bending.**

beneath

When something is **beneath** something else, it is below it or under it. We keep our brooms in the closet **beneath** the stairs. The dog's bed is **beneath** the table.

Phil and Terry exercise by **bending** and touching their toes.

beret

A **beret** is a soft, round, flat cap. My grandfather wears a plaid scarf and a **beret** on chilly days. ▲ **berets.**

berry

A **berry** is a small fruit that we can eat. A **berry** has many seeds. We went to Mr. Cole's farm to pick **berries.** ▲ **berries.**

We sat **beside** each other to read.

beside

Beside means next to a person or thing. Tim stood **beside** Donna in line. Richard and Evelyn are **beside** each other in the photograph.

best

Best means better than all the others. Of all the animals at the zoo, I like the monkeys **best.** Jeff won the race because he was the **best** runner.

better

Better means more of something good. Nancy is a good swimmer, but Lucy is **better.** Which is the **better** book? I play the piano **better** now than I did last year. Bob is feeling **better** today.

between

Between means in the middle of two other things. In the alphabet, **s** comes **between** **r** and **t**. The dog sat **between** us in the truck. Mom told us not to eat any cookies **between** meals.

Joey and Max put the dog **between** them to give it a bath.

bicycle

A **bicycle** is something to ride on. It has two wheels with one in front of the other. You use your feet to make the wheels turn. **Bike** is a short word for **bicycle.** ▲ **bicycles.**

big

Big means large in size or amount. The box was too **big** for Carlo to pick up. We live in a **big** city. ▲ **bigger, biggest.**

bill

A **bill** is the hard part of a bird's mouth. **Bill** is another word for **beak**. ▲ **bills.**

biography

A **biography** is a true story of someone's life written by another person. ▲ **biographies.**

bird

A **bird** is an animal with wings. **Birds** are covered with feathers and have two legs. Most **birds** can fly. **Birds** lay eggs. Chickens, robins, and penguins are **birds.** ▲ **birds.**

We sang "Happy Birthday" to Tommy on his **birthday.**

birthday

Your **birthday** is the day and month when you were born. Keith and I have the same **birthday.** ▲ **birthdays.**

bite

1. **Bite** means to cut something with the teeth. The dog tried to **bite** the stick I threw her. Jesse **bit** into the apple.
▲ **bit, bitten** or **bit, biting.**
2. A **bite** is a piece you get when you **bite.** Jack took a **bite** of the banana. ▲ **bites.**

black

Black is a very dark color. These letters are **black.** The opposite of **black** is **white.**

blame

Blame means to say that a person has done something wrong or bad. Mother **blamed** me for letting the bird out of its cage.
▲ **blamed, blaming.**

Who took a **bite** out of Will's sandwich?

39

blanket

A **blanket** is a cover that people use on a bed to keep them warm. Some **blankets** are made of wool or cotton. ▲ **blankets.**

bleed

Bleed means to lose blood from the body. Tom **bled** when he fell and cut his chin. ▲ **bled, bleeding.**

The wind **blew** so hard that we had trouble walking.

blew

Blew comes from the word **blow.** The wind **blew** the door shut.

blind

People who are **blind** cannot see. **Blind** people have a special alphabet that they read by feeling with their hands.

block

1. A **block** is hard and has flat sides. Kim built a house with her toy **blocks**.
2. A **block** is an area with four streets around it. A **block** is also the part between two streets. Ed lives on my **block**. ▲ **blocks**.

blood

Blood is the red liquid in your body. Your heart helps your **blood** move to all parts of your body.

The flowers are **blooming** outside the window.

bloom

Bloom means to have flowers. Cherry trees **bloom** in the spring. ▲ **bloomed, blooming**.

blouse

A **blouse** is a piece of clothing worn on the top part of the body. ▲ **blouses**.

blow

1. **Blow** means to put air into something. Will you help us **blow** up these balloons?
2. **Blow** also means to move with air. Hold on to your umbrella or the wind will **blow** it away. ▲ **blew, blowing**.

blue

Blue is a color. When there are no clouds during the day, the sky is **blue**.

board

1. A **board** is a long, flat piece of wood. **Boards** are used to build houses and other things.
2. A **board** is also a flat piece of thick paper or other material used for a game. Get the **board** and we'll play checkers. ▲ **boards**.

Janet is **blowing** up a beach ball for the game.

Jackie likes to sail her **boat** in the pond at the park.

boat

A **boat** is something that is used to travel on water. Some **boats** are moved by the wind blowing on sails. Other **boats** are moved by motors. ▲ **boats.**

body

A **body** is all of a person or an animal. An elephant has a huge, heavy **body.** Snakes have long, thin **bodies.** ▲ **bodies.**

boil

1. Boil means to make water very hot. When water **boils,** little bubbles come to the top. **2. Boil** also means to cook something in water that is **boiling.** John **boiled** an egg for breakfast. ▲ **boiled, boiling.**

bone

A **bone** is the hard part of a person's body under the skin and muscles. People have big, long **bones** in their legs and many tiny bones in their feet. Vinny broke a **bone** in his arm when he fell on the ice. ▲ **bones.**

book

A **book** is made up of pieces of paper that are sewed or pasted together at one edge. The pages of a **book** have words and pictures on them for people to read and look at. This dictionary is a **book.** There are many **books** in our school library. ▲ **books.**

boom

A **boom** is a deep, hollow sound. During the storm we heard **booms** of thunder. ▲ **booms.**

boost

Boost means to push up. Tommy **boosted** his friend into the tree so that he could reach the apple. ▲ **boosted, boosting.**

Nan is **boosting** Liz so that she can see what is going on.

boot

A **boot** is a kind of shoe. **Boots** usually cover the foot and the lower part of the leg. **Boots** are often worn in rain or snow. ▲ **boots.**

born

When people or animals are **born,** it means that they begin to live. My baby brother was **born** last month. When the puppies were **born,** their eyes were closed.

borrow

Borrow means to take something to use for a while. Hector let me **borrow** his roller skates. Ann **borrowed** a book from me. ▲ **borrowed, borrowing.**

both

Both means two people or two things. **Both** children won a prize. I like **both** apples and bananas.

Both boys are drawing the same person.

bother

Bother means to give trouble to or annoy someone. Erin's little sister **bothers** her when she is on the phone. ▲ **bothered, bothering.**

bottle

A **bottle** is something that is used to hold liquids. **Bottles** may be made of glass or plastic. ▲ **bottles.**

bottom

The **bottom** is the lowest part of something. The rock sank to the **bottom** of the pool. ▲ **bottoms.**

bought

Bought comes from the word **buy**. We **bought** food for the picnic.

bounce

Bounce means to move back after hitting something. Cal threw the ball and it **bounced** off the sidewalk. ▲ **bounced, bouncing**.

Bouncing up and down is lots of fun.

bow

1. A **bow** is a special kind of knot. It is made with a ribbon or string. Ricky tied a big red **bow** on the present.
2. A **bow** is also a thin piece of wood with a string tied from one end to the other. It is used for shooting arrows. ▲ **bows.**

bowl

A **bowl** is a dish with high sides that is used to hold food or liquid. Martha gave the dog a **bowl** of water. ▲ **bowls.**

box

A **box** is used to hold things. **Boxes** are often made of wood or heavy paper. ▲ **boxes.**

boy

A **boy** is a child who will grow up to be a man. **Boys** are male children. ▲ **boys.**

brace

1. A **brace** is something that holds parts together or keeps a thing from shaking. Andy wore a metal **brace** on his weak leg to help him walk.
2. Braces are also metal wires that are put on teeth to help them grow straight. ▲ **braces.**

bracelet

A **bracelet** is a chain or a large ring that is worn around your arm as jewelry. ▲ **bracelets.**

braid

1. When you **braid** your hair, you divide it into three parts and then put one part over the other until you get a long strip. ▲ **braided, braiding.**
2. A long strip of hair that is **braided** is called a **braid.**
▲ **braids.**

All the girls have **braids.**

brain

The **brain** is a part of the body that is inside the head of people and animals. It lets us think, learn, and remember. ▲ **brains.**

brainstorm

1. Brainstorm means to get together in a group and collect ideas from each person to try to find an answer to a problem. We **brainstormed** for a long time and finally thought of a good name for our team.
▲ **brainstormed, brainstorming.**
2. A **brainstorm** is a sudden, clever idea.
▲ **brainstorms.**

Marcia is doing her best to be **brave.**

brake

A **brake** is something that makes a bicycle, a car, or a train go slower or stop. You make some **brakes** work with your hands, like those on many bicycles. Other **brakes** work with the feet. Mom put her foot on the **brake** to make the car stop. ▲ **brakes.**

branch

A **branch** is the part of a tree or bush that grows out from the trunk. Leaves grow on **branches.** ▲ **branches.**

brave

If you are **brave,** it means that you have courage. The **brave** child climbed the tree to get the kitten. ▲ **braver, bravest.**

bread

Bread is a food that is baked. It is usually made by mixing flour, milk, and other things. **Bread** is used to make sandwiches and toast. ▲ **breads.**

break

1. When something **breaks,** it divides into pieces. If you drop that mirror, it will **break.** 2. When something **breaks,** it stops working. Our oven is **broken** and doesn't get hot. Sherman **broke** his toy truck when he threw it. ▲ **broke, broken, breaking.**

breakfast

Breakfast is the first meal of the day. We eat **breakfast** in the morning. I like cereal and a banana for **breakfast.** ▲ **breakfasts.**

breath

Breath is the air you take in and let out when you breathe. When it is very cold, you can see your **breath.** ▲ **breaths.**

Caroline didn't mean to **break** the window.

breathe

When you **breathe,** you take air into your body and let it out again. You **breathe** through your nose and mouth.
▲ **breathed, breathing.**

breeze

A **breeze** is a soft, gentle wind. The ocean **breeze** made us feel cool. ▲ **breezes.**

brick

A **brick** is a block of clay that has been baked in an oven or in the sun. Our chimney is made of **bricks.** ▲ **bricks.**

The ship has just gone under the tall **bridge.**

bridge

A **bridge** is something that is built across water. **Bridges** help people to get from one side of the water to the other. ▲ **bridges.**

bright

When something is **bright,** it gives out light or is filled with light. The sun made the room **bright.** ▲ **brighter, brightest.**

Bobby is **bringing** in the laundry for his aunt.

bring

Bring means to take someone or something with you. Jess asked if she could **bring** her friend Sally to the party. Will you please **bring** me the newspaper?
▲ **brought, bringing.**

broke

Broke comes from the word **break.** I dropped the glass and **broke** it.

broken

1. When something is **broken,** it is in pieces. The **broken** plate could not be fixed.
2. When something is **broken,** it also means that it doesn't work. We took the **broken** television set back to the store to be fixed.

broom

A **broom** is a brush with a long handle. It is used to sweep the floor or ground. Mr. Kelly uses a wide **broom** to sweep the leaves from his sidewalk. ▲ **brooms.**

brother

Your **brother** is a boy who has the same mother and father as you do. ▲ **brothers.**

brought

Brought comes from the word **bring.** Everyone at the party **brought** a birthday present for Harry.

brown

Brown is the color of the earth. Some people have **brown** hair and **brown** eyes.

The **broken** toaster burned the toast again.

brush

1. A **brush** is something used for cleaning or painting. **Brushes** have hairs or wires that are usually attached to a handle. A toothbrush is a special kind of **brush**. ▲ **brushes**.

2. Brush also means to clean or make something neat. Maria likes to **brush** and braid her sister's long hair. Jim **brushed** his dog at least once a week.
▲ **brushed, brushing**.

bubble

A **bubble** is a round drop of something filled with air. Mike and Sarah blew soap **bubbles**.
▲ **bubbles**.

Keith made the biggest **bubble** I have ever seen.

bucket

A **bucket** is a strong, round container with an open top and a flat bottom. The children filled their **buckets** with water to help wash the car. Another word for **bucket** is **pail**.
▲ **buckets**.

bug

A **bug** is an insect. Ants, bees, and mosquitoes are kinds of **bugs**. ▲ **bugs.**

build

Build means to make something. We are going to **build** a castle out of sand. Eben **built** a large cage for his rabbit.
▲ **built, building.**

TABLE # 3
A Desert

The students are **building** a model of a desert for the science fair.

building

A **building** is something built to live, work, or do things in. Houses, schools, churches, offices, and stores are **buildings**. ▲ **buildings.**

bulb

1. A **bulb** is the part of a plant under the ground from which a whole new plant will grow. Tulips grow from **bulbs**. Onions are **bulbs** you can eat.
2. A **bulb** can also be anything that has a part that is round. A **bulb** that is used in a lamp is called a **light bulb**. ▲ **bulbs.**

bulldozer

A **bulldozer** is a machine that is used to move rocks and dirt. **Bulldozers** get the land ready before roads and buildings are built. ▲ **bulldozers.**

bully

A **bully** is a person who likes to frighten people or be mean to them. ▲ **bullies.**

bump

1. Bump means to hit something suddenly. Carmen **bumped** into the chair with her knee. The table shook when I **bumped** into it. ▲ **bumped, bumping.**
2. A **bump** is also a place that is higher and rounder than the area around it. Johnny rode his bicycle over the **bump** in the road. The insect bite left a **bump** on Stephanie's arm. ▲ **bumps.**

bumper

A **bumper** is a heavy bar across the front or back of a car or truck that protects it when it hits something. ▲ **bumpers.**

bunch

A **bunch** is a group of things that are together. Mom picked a **bunch** of flowers from the garden. Sandra bought two **bunches** of carrots and one **bunch** of bananas. ▲ **bunches.**

bunny

A **bunny** is a small animal with long ears, a small tail, and soft fur. Another word for **bunny** is **rabbit.** ▲ **bunnies.**

A **bulldozer** is a machine that does big jobs quickly and easily.

Carlo bought a **bunch** of grapes to eat in the park.

The meat is **burned**. I think we will be going out for dinner.

burglar
A **burglar** is a person who gets into a house, store, or other place and steals things. **Burglars** stole jewelry from the hotel room. ▲ **burglars.**

burn
1. **Burn** means to be on fire. We **burn** wood in the fireplace to keep us warm on a cold day.
2. **Burn** also means to hurt yourself by touching something hot. Jean **burned** her hand on the stove. ▲ **burned, burning.**

bury
Bury means to put in the earth or the sea. Jan's dog is **burying** its bone in our backyard. ▲ **buried, burying.**

bus
A **bus** is like a large automobile with rows of seats for many people. ▲ **buses.**

bush
A **bush** is a plant with many branches. It is smaller than a tree. Roses and some kinds of berries grow on **bushes.** ▲ **bushes.**

business
1. **Business** is the work that a person does to earn money. My father's **business** is selling jewelry.
2. A **business** is also a factory, a store, a farm, or any other place where people work to earn money. ▲ **businesses.**

busy
When people are **busy,** they are doing something. Roberta can't come out to play because she's **busy** doing her homework. ▲ **busier, busiest.**

We are all **busy** getting ready for our trip.

but

1. We use **but** when we talk about how things are different. Dick is tall, **but** his brother is taller.
2. We also use **but** to mean except. Everyone **but** Kate liked the movie.

butter

Butter is a soft, yellow food that is made from cream or milk. People put **butter** on bread or use it to cook with.

butterfly

A **butterfly** is an insect that has four large wings with bright colors. A **butterfly's** body is very thin.
▲ **butterflies.**

button

1. A **button** is a small thing used to keep clothes together. Shirts, jackets, blouses, and some sweaters have **buttons.**
2. A **button** is also something small that is turned or pushed to make something else move. Push the **button** if you want to turn on the lamp. ▲ **buttons.**

Butterflies are beautiful.

buy

When you **buy** something, it means you give money for it. We **bought** food at the supermarket. ▲ **bought, buying.**

by

1. By means near something. My dog stands **by** the door when she wants to go out. We drove **by** my friend's house.
2. By also means not later than. We have to be at school **by** 8 o'clock.

Chorus of Camels

cab

A **cab** is a car that people pay to ride in. Aunt Jo took a **cab** to the airport. Another word for **cab** is **taxi**. ▲ **cabs**.

cabin

A **cabin** is a small house built of rough boards or logs. There are **cabins** all around the lake. ▲ **cabins**.

cactus

A **cactus** is a plant that grows in the desert. **Cactuses** have sharp needles instead of leaves. **Cactuses** grow in many shapes, and some have large, bright flowers. ▲ **cactuses** or **cacti**.

cafeteria

A **cafeteria** is a kind of restaurant. In **cafeterias,** you choose your food at a counter and carry it to a table. Rachel eats soup and a sandwich for lunch in the school **cafeteria**. ▲ **cafeterias**.

cage

A **cage** is something to keep animals in. The sides of a **cage** are made of wire or bars. Birds are kept in **cages**. ▲ **cages**.

cake

A **cake** is a sweet food that is baked in an oven. It is often made with flour, butter, eggs, and sugar. ▲ **cakes**.

calendar

A **calendar** is something that shows all the days, weeks, and months of the year. Josh marked the day of the party on the **calendar** so that he wouldn't forget. ▲ **calendars**.

The **calf** is between the two cows.

calf¹

A **calf** is a baby cow. A baby seal, elephant, or whale is also called a **calf.** ▲ **calves.**

calf²

The **calf** is a part of the leg. The **calf** is at the back of the leg, a little below the knee. ▲ **calves.**

call

1. **Call** means to say something in a loud voice. Dad **called** us when dinner was ready.
2. **Call** also means to give a name to someone or something. We decided to **call** our new cat "Jojo."
3. **Call** also means to talk with someone by telephone. We always **call** Grandma on her birthday. ▲ **called, calling.**
4. A **call** is the sound made by a bird or another animal. The **call** of a robin is different from the **call** of an owl.
5. When we call someone on the telephone, we are making a **call.** ▲ **calls.**

came

Came comes from the word **come**. Sam's mother **came** to school to take us home.

camel

A **camel** is a large animal with a long neck, long legs, and either one or two big humps on its back. **Camels** live in the desert and can go for a long time without water.
▲ **camels**.

camera

A **camera** is a kind of box for taking photographs or movies. A **camera** has a hole that you look through to see what will be in the picture. ▲ **cameras**.

camouflage

Camouflage is a way of hiding something by making it look like the things around it. The skin or fur of some animals is a **camouflage**. The fox's white fur was a good **camouflage** because it could not be seen in the snow.
▲ **camouflages**.

Migdalia is showing her sister how to use her new **camera**.

The tiger's stripes are its **camouflage**. Can you find the tiger in the grass?

Our family likes to **camp** in the woods.

camp

1. A **camp** is a place where people live in tents or cabins. Mike learned to dive at **camp** last summer. ▲ **camps.**

2. **Camp** also means to go to a place where you can cook, sleep, and live outdoors. Marcia and her family **camped** in the mountains on their vacation. A person who goes **camping** or stays at a **camp** is called a **camper.** ▲ **camped, camping.**

can¹

1. If you **can** do something, it means that you know how to do it. I **can** ride a bicycle. **Can** you speak more than one language?

2. **Can** also means that you are able to do something. Mario **can** run faster than his brother. **Can** you come to my party next Saturday? ▲ **could.**

can²

A **can** is a container made of metal. **Cans** are used to hold food and other things. Mom bought two **cans** of white paint. ▲ **cans.**

candle

A **candle** is a wax stick. It has a string through it that is burned to make a light. The family lit eight **candles** on the last night of Hanukkah. ▲ **candles.**

We like to make **candles** in different shapes and colors.

candy

Candy is a sweet food that may be soft or hard. Some **candies** are made of chocolate and have nuts or fruit inside. ▲ **candies.**

cannot

If you **cannot** do something, it means that you don't know how to do it or that you are not able to do it. Lisa **cannot** ride a horse until she has many more lessons. My brother **cannot** play in the baseball game tomorrow because he has a bad cold.

can't

Can't is a short word for "**cannot.**" My baby sister **can't** walk yet. The picnic table is so heavy I **can't** move it by myself.

cap

A **cap** is a small, soft hat. Nurses and police officers wear different kinds of **caps**. The children wore baseball **caps** to the big game. ▲ **caps.**

capital

1. A **capital** is a city where people in the government of a country or state meet to make laws and to work. Washington, D.C., is the **capital** of the United States. Do you know the **capital** of your state?

2. A **capital** is also a large letter of the alphabet. **E** and **M** are the **capitals** for the letters **e** and **m.** When we write a name or a sentence, we start with a **capital.** ▲ **capitals.**

We kept our **caps** on for the picture.

car

A **car** is a machine to ride in. It has four wheels and a motor to make it move. ▲ **cars.**

card

A **card** is a thick piece of paper that has words, numbers, or pictures on it. Maureen has her own library **card.** Matthew sent a birthday **card** to his friend Mickey. ▲ **cards.**

care

When you **care** about something, you have a good feeling about it. Max **cares** about his cat and feeds it and fills its water bowl twice every day. ▲ **cared, caring.**

Anna is enjoying the **cards** from her friends.

59

careful

If you are **careful,** it means that you are thinking about what you are doing. Tina is very **careful** not to spill the paint. She works **carefully.**

careless

Careless means that you are not thinking about what you are doing. Lee and Sal were **careless** and spilled the paint. They worked **carelessly.**

carnival

A **carnival** is a kind of fair that has food, games, and many things to amuse people. ▲ **carnivals.**

carpenter

A **carpenter** is a person who builds and fixes houses and other things made of wood. The **carpenter** built shelves and a seat under the window in my room. ▲ **carpenters.**

The **carpenters** are building shelves.

Kings and queens ride in **carriages** like this one.

carriage

A **carriage** is a kind of wagon on four wheels for carrying people. A baby rides in a **carriage** pushed by a person. ▲ **carriages.**

carrot

A **carrot** is a long, orange vegetable that grows in the ground. The root of the plant is the part that we eat. ▲ **carrots.**

carry

Carry means to hold a thing and move it. Mike **carried** the groceries for his mom. ▲ **carried, carrying.**

Billy has been picking **carrots.**

cart

A **cart** is a kind of wagon. Most **carts** have two wheels and are pulled. **Carts** at the supermarket have four wheels and are pushed. ▲ **carts.**

carton

A **carton** is a box made of very heavy paper. Ann bought a **carton** of milk. ▲ **cartons.**

cartoon

A **cartoon** is a picture that makes people laugh. There are **cartoons** in newspapers and magazines, in movies, and on television.
▲ **cartoons.**

carve

1. **Carve** means to cut out a shape. The artist **carved** animals from wood.
2. **Carve** also means to cut meat into pieces. It is almost time to **carve** the turkey.
▲ **carved, carving.**

case

A **case** holds or covers a thing. My glasses fit into a narrow **case.** ▲ **cases.**

castle

A **castle** is a very big building with high walls and towers. A long time ago, kings and queens lived in **castles.** ▲ **castles.**

I wonder why the frog wants to visit the **castle.**

cat

1. A **cat** is a small animal that has soft fur and a long tail. Mary has a pet **cat**.
2. Some kinds of **cats** are large and wild. Tigers and leopards are large, wild **cats**.
▲ **cats**.

catch

Catch means to take hold of something that is moving. Karen ran to **catch** the ball.
▲ **caught, catching**.

catcher

A **catcher** is a person or thing that **catches**. The **catcher** in a baseball game is behind the person who is ready to hit the ball.
▲ **catchers**.

caterpillar

A **caterpillar** looks like a worm with fur. **Caterpillars** come from eggs and will become butterflies.
▲ **caterpillars**.

catsup

Catsup is a thick liquid made from tomatoes. It is eaten on other foods. Another way to spell **catsup** is **ketchup**.

cattle

Cattle are large animals raised for milk and meat on dairy farms and ranches. Cows are **cattle**.

caught

Caught comes from the word **catch**. Michael **caught** the pencil before it rolled off the top of his desk. Elizabeth **caught** a black and orange butterfly in a net.

Ginger is the **catcher** on our baseball team.

One of the boys has just **caught** a fish.

cause

1. Cause means to make something happen. If you don't hurry, you will **cause** us to be late for school. ▲ **caused, causing.**
2. A **cause** is a person or thing that makes something happen. A car going too fast was the **cause** of the accident. What was the **cause** of the fire? ▲ **causes.**

cave

A **cave** is an opening under the ground or in the side of a mountain. ▲ **caves.**

We walked through the large **cave** and saw rocks in many strange shapes.

cavity

A **cavity** is a hole in a tooth. After my dentist showed me how to brush my teeth, I got fewer **cavities.** ▲ **cavities.**

ceiling

A **ceiling** is the part of a room that is over your head. There is a light hanging from the kitchen **ceiling.** ▲ **ceilings.**

celebrate

When you **celebrate** something, you show that it is important in a special way. Our town **celebrated** the Fourth of July with a parade and fireworks. ▲ **celebrated, celebrating.**

Our family **celebrated** Grandma and Grandpa's 50th wedding anniversary.

center

Center means middle. Cassie stood in the **center** of the circle for the game. We put the flowers in the **center** of the table. ▲ **centers.**

cereal

Cereal is a food often made from wheat, corn, or rice. We like **cereal** for breakfast. ▲ **cereals.**

certain

Certain means that you are very sure about something. Are you **certain** that you closed the door?

chain

A **chain** is a row of rings that are joined together. Margaret wore a heart on a **chain** around her neck. ▲ **chains.**

chair

A **chair** is a piece of furniture with four legs and a back. People sit on **chairs.** ▲ **chairs.**

Meg is using a **chain** to keep her bike safe.

This shows a caterpillar **changing** into a butterfly.

chalk

Chalk is a small stick that is used for writing or drawing. Our new teacher wrote her name on the chalkboard with yellow **chalk.** ▲ **chalks.**

chalkboard

A **chalkboard** is a hard, smooth board made of a special material that can be written on and erased. **Chalkboards** may be black or green. The special crayon used to write on a **chalkboard** is called **chalk.** ▲ **chalkboards.**

chance

1. A **chance** is a time to do something. Each child will have a **chance** to ride the pony. Nikki has a **chance** to go to the circus next month.
2. **Chance** also means that something might happen. There is a **chance** that it may snow tomorrow. ▲ **chances.**

change

Change means to make or become different. I have to **change** my clothes before I go out to play. Do you think Myra will **change** her mind and come with us? Suddenly, the weather **changed,** and it began to rain. ▲ **changed, changing.**

channel

A television has many **channels.** Each **channel** can carry a different program. One **channel** has science programs for children. Angela changed the **channel** on the television so that we could watch cartoons. ▲ **channels.**

chant

A **chant** is a singing or shouting of words again and again. Each team yelled a **chant** before the football game began. ▲ **chants.**

chapter
A **chapter** is a main part of a book. Jill's book has 10 **chapters.** ▲ **chapters.**

character
A **character** is a person in a book, play, story, or movie. ▲ **characters.**

Cinderella is a **character** in a fairy tale.

charge
1. **Charge** means to ask an amount of money as a price for something. How much did the store **charge** for fixing the radio?
2. **Charge** also means to buy something and pay for it later. ▲ **charged, charging.**

chase
Chase means to run after something and try to catch it. My dog **chased** the car down the road. ▲ **chased, chasing.**

cheap
Cheap means that something costs very little. These cars are the **cheapest** toys in the store. ▲ **cheaper, cheapest.**

check

1. Check means to find out if something is the way it should be. The teacher told us to **check** our spelling. Dad has the car **checked** before we take a trip. ▲ **checked, checking.**
2. A **check** is also a mark to show that something has been looked at or is correct. A **check** looks like this: √. Amy put a **check** next to each answer that was correct.
▲ **checks.**

Edith and her grandfather like to play **checkers.**

checkers

Checkers is a game for two people played on a board, with 12 pieces for each person. George and his friends like to play **checkers.**

checkup

A **checkup** means a careful look to see if somebody or something is all right. Lila went to the doctor for a **checkup** last week.
▲ **checkups.**

cheek

Your **cheek** is the part of your face that is under your eyes. Terry's **cheeks** became red when he played in the snow. ▲ **cheeks.**

cheerful

When you are **cheerful,** it means that you feel happy. The **cheerful** boy whistled while waiting for the bus.

cheese

Cheese is a kind of food that is made from milk. ▲ **cheeses.**

cherry

A **cherry** is a small, round, red fruit. **Cherries** grow on trees. ▲ **cherries.**

chess

Chess is a game for two people played on a board, with 16 pieces for each person. Mom showed me how different **chess** pieces move in different ways.

chest

1. Your **chest** is the front part of your body just below the shoulders. Your heart is in your **chest.**
2. A **chest** is also a big box that holds things. Grandma keeps her blankets in a wood **chest.** Bill put the hammer back in the tool **chest.**
▲ **chests.**

chew

Chew means to cut something with the teeth. One of my new slippers had a lot of holes after the dog **chewed** it.
▲ **chewed, chewing.**

chicken

A **chicken** is a bird. **Chickens** lay eggs that people eat. People also eat meat from **chickens.** ▲ **chickens.**

Sue knew she would find her bear in her toy **chest.**

Baby **chickens** stay close to the mother hen.

chief

A **chief** is a person who is the leader of a group. Each year the **chief** of police gives medals to the bravest police officers. ▲ **chiefs.**

child

A **child** is a young girl or boy. Twelve **children** played in the school band. ▲ **children.**

We felt a **chill** in the air as we waited for the bus.

chill

A **chill** is a feeling of cold. There was a **chill** in the air this morning. ▲ **chills.**

chimney

A **chimney** is something that carries smoke away from a fireplace or a furnace to the outdoors. ▲ **chimneys.**

chin

The **chin** is the part of your face between your mouth and your neck. My Dad's beard covers his **chin.** ▲ **chins.**

chocolate

Chocolate is a food used in making candies, cakes, and other sweet things to eat. ▲ **chocolates.**

choose

Choose means to pick out something you want to have. Billy **chose** a red balloon with his name on it.
▲ **chose, chosen, choosing.**

chorus

A **chorus** is a group of people who sing or dance together. Mark and Anna sing in the **chorus** at school. ▲ **choruses.**

Christmas

Christmas is a Christian holiday celebrated on December 25. Many people go to church and give presents on **Christmas.**

church

A **church** is a building where Christian people go to pray and sing. ▲ **churches.**

circle

A **circle** is a shape that is round. A ring is a **circle.** ▲ **circles.**

circus

A **circus** is a show put on by people and animals. **Circuses** travel from one town to another.
▲ **circuses.**

The Ramirez family is **choosing** a puppy to take home with them.

The red tube is in the shape of a **circle.**

Cities have many tall buildings where people live and work.

Bobby is making a head out of **clay.**

city

A **city** is a place where a lot of people live and work. **Cities** have many tall buildings. A **city** is bigger than a town. ▲ **cities.**

class

A **class** is a group of people who learn together in a school. Our science **class** is learning all about clouds. ▲ **classes.**

classroom

A **classroom** is a room where a class works with a teacher. ▲ **classrooms.**

claw

A **claw** is one of the sharp nails on the feet of birds, cats, and many other animals. ▲ **claws.**

clay

Clay is a kind of earth. Wet **clay** can be made into many different shapes. When **clay** is dried or baked, it becomes hard. ▲ **clays.**

clean

1. When something is **clean,** it does not have dirt on it. Leslie just washed her hands and now they are **clean.** I used soap to wash my brushes and they are **cleaner** than yours.
▲ **cleaner, cleanest.**
2. When you **clean** something, you wash it or make it neat. We **cleaned** our rooms before we went out to play.
▲ **cleaned, cleaning.**

clear

1. When something is **clear,** you can see through it. Glass is **clear.**
2. Clear can also mean that you understand something. This math problem is now **clear** because you explained it. ▲ **clearer, clearest.**

clever

When people are **clever,** they can think quickly. The **clever** child learned how to do the puzzle in a very short time.
▲ **cleverer, cleverest.**

Timothy and Jennifer **climb** the rocks in the park almost every Saturday.

climb

Climb means to move up something. People use their hands or feet when they **climb.** Mom had to **climb** a ladder to get the kite out of the tree. Toni **climbed** into bed and went right to sleep.
▲ **climbed, climbing.**

clock

We read the numbers on a **clock** to know what time it is. Some **clocks** have hands that move around. Other **clocks** show numbers that change as the time changes. ▲ **clocks.**

It's nice to sit **close** to someone you love.

close

1. When **close** sounds like nose, it means to shut something. Please **close** the door. ▲ **closed, closing.**
2. **Close** also means near. The child stayed **close** to its mother. We live much **closer** to school since we moved. ▲ **closer, closest.**

closet

A **closet** is a small room used for storing clothes and other things. A **closet** usually has a door. ▲ **closets.**

cloth

Cloth is material that is used to make clothes, blankets, and other things. Cotton **cloth** is made from plants, and wool **cloth** is made from the hair of animals. ▲ **cloths.**

clothes

People wear **clothes** to cover their bodies. Coats, dresses, pants, and jackets are kinds of **clothes.** Another word for **clothes** is **clothing.** We put on warm **clothing** to play outdoors in the winter.

cloud

A **cloud** is made of tiny drops of water that float high in the sky. There were dark **clouds** in the sky before the storm. ▲ **clouds.**

clown

A **clown** is a person who dresses in funny clothes and does tricks to make people laugh. The **clowns** at the circus wore paint on their faces. ▲ **clowns.**

club

A **club** is a group of people who meet together for fun or some special purpose. Our book **club** meets on Friday. ▲ **clubs.**

clue

A **clue** is something that helps us find the answer to a problem or mystery. The footprints were the **clue** that helped us catch the burglar. ▲ **clues.**

coach

A **coach** is a person who trains people who play sports. The **coach** made the basketball team practice every afternoon until the big game. ▲ **coaches.**

What **clues** tell you who ate the piece of cake?

The **coach** is telling the players what to do.

Tommy saves his **coins** in a clear, plastic bank.

coast

A **coast** is the land next to the sea. Fran and Tom walked along the **coast** looking at all the sea birds. ▲ **coasts.**

coat

A **coat** is a piece of clothing to wear over other clothes. People wear **coats** outdoors to keep warm. ▲ **coats.**

cocoon

A **cocoon** is a small, soft case that a caterpillar makes around itself. A caterpillar lives in a **cocoon** until it changes into a butterfly. ▲ **cocoons.**

coin

A **coin** is a piece of money that is made of metal. **Coins** usually have pictures and words or numbers on them. Nickels, dimes, and quarters are kinds of **coins.** ▲ **coins.**

cold

1. **Cold** means not warm or hot. Ice is very **cold.** It is **cold** outside in winter. The puppy wanted to come in because it was **cold.** ▲ **colder, coldest.**
2. When you have a **cold,** you feel sick and you may sneeze or cough a lot. ▲ **colds.**

collar

1. A **collar** is the part of a shirt or dress that fits around the neck.
2. A **collar** is also a short belt worn around an animal's neck. My dog's **collar** has my address on it. ▲ **collars.**

collect

Collect means to gather things together. I like to **collect** different kinds of rocks as a hobby. ▲ **collected, collecting.**

color

Red, blue, and yellow are the main **colors.** All other **colors** have some red, blue, or yellow in them. If we mix blue and yellow together, we get the **color** green. Orange is my favorite **color.** ▲ **colors.**

comb

A **comb** is a piece of plastic or metal with teeth in it. You use a **comb** in your hair to make it smooth. ▲ **combs.**

come

Come means to move toward a person or place. My cat **comes** to me when I call her. I hope you can **come** with me.
▲ **came, coming.**

comfortable

If something is **comfortable,** it feels nice. The chair is so **comfortable** that Dad falls asleep in it.

comic

1. **Comic** means funny. A mouse chasing a cat is a **comic** thing to see.
2. **Comics** are cartoons put in a row to tell a story. **Comics** are printed in newspapers and in thin paper books. ▲ **comics.**

company

Company is a person or a group of people who visit you. We had **company** for dinner on Thanksgiving.

Barbara likes to use all the **colors** when she paints.

We love to get **comfortable** and read our books.

Ginnie's book of photographs is almost **complete.**

compare

Compare means to look at people or things to see how they are alike or different. If you **compare** your book with mine, you will see that yours is much thicker.
▲ **compared, comparing.**

complete

1. When something is **complete,** it has all its parts. Our school library has a **complete** set of books by my favorite author.
2. Complete also means finished. Andrew can't go out until his homework is **complete.**

computer

A **computer** is a machine that can do many kinds of work very fast. People use **computers** to work with numbers or words or even to draw pictures. ▲ **computers.**

Michael, Josh, and Maria are working together on the **computer.**

concert

A **concert** is a show of music. The new school orchestra is going to give three **concerts** this year. ▲ **concerts.**

cone

1. A **cone** is a shape that has a round, flat bottom and a top that comes to a point.
2. A **cone** is also anything that has the shape of a **cone**. For Halloween, I made a witch's hat in the shape of a **cone**. ▲ **cones.**

confuse

1. Confuse means to mix up. That street sign is so **confusing** that drivers often take a wrong turn.
2. Confuse also means not to see how things are different. Many people often **confuse** me with my cousin, Jane. ▲ **confused, confusing.**

consonant

A **consonant** is a letter of the alphabet that is not a vowel. The **consonants** are **b, c, d, f, g, h, j, k, l, m, n, p, q, r, s, t, v, w, x, z,** and sometimes **y.** ▲ **consonants.**

container

A **container** is something that is used to hold things. Boxes and jars are **containers.** ▲ **containers.**

contest

A **contest** is a game or a race that people try to win. Sue won the swimming **contest.** ▲ **contests.**

cook

Cook means to use heat to make food ready to eat. Mom is **cooking** fish tonight.
▲ **cooked, cooking.**

Miranda likes her ice cream in a **cone.**

Tom and his father are **cooking** dinner.

cookie
A **cookie** is a small, flat, sweet food. Some **cookies** have chocolate in them. ▲ **cookies.**

Vicky and Toby are relaxing in a **cool** stream.

cool
When something is **cool,** it is more cold than hot. It feels good to swim in **cool** water on a very hot day. ▲ **cooler, coolest.**

copy
1. Copy means to make or do something that is like something else. Andy **copied** a picture of a lion to show me. ▲ **copied, copying.**
2. A **copy** is a thing that is just like something else. I'd like two **copies** of each photograph, please. ▲ **copies.**

corn
Corn is a long, yellow vegetable with a green cover. The **corn** seeds grow in rows and are the part of the plant that we eat.

Wendy has picked four ears of **corn.**

corner
A **corner** is a place where two lines or sides come together. Paul bumped his knee on the **corner** of the table. ▲ **corners.**

correct

1. Correct means without any mistakes. All the answers on my science test were **correct.**
2. Correct also means to mark mistakes in something. The teacher will **correct** all the spelling tests and give them back to us.
3. Correct also means to make something right that is wrong. We will **correct** the words that we spelled wrong.
▲ **corrected, correcting.**

cost

1. Cost is how much money you have to pay to buy something. What is the **cost** of that bicycle? ▲ **costs.**
2. Cost also means that you can buy something for a certain amount of money. My new shoes **cost** 20 dollars.
▲ **cost, costing.**

costume

A **costume** is clothing you wear to look like someone or something else. ▲ **costumes.**

Mr. Williams is helping us put on our **costumes** for the play.

cotton

Cotton is a kind of cloth that is made from the **cotton** plant. It is used to make clothes and other things.

Henry has put the apple he wants to buy on the **counter.**

couch

A **couch** is a soft piece of furniture that more than one person can sit on. ▲ **couches.**

cough

Cough means to make a noise by making air come out of the throat. ▲ **coughed, coughing.**

could

Could comes from the word **can. We could** ride to school, but we'd rather walk.

couldn't

Couldn't means "could not." The baby lamb **couldn't** walk well.

count

1. **Count** means to find out how many of something there are. Let's **count** how many apples we picked.
2. **Count** also means to say numbers in order. Can you **count** to 10?
▲ **counted, counting.**

counter

A **counter** is a long table. Things are sold at **counters** in stores. In some restaurants people can eat at a **counter.** ▲ **counters.**

country

1. **Country** means the land outside of cities and towns where there are woods and farms.
2. A **country** is an area of land and the people who live there. A **country** has its own government. The United States is a **country.**
▲ **countries.**

courage

When you do something even though you are afraid, you show **courage.** Firefighters have a lot of **courage.**

cousin

A **cousin** is the child of an aunt or uncle. My **cousin** and I have the same grandfather.
▲ **cousins.**

cover

1. Cover means to put one thing on top of another. We always **cover** the bird's cage at night. ▲ **covered, covering.**
2. A **cover** is something that is put over another thing. The **cover** of that book has a picture of a rocket on it. Please put the **cover** on the pot of soup. ▲ **covers.**

cow

A **cow** is a female animal. People get milk and meat from **cows.** ▲ **cows.**

cowboy

A **cowboy** is a man who takes care of cattle on a ranch. **Cowboys** ride horses and sometimes do tricks in shows that are called rodeos.
▲ **cowboys.**

cowgirl

A **cowgirl** is a woman who takes care of cattle on a ranch. **Cowgirls** ride horses and sometimes do tricks in shows that are called rodeos.
▲ **cowgirls.**

crack

A **crack** is a narrow open space. When something has a **crack,** it is broken but it does not fall into pieces. There was a **crack** in the mirror after I dropped it.
▲ **cracks.**

Camilla and Luis dressed up like a **cowgirl** and a **cowboy** for the rodeo.

cracker

A **cracker** is a small, hard, flat food that is baked. **Crackers** are like cookies, but they are not sweet. ▲ **crackers.**

Cranes are used for lifting and moving heavy things.

crane

A **crane** is a large machine with a long arm that can be moved up and down and in a circle. **Cranes** are used for lifting and moving heavy things. ▲ **cranes.**

crash

1. **Crash** means to fall or break and make a very loud noise. The lamp **crashed** to the floor when the dog ran into the table.
▲ **crashed, crashing.**
2. **Crash** also means a loud noise. We heard a **crash** when the ball broke the window.
▲ **crashes.**

crawl

Crawl means to move slowly on your hands and knees. The baby is just beginning to learn to **crawl.** ▲ **crawled, crawling.**

crayon

A **crayon** is a wax stick that is used for writing and drawing. **Crayons** are made in many different colors. ▲ **crayons.**

cream

Cream is the thick part of milk. Butter is made from **cream.** My dad likes **cream** in his coffee.

creep

When something **creeps,** it moves slowly and quietly along the ground. A spider **crept** across the floor. ▲ **crept, creeping.**

cried

Cried comes from the word **cry.** Chris **cried** when he fell down and hurt his knee.

crime

A **crime** is anything that is against the law. To steal something is a **crime.** ▲ **crimes.**

crocodile

A **crocodile** is a large animal that lives in the water. It has short legs and a long tail. It also has sharp teeth. ▲ **crocodiles.**

cross

Cross means to go from one side of something to the other. We were careful when we **crossed** the street. ▲ **crossed, crossing.**

crowd

A **crowd** is a large group of people in one place. The **crowd** waited for the game to start. ▲ **crowds.**

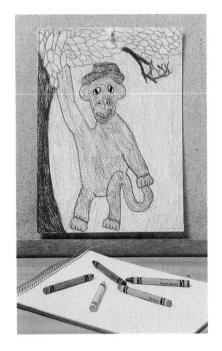

Jessie used **crayons** to draw this picture.

Kim is using the rocks to **cross** the stream.

85

crown

A **crown** is a special kind of hat that is worn by kings and queens. **Crowns** are often made of gold or silver and have beautiful stones in them. ▲ **crowns.**

cruel

If people are **cruel,** it means that they are ready to hurt others. ▲ **crueler, cruelest.**

crutch

A **crutch** helps a person with weak legs to walk. A **crutch** is a pole with a soft top that fits under the arm. ▲ **crutches.**

cry

Cry means to have tears come out of your eyes. ▲ **cried, crying.**

The **cubs** feel warm and safe next to their mother.

cub

A **cub** is a very young bear, wolf, lion, or tiger. ▲ **cubs.**

cube

A **cube** is a solid shape like a block. It has six equal, square sides. ▲ **cubes.**

cup

1. A **cup** is a small bowl that has a handle on it. **Cups** are used for drinking.

2. A **cup** is also a container for measuring things. The recipe for bread says to add 4 **cups** of flour and 1 **cup** of water. ▲ **cups.**

curious

A **curious** person wants to know or learn something. My brother and I were **curious** about our new neighbors. Mario was **curious** about how birds fly.

curl

A **curl** is a piece of hair that has the shape of a little circle. Sally has **curls** all over her head. ▲ **curls.**

curve

A **curve** is a line that bends. It has no straight parts or corners. The letter **C** is a **curve.** ▲ **curves.**

customer

A **customer** is a person who buys something. There were many **customers** at the grocery store. ▲ **customers.**

cut

1. Cut means to divide something into pieces by using a knife, scissors, or other sharp thing. Hal **cut** the pizza into eight pieces.

2. Cut also means to make something shorter by taking away a part. The barber **cut** my hair last week.

3. Cut also means to hurt yourself on something sharp. Amy **cut** her foot on a rock. ▲ **cut, cutting.**

The bottom of the swing is in the shape of a **curve.**

Jan and Allison are **cutting** out the pictures they drew.

Dd

dad
Dad is a name for your father. Some children also call their father **Daddy.**
▲ **dads.**

dairy
A **dairy** is a place where milk is put into bottles or cartons. It is also a place where butter, cheese, and other foods are made from milk. A farm where cows are raised for their milk is sometimes called a **dairy farm.**
▲ **dairies.**

daisy
A **daisy** is a flower with a round yellow center and white petals.
▲ **daisies.**

dam
A **dam** is a wall that is built across a river to hold back water. When the water is held back, it makes a lake. Beavers build **dams** in rivers with sticks and mud. ▲ **dams.**

damp
When something is **damp,** it is a little wet. Michael used a **damp** napkin to wipe up the milk that spilled.
▲ **damper, dampest.**

dance
1. **Dance** means to move your body to music. At the party, we played music and **danced.** A person who **dances** is called a **dancer.** ▲ **danced, dancing.**
2. A **dance** is the way you move your body to music. My friend showed me how to do a **dance** that she learned in another country. ▲ **dances.**

Dancing Dogs

danger

Danger means that something could happen to hurt you. The bird escaped **danger** by flying away from the cat. We knew not to swim because a big sign at the end of the beach said **DANGER—DEEP WATER.** ▲ **dangers.**

dangerous

When something can hurt you, it is **dangerous.** It is **dangerous** to cross the street without looking both ways. Riding a bicycle at night without lights is **dangerous.**

dark

1. When it is **dark,** there is little or no light. It is **dark** outside at night. During the day, sometimes it is **dark** before a storm.
2. **Dark** is also a way to talk about color. Black is a **dark** color.
▲ **darker, darkest.**

Jimmy and Tina saw the **DANGER** sign and knew they had to be careful.

dash

Dash means to move fast. The chicken **dashed** for cover when it started to rain. ▲ **dashed, dashing.**

date¹

A **date** is the day of the month or the year when something happens. Amy marked the **date** of her birthday on the calendar. ▲ **dates.**

date²

A **date** is a dark, sweet fruit that grows on trees. ▲ **dates.**

How many **daughters** are there in this picture of Claire and her family?

daughter

A **daughter** is the female child of a mother and a father. A **daughter** can be a young girl or a grown-up woman. Claire is the **daughter** of her mother and father. Claire's mother is the **daughter** of Claire's grandmother and grandfather. ▲ **daughters.**

day

1. **Day** is the time when it is light outside. On our vacation, we played and swam during the **day** and slept in a tent at night.
2. A **day** is also part of a week. There are seven **days** in one week. Tuesday is the third **day** of the week. ▲ **days.**

dead

When something is **dead,** it is no longer alive. We found a **dead** mouse in the barn. Trees look **dead** in the winter when they have no leaves.

deaf

Deaf means not able to hear.
▲ **deafer, deafest.**

decide

When you **decide** to do something, you choose to do one thing instead of another. For breakfast José **decided** to have cereal instead of eggs. Our town **decided** to put a traffic light in front of the school.
▲ **decided, deciding.**

deck

1. A **deck** is a set of cards that people use in playing games. Most **decks** have 52 cards, and they are all different.
2. A **deck** is also the floor on a ship or a boat. A **deck** may have a roof or cover over it or be all open. There may be many **decks** on a large ship. ▲ **decks.**

Paul is putting circles around the **days** of his vacation.

deep

Deep means very far down. The dog dug a **deep** hole in the ground to hide its bone. ▲ **deeper, deepest.**

deer

A **deer** is an animal with four legs, a small tail, and brown fur. Some **deer** have big horns. A **deer** runs very fast and lives in the woods. ▲ **deer.**

define

When you **define** something, you give the meaning of it. A dictionary **defines** words. Do you know how to **define** the words "camouflage" and "draw"? ▲ **defined, defining.**

delicious

If something is **delicious,** it tastes or smells very good. The bread smelled **delicious** as it baked in the oven.

den

A **den** is a place where wild animals rest or sleep. The bear used a cave as a **den** during the winter. ▲ **dens.**

dentist

A **dentist** is a doctor who takes care of people's teeth. The **dentist** showed the children how to brush their teeth. ▲ **dentists.**

describe

Describe means to give a picture of something in words. Grandma asked Ben to **describe** the fish he caught. Ben **described** it as 6 inches long, with thin stripes on its body from head to tail. ▲ **described, describing.**

The **deer** is growing horns.

91

The **desert** is filled with many kinds of cactuses.

desert

A **desert** is a hot place with very little water and a lot of sand. ▲ **deserts.**

desk

A **desk** is a kind of table for writing or doing work. Some **desks** have drawers. ▲ **desks.**

dessert

Dessert is food that is eaten after lunch or dinner. Today we had fruit salad for **dessert.** ▲ **desserts.**

detective

A **detective** is someone who tries to find out things. The **detective's** job was to find out who stole the jewelry. ▲ **detectives.**

dial

1. A **dial** is the front part of an instrument. A **dial** has numbers or letters on it and a kind of arrow that points to them. Many clocks have **dials** that show the time.
2. A **dial** is also the disk on a radio or television that is used to choose a program. ▲ **dials.**

Harry is turning the **dial** on his radio.

diamond

1. A **diamond** is a hard, clear, shiny stone. Some rings have **diamonds** in them.
2. A **diamond** is also a shape. It has four sides and four corners and looks like this ◆. A baseball field is shaped like a **diamond**. ▲ **diamonds**.

dictionary

A **dictionary** is a book that shows how words are spelled and what they mean. This book is a **dictionary**. ▲ **dictionaries**.

did

Did comes from the word **do. Did** you go to the supermarket? Yes, I **did.**

didn't

Didn't means "did not." The footprints on the floor show that Alex **didn't** wipe his feet before going into the house.

Mary Jo is looking up a word in the **dictionary.**

die

Die means to stop living. Flowers **die** if they don't get enough water. ▲ **died, dying.**

different

When something is **different,** it is not the same as something else. Cold water is **different** from hot water. A duck is **different** from a deer.

dig

Dig means to make a hole in something. Sally likes to **dig** in the sand at the beach. ▲ **dug, digging.**

dining room

A **dining room** is a room to eat in. The hotel has a **dining room** where all the guests can eat. At camp, everyone ate their meals in a large **dining room.** ▲ **dining rooms.**

dinner

Dinner is the biggest meal we eat each day. Most of the time we eat **dinner** at 6 o'clock in the evening. On holidays we eat **dinner** in the afternoon. ▲ **dinners.**

dinosaur

A **dinosaur** was an animal that lived millions of years ago. Some **dinosaurs** were huge. There are no **dinosaurs** alive today. ▲ **dinosaurs.**

This **dinosaur** is called a tyrannosaurus.

direction

1. A **direction** is the way you go to get to another place. If we keep walking in this **direction,** we will get to the park.
2. A **direction** is also the way that something points. That sign points in the **direction** of the zoo. ▲ **directions.**

dirt

Dirt is dust or mud or something else that makes things not clean. Don't forget to wash the **dirt** off your hands before you sit down for dinner. When something has **dirt** on it, it is **dirty.** Mike got his clothes **dirty** playing football in the mud.

disappear

When something **disappears,** it cannot be seen anymore. When you stand up, your lap **disappears.** The sun has **disappeared** behind a cloud.
▲ **disappeared, disappearing.**

Scruffy is making Debbie's sweater **disappear.**

disappoint

When something **disappoints** you, you are unhappy because it did not happen. Megan and Todd were **disappointed** when it rained and they could not ride their new bikes. ▲ **disappointed, disappointing.**

discover

Discover means to find something or learn something for the first time. You will **discover** how to make orange paint if you mix red and yellow paints together. The baby smiled when she **discovered** that she could stand all by herself. ▲ **discovered, discovering.**

disguise

1. **Disguise** means to hide something by making it look like something else. The children wore masks and costumes to **disguise** themselves on Halloween.
▲ **disguised, disguising.**
2. A **disguise** is something that hides or changes the way you look. Jim wore a funny nose and glasses as a **disguise.** ▲ **disguises.**

Do you think that Jim's **disguise** is working?

95

dish

A **dish** is a plate or bowl to put food on. Our kitten has a special **dish** of its own. Sal and Terry washed all the **dishes** after the party. ▲ **dishes.**

disk

1. A **disk** is something that is flat, thin, and round. Coins and plates and records are **disks. 2.** A **disk** is also a flat, thin piece of plastic or metal that is used to store information for a computer. ▲ **disks.**

distance

Distance means the space between two things. The **distance** between my bed and my sister's bed is about 3 feet. Karl lives a long **distance** from his grandmother and flies on an airplane to visit her. ▲ **distances.**

dive

Dive means to go into the water with your head first. When Maria and Carlos took swimming lessons, they learned how to **dive.** A person who **dives** is called a **diver.** The **divers** took pictures of animals that live in the ocean. ▲ **dived** or **dove, diving.**

Lou has **divided** the apple in half and is sharing it.

divide

Divide means to break something into parts. The children **divided** into two teams for the game. We **divided** the fruit among us. A fence **divides** the yard into two parts. ▲ **divided, dividing.**

divorce

Divorce means to end a marriage by law. After their mother and father were **divorced,** Susie and Tom lived part of the time with each parent. ▲ **divorced, divorcing.**

dizzy

When you are **dizzy,** you have the feeling of spinning and being about to fall. The children ran in circles until they were **dizzy.** ▲ **dizzier, dizziest.**

do

What **do** you plan to **do** after you finish practicing the piano? **Did** you get that book from the library? I am **doing** the best I can. ▲ **did, done, doing.**

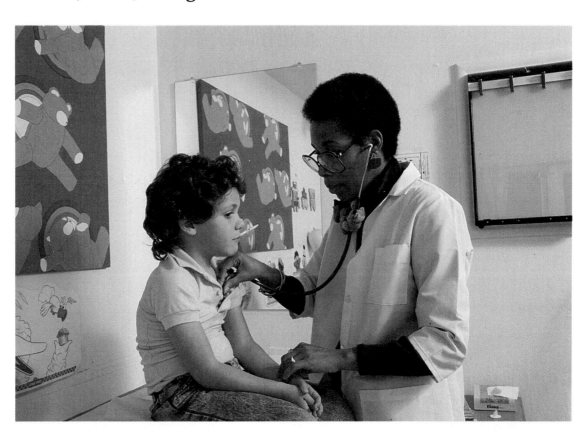

The **doctor** is listening to Roberto's heart.

doctor

A **doctor** is a person who helps sick people get well and stay well. Roberto went to the **doctor** for a checkup before he went to camp. ▲ **doctors.**

does

Does comes from the word **do.** Rebecca **does** her homework after dinner every night. **Does** Leroy like to swim? He says he **does.**

Barbara's **dog** will guide her across the street.

John has discovered a **door** to the attic.

doesn't

Doesn't means "does not." Margo's dog loves the water, but Albert's dog **doesn't** like it at all.

dog

A **dog** is an animal that has four legs and barks. A young **dog** has soft fur and is called a **puppy.** Some **dogs** can be trained to help people. ▲ **dogs.**

doll

A **doll** is a toy that looks like a baby, a child, or a grown-up. Jenna pretends that her **doll** is her baby. ▲ **dolls.**

done

1. **Done** comes from the word **do.** What have you **done** with the book I gave you?
2. **Done** also means finished. Donald is **done** with his homework.

don't

Don't means "do not." I **don't** know when the game starts, but I'll ask.

door

1. A **door** is something that closes off a space. A **door** opens and shuts so that people can go in and out. The elevator **door** closed after everyone was inside.
2. Sometimes a ceiling or wall or floor has a small **door** in it. This kind of **door** is often called a **trapdoor.** ▲ **doors.**

dot

A **dot** is a small spot. Mary bought a new umbrella with green **dots** on it. When you write the letters **i** and **j,** you put a **dot** over them. ▲ **dots.**

double

1. Double means to make twice as much of something. I hope I can **double** the amount I save this year. ▲ **doubled, doubling.**

2. Double also means two of the same thing or twice as much. The children formed a **double** line to go into school.

doubt

1. Doubt means to not be certain. We **doubted** that our team would win the trophy.
▲ **doubted, doubting.**

2. A **doubt** is a feeling of not believing or of not being certain. Jeffrey had **doubts** about getting on the soccer team. ▲ **doubts.**

dove

Dove comes from the word **dive.** The dog **dove** into the water to get the stick I threw.

down

Down means to move from a higher place to a lower place. The cat jumped **down** from the tree. You can put your books **down** on the table.

The children enjoy going **down** the slide.

dozen

Dozen means twelve of anything. Carol bought a **dozen** eggs at the store.
▲ **dozen** or **dozens.**

drag

Drag means to pull something slowly along the floor or the ground. Bud **dragged** the heavy table across the room. The dog came in **dragging** its leash behind it.
▲ **dragged, dragging.**

dragon

A **dragon** is a make-believe animal that is big and scary. Some **dragons** have wings and long tails, and some breathe fire. ▲ **dragons.**

Many people are helping to hold up the **dragon.**

drain

1. Drain means to take water or another liquid away from something. We **drained** the can of peas. ▲ **drained, draining.**
2. A **drain** is a kind of pipe that is used to take water or another liquid away from something. Lisa took a bath and then let the water go down the **drain.** ▲ **drains.**

drank

Drank comes from the word **drink.** Sarah **drank** all of her milk.

draw

Draw means to make a picture of something with a pencil or crayon. I **drew** a picture of my cat. ▲ **drew, drawn, drawing.**

drawbridge

A **drawbridge** is a kind of bridge that can be moved or opened, so that tall ships can pass under it. It's fun to watch the boats go by when the **drawbridge** is raised.

drawer

A **drawer** is a box inside a piece of furniture. A **drawer** can be pulled out or pushed in. My sweaters are in the bottom **drawer**.
▲ **drawers.**

drawing

A **drawing** is a picture that someone has made using a pencil or crayon. Yesterday I made a large **drawing** of an elephant and a giraffe.
▲ **drawings.**

drawn

Drawn comes from the word **draw**. Patrick has **drawn** a picture of some brown and white cows that are eating grass in a meadow.

dream

1. A **dream** is a picture in your mind that you have when you are asleep. Last night Carol had a **dream** that she could fly. ▲ **dreams.**
2. When you **dream,** there is a picture in your mind while you are asleep. Alfredo **dreamed** that he rode a dinosaur. I was **dreaming** about my pet hamster when Dad woke me up.

▲ **dreamed** or **dreamt, dreaming.**

The **drawbridge** is raised to let the boat go by.

Mark gave his grandfather a new **drawing**.

Annie is learning how to **dress** herself.

dress

1. A **dress** looks like a blouse and a skirt that are made in one piece. Girls and women wear **dresses**. ▲ **dresses**.
2. **Dress** also means to put on your clothes. ▲ **dressed, dressing.**

dresser

A **dresser** is a piece of furniture that has drawers. People usually put their clothes in **dressers**. My jewelry and mirror are on top of my **dresser**. ▲ **dressers**.

drew

Drew comes from the word **draw**. We **drew** pictures of each other in art class today.

dried

Dried comes from the word **dry**. The hot sun **dried** the puddles on the sidewalk.

drill

1. **Drill** means to cut a hole in wood, plastic, and other hard materials. Tyler and Derek measured the wood carefully before **drilling** any holes. ▲ **drilled, drilling.**
2. The word **drill** can also mean a tool used for **drilling**.
3. A **drill** is also a way of training people by having them do something over and over again. A spelling **drill** helps us learn to spell new words. In a **fire drill**, people learn what to do if there is a fire. ▲ **drills.**

drink

Drink means to put a liquid into your mouth and swallow it. Milk and juice are foods that we **drink**. Tim **drank** all of his milk at breakfast. Rosy has **drunk** only half of her juice, but all of her milk.
▲ **drank, drunk, drinking.**

Derek is **drilling** a hole in a piece of wood.

drip

Drip means to fall in drops. The painter tried not to **drip** paint on the rug.
▲ **dripped, dripping.**

drive

Drive means to use a car, truck, bus, or train and make it go. Mrs. Marina **drives** us to school in the morning on her way to work. A person who **drives** is called a **driver**.
▲ **drove, driven, driving.**

Jane's dad is showing her how to fix a faucet that is **dripping**.

drop

1. **Drop** means to let something fall. Walter cried when he **dropped** his ice-cream cone.
▲ **dropped, dropping.**
2. A **drop** is a tiny amount of liquid. There were **drops** of rain on the flowers. ▲ **drops.**

drove

Drove comes from the word **drive**. The farmers **drove** to town to sell their fruit.

drown

Drown means to die by staying under water and not getting air to breathe. Someone at the beach swam out too far and almost **drowned**.
▲ **drowned, drowning.**

drug

1. A **drug** is a medicine that can help make a sick person feel better. **Drugs** can be pills or liquids.
2. There is another kind of **drug** that is not a medicine. It can hurt a person's body and make that person sick. ▲ **drugs.**

Katie is **dropping** a letter in the mailbox.

drugstore

A **drugstore** is a store where people buy medicine, bandages, and many other small things. Mom bought me a toothbrush at the **drugstore.** ▲ **drugstores.**

drum

A **drum** is a musical instrument that makes a sound when it is hit. Cliff plays the **drum** in the school band. A person who plays the **drum** is called a **drummer.** ▲ **drums.**

drunk

Drunk comes from the word **drink.** The baby has **drunk** all of her juice.

dry

1. **Dry** means without water. When something is **dry,** it is not wet. It didn't rain for three weeks, and the garden got very **dry.** ▲ **drier, driest.**
2. **Dry** also means to make something **dry.** We left our beach towels out in the sun to **dry.** ▲ **dried, drying.**

The **ducks** are standing near the water.

duck

A **duck** is a bird that lives in the water. There is a family of **ducks** in the pond at the park. ▲ **ducks.**

dug

Dug comes from the word **dig**. The workers have **dug** a large hole in the ground where the new store is to be built.

dull

1. When something is **dull,** it is not sharp. The knife is so **dull** that I can't cut the meat.
2. Dull means not interesting. The program was so **dull** that I didn't want to watch the end of it. ▲ **duller, dullest.**

Rosa is **dumping** some more dirt in the garden.

dump

Dump means to drop things in a pile. The truck is going to **dump** the dirt on the side of the road. ▲ **dumped, dumping.**

during

During means at the same time as something else. We go camping every summer **during** July and August. Please try not to talk **during** the concert.

dust

Dust means small pieces of dirt. The car raised a lot of **dust** as it rode down the dirt road. You can use a broom to sweep the **dust** from the floor. When something is **dusty,** it is covered with **dust.**

The car created a lot of **dust** as it went by.

dying

Dying comes from the word **die**. The plant in our classroom is **dying** because we forgot to water it before vacation.

Ee

Elephant Exercising

each
1. Each means every one of a group of people, animals, or things. **Each** student has a pencil and paper.
2. Each also means for one. These pencils cost 10 cents **each.**

eagle
An **eagle** is a large bird with long wings and strong claws. When **eagles** hunt for food, they can see things very far away. ▲ **eagles.**

ear¹
An **ear** is the part of the body that you hear with. There is one **ear** on each side of your head. Rabbits have very long **ears.** ▲ **ears.**

ear²
An **ear** is the part of a corn plant on which the seeds grow. Frank had two **ears** of corn at the picnic. ▲ **ears.**

early
1. Early means near the time when something begins. Tanya wakes up **early** in the morning. Her father wakes up **earlier** to get ready for work. Tanya's baby brother wakes up **earliest** of all.
2. Early also means before the usual time. We had dinner **early** because we were going to a puppet show.
▲ **earlier, earliest.**

earn
Earn means to get money or something else for work that you do. Megan **earns** a dollar when she cuts the lawn. Billy **earned** high marks in school by working hard. ▲ **earned, earning.**

earth

1. The **earth** is the planet we live on. The **earth** moves around the sun, and the moon moves around the **earth.** It takes one year for the **earth** to go around the sun.

2. Earth also means dirt. The farmer dug up the **earth** to make it loose enough to plant seeds for a garden.

earthquake

When there is an **earthquake,** large pieces of the earth move and the ground shakes. Small **earthquakes** can cause things to shake and break. Big **earthquakes** can cause buildings to fall down.
▲ **earthquakes.**

easily

Easily means in an easy way. When something can be done **easily,** it can be done without hard work. Melinda can touch her toes **easily.** Now that Anthony knows the alphabet, he is able to find words in the dictionary **easily.**

This is how the **earth** looks from outer space.

east

East is the direction that you face to see the sun rise in the morning. On a map, if north is at the top, **east** is on the right. We go to school on the **east** side of town. **East** is the opposite of **west.**

Easter

Easter is a Christian holiday that is celebrated on a Sunday either in late March or in early April. Sometimes children paint eggs bright colors for **Easter.**

Look how **easy** it is to find Erin in the picture.

When people go to the **edge** of the railing, they can see how the water falls.

easy
When something is **easy,** it is not hard to do. It is **easy** to see the chalkboard with my new glasses. ▲ **easier, easiest.**

eat
Eat means to put food into your mouth and to chew it and swallow it. The giraffe **ate** leaves from the tree. ▲ **ate, eaten, eating.**

echo
An **echo** is a sound that is repeated. We hear an **echo** when a sound bounces off something hard, like stone or a wall. After Joan shouted "hello" in the cave, she heard the **echo** of her voice. ▲ **echoes.**

edge
An **edge** is the line or place where something ends. The dime rolled off the **edge** of the table. I live near the **edge** of a lake. ▲ **edges.**

egg
An **egg** is the beginning of some kinds of living things. Birds, insects, fish, and frogs are hatched from **eggs.** Some people eat **eggs** from chickens. ▲ **eggs.**

either

We use the word **either** when we talk about two of anything, and we mean one or the other. Rosie wanted **either** a yellow or a white shirt. Tom didn't like **either** jacket.

elbow

The **elbow** is the part of the body where the arm bends. My **elbow** hurt when I bumped it. ▲ **elbows.**

election

When people vote in an **election,** they are choosing someone to do something. In the United States there is an **election** for president every four years. ▲ **elections.**

electricity

Electricity is a kind of energy that can make light and heat. It can also make motors go. A machine that uses **electricity** to work is **electric.** Television sets are **electric.**

This is a family of **elephants.**

elephant

An **elephant** is the biggest and strongest animal that lives on land. It has thick gray skin and a long nose called a trunk.
▲ **elephants.**

elevator

An **elevator** is a small room or cage that goes up and down in a building. Sometimes an **elevator** is on the outside of a building. **Elevators** are used to carry people or things from one floor to another. ▲ **elevators.**

else

1. Else means other or different. What **else** would you like to play instead of baseball?
2. Else also means if not. Eat your breakfast or **else** you will be hungry before lunch.

emergency

Sometimes something important or dangerous happens very fast, and we must act immediately. This is called an **emergency**. Police officers, doctors, and firefighters help people with **emergencies**. ▲ **emergencies**.

empty

When something is **empty,** there is nothing in it. After the puppy ate its food, its dish was **empty. Empty** is the opposite of **full.**

end

1. The **end** is the last part of something. The principal's office is at the **end** of the hall. We left the beach at the **end** of the day. ▲ **ends**.
2. End also means to stop. The teacher **ended** the lesson just before lunch.
▲ **ended, ending.**

We're at the **end** of a long and wonderful parade.

enemy

1. An **enemy** is a person who hates someone else. The cruel ruler had many **enemies.**
2. An **enemy** is also a country that is at war with another country. The two countries that were **enemies** are now friends. ▲ **enemies.**

energy

Energy makes things move and makes machines work. Light, heat, and electricity are kinds of **energy.** When you run and jump, you use your own **energy.**

engine

1. An **engine** is a machine that uses energy to make other machines work. The **engine** of a car makes it move.
2. An **engine** is also the first car of a train that pulls the other cars. An **engineer** drives the **engine** of a train. ▲ **engines.**

English

English is the name of the language that is spoken in the United States and many other countries.

Marta is looking for the right **envelope** for her card.

enjoy

When you **enjoy** something, it makes you feel good. Sam is **enjoying** reading about outer space. When you **enjoy** yourself, it means that you have a good time. Mary and Emily **enjoyed** themselves at the circus.
▲ **enjoyed, enjoying.**

enough

Enough means that there is as much of something as you need. There was **enough** food for everyone at the picnic. I have saved **enough** money for a new bat.

enter

Enter means to go into a place. You **enter** a room through a door. We **entered** the garden through a gate. ▲ **entered, entering.**

envelope

An **envelope** is a folded piece of paper for holding things. People mail letters and cards in **envelopes.** ▲ **envelopes.**

environment

The **environment** is the air, the water, the earth, and all the other things around us.
▲ **environments.**

equal

1. **Equal** means the same. If you have two peaches and two oranges, you have an **equal** number of peaches and oranges.
2. **Equal** also means to be the same as. Six plus four **equals** ten. Another way of writing this is: $6 + 4 = 10$. ▲ **equaled, equaling.**

erase

When you wipe off marks that were made with pencil or chalk, you **erase** them. Guy **erased** everything on the chalkboard.
▲ **erased, erasing.**

George has **equal** amounts of carrots and potatoes for his vegetable soup.

eraser

An **eraser** is something we use to make marks disappear. I need some pencils with **erasers** on them. You can take chalk marks off the chalkboard with an **eraser.** ▲ **erasers.**

escalator

An **escalator** is a set of stairs that move up or down. Tom and his mother took an **escalator** to the third floor of the store. ▲ **escalators.**

escape

Escape means to get away from something. The parrot **escaped** from its cage. People knew that a hurricane was coming and were able to **escape** without getting hurt. ▲ **escaped, escaping.**

When people shop here, they take the **escalator** to get from one floor to another.

even

1. When something is **even,** it is flat or straight. The floor of the room is **even.** Let me see if your skirt is **even** all the way around.
2. Even can also mean the same height. The snow is so high that it is **even** with the top of the car.
3. If a number is **even,** it means that it can be divided into groups of 2. The numbers 2, 4, 6, 8, and 10 are **even** numbers.

evening

Evening is the time of day when it starts to get dark. **Evening** is between afternoon and night. We eat dinner at 6 o'clock in the **evening.** ▲ **evenings.**

ever

Ever means at any time. Did you **ever** fly in an airplane? Yesterday was the first time I **ever** went to the circus.

every

Every means all or each one of a group. **Every** goat was eating grass. **Every** person in our class went on the trip.

everybody

Everybody means all the people in a group. **Everybody** left the building during the fire drill. **Everyone** is another word for **everybody. Everyone** smiled for the class picture.

Everybody wants to answer the question.

everything

Everything means all the things in a group. Bud ate **everything** on his plate.

everywhere

Everywhere means in all places. Betty looked **everywhere** in the house for her shoes.

evil

Something that is **evil** is very, very bad. **Evil** people hurt other people on purpose. The **evil** witch in the story turned the prince into a frog.

excellent

Excellent means very, very good. Jim and Lisette are **excellent** ice skaters. Carol knows how to add and subtract. She is doing **excellent** work in mathematics.

Timothy's grandparents are **excellent** dancers.

except

Except means that something or someone has been left out. Everyone **except** Joe liked the movie. I put everything in my backpack **except** my lunch money and my keys.

excited

When you are **excited,** you are very happy about something. It's hard for you to think about anything else. June was **excited** when she saw her new kitten. Willis was too **excited** about Christmas to go to sleep.

All the geese are white **except** one.

excuse

1. **Excuse** means to allow someone not to do something. The teacher **excused** Jill from the class to see the school nurse. I was **excused** from gym class because I hurt my knee.
2. **Excuse** also means to forgive. Please **excuse** me for leaving early. ▲ **excused, excusing.**
3. An **excuse** tells why someone did or did not do something. Jimmy's cold and sore throat were his **excuse** for not being in school on Monday. ▲ **excuses.**

exercise

1. Exercise is something done to help the body stay healthy and strong. Swimming is good **exercise.** ▲ **exercises.**

2. When people **exercise,** they use their muscles. ▲ **exercised, exercising.**

exit

An **exit** is the way out of a place. The back door of a bus is an **exit.** During the fire drill we learned where all the **exits** in the building are. ▲ **exits.**

At the end of the movie, we left through the **exit.**

expect

Expect means to look forward to something or to think that something will happen. We are **expecting** 50 people to come to the family picnic on Sunday. ▲ **expected, expecting.**

expensive

Expensive means that something costs a lot of money. I bought the blue pen because it was less **expensive** than the red one.

explain

When you **explain** something, you help another person understand it. Rosa **explained** her poem to the class. ▲ **explained, explaining.**

116

explode

Explode means to break open suddenly and with a loud noise. When the fireworks **exploded,** there were bright and beautiful lights in the sky.
▲ **exploded, exploding.**

explore

Explore means to look around a place and discover new things. Nancy and Robert couldn't wait to **explore** their new neighborhood.
▲ **explored, exploring.**

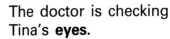
This person is **exploring** life under the water.

explorer

An **explorer** is a person who travels to places that are far away to discover new things. **Explorers** look on land, under water, and in space. The astronauts who went to the moon were **explorers.** ▲ **explorers.**

explosion

When something **explodes,** it is called an **explosion.** An **explosion** of gas broke the windows in our building. ▲ **explosions.**

The doctor is checking Tina's **eyes.**

extra

Extra means more than you need. I keep **extra** batteries for my radio.

eye

An **eye** is the part of the body that you see with. People have two **eyes.** Most animals also have two **eyes.** The baby closed his **eyes** and went to sleep. ▲ **eyes.**

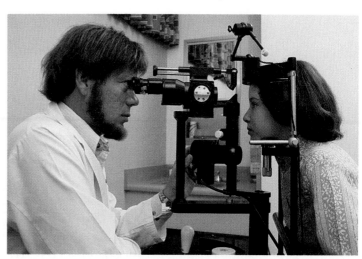

F f

Five Funny Frogs

face

1. The **face** is the front part of your head. Your eyes, nose, and mouth are on your **face**. ▲ **faces**.
2. **Face** also means to turn your **face** toward something. When you **faced** the sun early this morning, you were **facing** east. ▲ **faced, facing**.

fact

A **fact** is something that is true. It is a **fact** that there are 50 states in the United States. ▲ **facts**.

factory

A **factory** is a building or a group of buildings where something is made. Cars are made in **factories**. ▲ **factories**.

fair¹

When you are **fair,** you behave toward each person in the same way. Janice was **fair** when she gave each person an apple. ▲ **fairer, fairest**.

fair²

A **fair** is also a place where people show and sell things they have grown or made. Many **fairs** have games, too. Benito won first prize for his pet pig at the state **fair**. Ida won a toy bear in a game at the **fair**. ▲ **fairs**.

fairy

A **fairy** is a tiny, make-believe person who can make magical things happen. **Fairies** can fly. Donna likes to read stories about **fairies**. A **fairy tale** is a story about magical people and animals and the things that happen to them. ▲ **fairies**.

fall

1. Fall means to come down from a place. Snow was **falling** from the sky.
▲ **fell, fallen, falling.**

2. When something or someone comes down suddenly to the floor or ground, it is called a **fall.** Henry had a bad **fall** from his bicycle.

3. Fall is also a season of the year. Fall comes after summer and before winter. Many people call this season **fall** because it is the time when leaves **fall** from the trees. Another word for **fall** is **autumn.** ▲ **falls.**

false

When something is **false,** it is not true or correct. Do you think it is true or **false** that you live in the United States? The idea that plants do not need light is **false.**
▲ **falser, falsest.**

family

1. A **family** is usually a mother, a father, and their children. Some **families** are made up of children and one of their parents. Grandparents, aunts, uncles, and cousins are also part of a **family.**

2. Animals, plants, or any group of things that are alike in some way may also belong to a **family.**
▲ **families.**

There are three people in our **family.**

famous

When people or things are **famous,** many people know about them. Thomas Edison became **famous** when he invented the electric light. New York City is **famous** for its skyscrapers. The Statue of Liberty is a **famous** statue.

fantasy

Fantasy is anything that is not real. Books about people who live on other planets are **fantasies. Fantasy** is the opposite of **reality**.
▲ **fantasies.**

far

1. When something is **far,** it is not close. We can see the moon, but it is **far** away.
2. We also use the word **far** when we talk about the space between two places. How **far** is your school from your house? Toby lives **farther** away from the store than I do.
▲ **farther, farthest.**

Uncle Mark has a small herd of cows on his **farm.**

farm

A **farm** is a place where people raise animals and plants. Much of the food we eat comes from **farms.** A person who lives and works on a **farm** is called a **farmer.** ▲ **farms.**

farther

Farther comes from the word **far.** Rae's paper airplane flew **farther** than Tommy's did.

fast

Fast means to go quickly. The children could not catch the bunny because it ran **faster** than they did. ▲ **faster, fastest.**

fat

When something is **fat,** it weighs more than it should. Our cat Tubby is the **fattest** cat in the neighborhood. ▲ **fatter, fattest.**

father

A **father** is a man who has one or more children. My **father** made a special dinner for my mother on her birthday. ▲ **fathers.**

faucet

A **faucet** is something you use to turn water on and off. A sink and a bathtub both have **faucets.** ▲ **faucets.**

David is using the outdoor **faucet** to get some water.

fault

When you have done something wrong, it means that it is your **fault.** It was my **fault** that the baseball broke the window because I threw the ball. ▲ **faults.**

favor

1. A **favor** is something kind that you do for someone else. I did Jane a **favor** by taking her books back to the library.
2. A **favor** is also something given to everyone at a party. All the children got balloons as **favors** at Leon's party. ▲ **favors.**

favorite

Favorite means to be liked best. Christopher always wears his **favorite** cap.

Bears are Caroline's **favorite** animal.

fear

1. Fear is a feeling you have when you think danger or pain is near. Marge has a **fear** of very high places. ▲ **fears.**

2. When you are afraid of something, you **fear** it. George **feared** the dog that was barking. ▲ **feared, fearing.**

feast

A **feast** is a large, special meal that is usually made for many guests. The table was piled high with food for the holiday **feast.** ▲ **feasts.**

feather

A **feather** is something that grows from a bird's skin. **Feathers** cover most of a bird's body and keep it warm and dry. Joy's parrot has red and green **feathers.** ▲ **feathers.**

feed

Feed means to give food to an animal or a person. Raul **feeds** his pet rabbit carrots. Jill **fed** her baby brother. A container used for feeding is called a **feeder.** In the winter we put seeds in the **feeder** for the birds. ▲ **fed, feeding.**

The mother bird has a worm to **feed** her babies.

feel

1. Feel means to learn about something because you touch it or it touches you. I can **feel** the rain on my face. I **felt** the kitten's soft fur.

2. Feel also means to know how you are. Do you **feel** sick? Jimmy is **feeling** happy today because he is going to the circus.
▲ **felt, feeling.**

3. Feel also means the way that something seems when you touch it. Jan likes the **feel** of cotton.

feeling

A **feeling** is a way of knowing how you are. **Feelings** tell you when you are afraid, happy, excited, sad, tired, or angry. Sometimes my **feelings** get hurt when someone yells at me.
▲ **feelings.**

Snowball's fur **feels** soft.

feet

Feet means more than one **foot.** You have two **feet,** and an elephant has four **feet.**

fell

Fell comes from the word **fall.** A branch **fell** from the tree. The streets are very wet because a lot of rain **fell** last night.

felt

Felt comes from the word **feel.** Vincent **felt** tired after running so far.

female

A **female** is a girl or a woman. Mothers and aunts are **females.** An animal may be a **female,** too.
Our cat Matilda is a **female.**
▲ **females.**

Gwen **fell** down while she was roller-skating.

123

fence

A **fence** is built around something to keep things out or in. This **fence** keeps rabbits out of our vegetable garden. There is a **fence** around our backyard to keep the dog from getting out. ▲ **fences.**

fern

A **fern** is a plant with many thin leaves and no flowers. There are **ferns** growing in the forest. ▲ **ferns.**

This **ferry** takes many people across the river.

ferry

A **ferry** is a boat that carries people and cars across water. We took a **ferry** to the island. ▲ **ferries.**

festival

A **festival** is a special time to celebrate. Most **festivals** take place once a year and may last for one or more days. **Festivals** often have feasts, dances, and parades. ▲ **festivals.**

fever

When you have a **fever,** your temperature is high and your body feels hot. If you have a **fever,** you are sick. ▲ **fevers.**

few

Few means not many of something. I have a **few** pages left to read. We went on a trip for a **few** days.
▲ **fewer, fewest.**

fiction

Fiction means stories that are written about people and things that are not real. The characters in **fiction** are make-believe and imagined by an author.

field

1. A **field** is an area of land that has no trees. It is used for growing grass or food. We planted corn in this **field.**
2. A **field** is also an area of land where some games are played. Football is played on a football **field.** ▲ **fields.**

fierce

When something is **fierce,** it is wild and dangerous. A hungry lion is **fierce.** This storm is the **fiercest** storm I've ever seen. ▲ **fiercer, fiercest.**

fight

1. When people **fight,** they are angry at each other. People who **fight** yell at each other and sometimes hit one another. Cathy was punished when she **fought** with other children at school.
▲ **fought, fighting.**
2. When people are angry and yell at each other, we call that a **fight.** I had a **fight** with my sister today. ▲ **fights.**

There are only a **few** pieces of chicken left on the plate.

The scarecrow is standing in a **field** of lettuce.

125

The man is **filling** the balloons.

fill

Fill means to make something full. Bobby **filled** his pail with sand. ▲ **filled, filling.**

fin

A **fin** is one of the thin, flat parts of a fish. A fish has **fins** on both sides of its body. It uses its **fins** to swim and balance itself in water. ▲ **fins.**

finally

Finally means at the end. After riding for 3 hours in a bus, we **finally** reached our camp in the mountains.

find

Find means to see or discover something. Sometimes people **find** things that they have lost. Other times they **find** things that they have not seen before. Jean couldn't **find** the dime she dropped. Jerry likes **finding** good books in the library. ▲ **found, finding.**

fine

1. When something is **fine,** it means it is good. This is a **fine** day for playing baseball. 2. **Fine** also means very well. Dot felt sick yesterday, but today she feels **fine.** ▲ **finer, finest.**

finger

A **finger** is a part of your hand. You have five **fingers** on each hand. One of these **fingers** is your thumb. A **fingernail** is the hard part on the end of each **finger.** ▲ **fingers.**

We **find** some of our best shells on this beach.

finish

Finish means to get to the end of something. I am almost **finished** with the letter I am writing. ▲ **finished, finishing.**

fire

A **fire** is the flame, heat, and light made by something that is burning. A **fire** burned down the old factory. ▲ **fires.**

fire engine

A **fire engine** is a truck that carries a ladder and other things to help firefighters put out a fire. Firefighters ride to fires in **fire engines.** ▲ **fire engines.**

firefighter

A **firefighter** is a person whose job it is to put out fires. **Firefighters** help people escape from burning buildings. They use very long ladders to put out fires in tall buildings. ▲ **firefighters.**

Two **fire engines** were sent to this fire.

firefly

A **firefly** is a small bug that gives off light. At night, **fireflies** look like very tiny lights going on and off. ▲ **fireflies.**

fireplace

A **fireplace** is an open place that is used for building fires indoors. A **fireplace** has a chimney to carry away the smoke. When we come home from skiing, my family and I like to build a fire in the **fireplace** to make ourselves warm. ▲ **fireplaces.**

The **fireworks** are lighting up the sky.

fireworks

Fireworks make loud noises and bright shows of light. **Fireworks** are used at special times. Our town exploded **fireworks** at night to celebrate the Fourth of July.

first

When something is **first,** it comes before everything else. John finished **first** in the race. **A** is the **first** letter of the alphabet.

first aid

Sometimes a person has an accident or gets sick suddenly. **First aid** is the help we give this person before the doctor comes.

fish

1. A **fish** is an animal that lives in the water. ▲ **fish** or **fishes.**
2. **Fish** also means to catch **fish.** The children like to **fish** close to shore. People who **fish** are called **fishermen.** Some **fishermen** catch **fish** and then sell them. ▲ **fished, fishing.**

fist

When you close your hand into a tight ball, you make a **fist.** The doctor asked if Loren could make a **fist** with her sore hand. ▲ **fists.**

fit

Fit means to be the right size. When something **fits,** it is not too big or too small. Mike's jacket **fits** his older brother, too. Six people can **fit** into our new car.
▲ **fitted, fitting.**

fix

Fix means to make something work again. Carol **fixed** her sister's wagon when the wheel fell off. Now that Dad has **fixed** my radio, I can listen to music again.
▲ **fixed, fixing.**

flag

A **flag** is a piece of cloth with different colors on it. Some **flags** have pictures on them. Every country has its own **flag.** The **flag** of the United States is red, white, and blue. **Flags** fly on poles called **flagpoles.** ▲ **flags.**

flame

A **flame** is the light you see in a fire. The **flame** of a candle is very small. ▲ **flames.**

flashlight

A **flashlight** is a light that is small enough to carry in your hand. We keep a **flashlight** in our room to use if the lights in our house go out.
▲ **flashlights.**

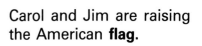

Carol and Jim are raising the American **flag.**

Jeff used his **flashlight** to see what was making the noise.

129

The top of the table is **flat.**

flat
If something is **flat,** it has no bumps or holes. Walls and floors are **flat.**
▲ **flatter, flattest.**

flavor
The **flavor** of something is the way it tastes. Karen squeezed lemon juice on her fish to give it more **flavor.** ▲ **flavors.**

flew
Flew comes from the word **fly.** The birds **flew** away from the barking dog.

float
1. **Float** means to stay on top of the water. Ray has a toy boat that **floats.**
2. **Float** also means to move slowly in the air. The baby let the balloon go, and it **floated** high above the house.
▲ **floated, floating.**

flood
1. A **flood** is what happens when an area of dry land is covered with water. **Floods** often happen in the spring when the snow melts and there is a lot of rain. ▲ **floods.**
2. **Flood** means to cover with water. Last spring it rained so much that the river **flooded** the whole town. ▲ **flooded, flooding.**

floor
1. A **floor** is the part of a room that you walk on or stand on. There is a blue rug on the **floor** of our bedroom.
2. A **floor** is also a part of a building. Tall buildings have many **floors.** Mom's office is on the second **floor.** ▲ **floors.**

Richard likes to **float** on his raft.

flour

Flour comes from wheat. **Flour** is used to bake foods like bread and cake. We bought milk, eggs, margarine, and **flour** at the supermarket.

flower

A **flower** is the part of a plant that makes seeds. **Flowers** grow in many different colors. Most **flowers** bloom when the weather is warm. Some **flowers** are nice to smell. ▲ **flowers.**

flown

Flown comes from the word **fly.** The parrot has **flown** out of its cage. I've never **flown** in a plane before.

flu

When someone has the **flu,** that person has a fever and feels sick. When Charlie had the **flu,** his head and stomach hurt, and he ached all over. ▲ **flus.**

fly¹

A **fly** is an insect with two very thin wings. The fly we often see is called a **housefly.** ▲ **flies.**

fly²

1. Fly means to move through the air with wings. Ben **flew** in an airplane to visit his grandmother. Butterflies were **flying** around the flowers.

2. Fly also means to float in the air. We like to **fly** our kites in the park on a windy day. ▲ **flew, flown, flying.**

These **flowers** grow very tall.

Brian and Rosalie know how to **fold** paper into animal shapes.

fog

Fog is a cloud that is close to the ground. We couldn't see the road because of the **fog**. ▲ **fogs.**

fold

Fold means to bend. Rico showed me how to **fold** my tent and put it into a bag. Judy and Robert **folded** the blanket and put it in the closet. ▲ **folded, folding.**

follow

Follow means to go or come after something or someone. Spring **follows** winter. The baby bears **followed** their mother into the forest. ▲ **followed, following.**

The campers are **following** the leader because she knows which trail to take.

food

Food is what we eat. Everything that lives needs **food** to grow and to stay alive. Bread, milk, and vegetables are important **foods.** ▲ **foods.**

foot

A **foot** is the part of the body at the end of a leg. Alec wears special shoes on his **feet** to play soccer. ▲ **feet.**

That's our team in red carrying the **football.**

football

1. **Football** is a game played by two teams on a large field. Each team has 11 players. The players on one team throw the ball and run with it toward the other team's goal. The other team tries to stop them.
2. **Football** is also the name of the ball used in this game. ▲ **footballs.**

footprint

A **footprint** is a mark made by a foot or shoe. The children made **footprints** on the floor with their dirty boots. Did you see the **footprints** the deer left in the snow? ▲ **footprints.**

for

We went **for** a ride in the car. This box is **for** toys. Sarah got a puppy **for** her birthday.

133

Outside the **forest** the sun is shining, but inside the **forest** it's much darker.

forest

A **forest** is a large area of land covered by trees and other plants. Wild animals live in **forests**. ▲ **forests.**

forever

Forever means that something will never end. The boy and girl in the fairy tale wanted to stay young **forever.**

forgave

Forgave comes from the word **forgive.** Larry **forgave** his brother for taking his bike without asking.

forget

Forget means to not remember something. Josie was afraid she would **forget** my address, so she wrote it down.
▲ **forgot, forgotten, forgetting.**

forgive

Forgive means to stop being angry at someone. Annie's brother Frank tore her sweater and asked her to **forgive** him. Annie **forgave** her brother.
▲ **forgave, forgiven, forgiving.**

forgot

Forgot comes from the word **forget**. Tim's hands got cold because he **forgot** his mittens. The word **forgotten** also comes from the word **forget**. Suzanne ran back to the store because she had **forgotten** to buy some milk.

fork

A **fork** is a tool that we use for eating food. **Forks** have a handle at one end and two or more points at the other end. I eat meat and vegetables with a **fork.** ▲ **forks.**

forward

Forward means toward what is ahead. Bill stepped **forward** to get his prize. Mary and Pete are looking **forward** to seeing zebras at the zoo.

fossil

A **fossil** is what is left of an animal or plant that lived a long time ago. **Fossils** are found in rocks, earth, or clay. The bones and footprints of dinosaurs are **fossils.** ▲ **fossils.**

fought

Fought comes from the word **fight.** Dad said I should not have **fought** with my sister.

found

Found comes from the word **find.** Luke **found** a dime on the sidewalk.

Lucas **forgot** his umbrella, but Grace is sharing hers.

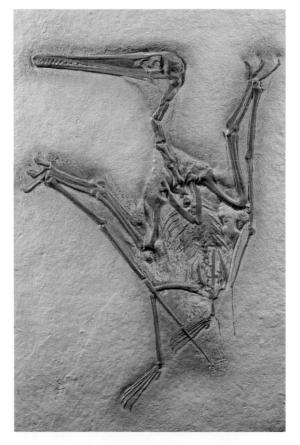

This **fossil** shows a flying reptile that lived millions of years ago.

Alexander was hot and thirsty and was happy to find this **fountain.**

fountain

A **fountain** is a stream of water that shoots up into the air. Some **fountains** are pretty to look at. Other **fountains** are used for drinking. ▲ **fountains.**

Fourth of July

The **Fourth of July** is an American holiday that celebrates the birthday of the United States. It is also called **Independence Day.**

fox

A **fox** is a wild animal. Most **foxes** look like small, thin dogs, but they have thick fur and a big tail. They also have large ears that are pointed and a long nose. ▲ **foxes.**

free

1. **Free** means that a person does not have to pay any money for something. The magic show in the park is **free.** There is a **free** toy in every box of that cereal.
2. **Free** also means not held back or kept in. The cat was **free** to walk around.
▲ **freer, freest.**

freeze

Freeze means to become solid when it is very cold. When water **freezes,** it changes into ice. We skated on the pond after it **froze.**
▲ **froze, frozen, freezing.**

fresh

1. When something is **fresh,** it has just been made, done, or gathered. We ate **fresh** tomatoes from June's garden. Our supermarket sells **fresh** fish. This bread was baked this morning and is very **fresh.**
2. **Fresh** also means not having salt. Water in rivers, lakes, and ponds is **fresh** water. Water in the ocean is salt water. ▲ **fresher, freshest.**

friend

A **friend** is someone you like very much and enjoy being with. Karen and Nancy are good **friends** and often play together. I made **friends** with my new neighbors. ▲ **friends.**

friendly

When people or animals are **friendly,** they are nice to you. When I went traveling, I met **friendly** people in every place. Jordan's dog is **friendlier** than mine. ▲ **friendlier, friendliest.**

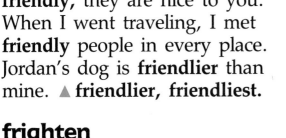

Heather's dog is **friendly.**

frighten

Frighten means to make a person or an animal afraid. I hope my Halloween costume will **frighten** the other children. The cat **frightened** the birds away. ▲ **frightened, frightening.**

frog

A **frog** is a small animal that lives in or near the water. **Frogs** have strong legs that they use to hop from place to place. The **frog** hopped into the water. ▲ **frogs.**

from

1. From means where something started or when it began. Our family moved **from** the city to the country. Freda is in school **from** 8 o'clock until 3 o'clock.
2. From also means having a person, place, or thing as a beginning. I got a letter **from** my friend at camp.
3. From also means a distance away. Denise's school is 2 miles **from** her house.

This **frog** lives in trees.

front

The **front** is the part that faces forward or comes first. Your chest is on the **front** of your body. There is an apple tree in **front** of Toby's house. ▲ **fronts.**

frown

1. **Frown** means to turn down the corners of your mouth. People **frown** when they are angry or when they are thinking hard. Bud **frowned** when his crayon broke.
▲ **frowned, frowning.**
2. When you are angry or thinking hard, you may have a **frown** on your face. ▲ **frowns.**

froze

Froze comes from the word **freeze.** The pond **froze** last night, and we were able to skate on it today. The word **frozen** also comes from the word **freeze.** The cold weather has **frozen** the pipes in our house.

fruit

A **fruit** is a part of a plant that holds the seeds. Apples, peaches, and oranges are kinds of **fruit.** We cut up **fruit** and made a salad. ▲ **fruit** or **fruits.**

full

When something is **full,** it holds as much as it can. Nothing else can be put into something that is **full.** The bus was so **full** that no one else could get on. We also say that the moon is **full** when we can see all of its round shape. ▲ **fuller, fullest.**

fun

When you are having **fun,** it means that you are having a good time. When you laugh and play, you are having **fun.** Louisa thought it was **fun** to ride on her sled.

You can find many kinds of **fruit** at this market.

Philip has **fun** playing in the water with Sparky.

138

funeral

A **funeral** is a time when people get together after someone dies. **Funerals** give people a chance to show how sad they feel and to share their feelings with friends and family. ▲ **funerals.**

funny

When something is **funny,** it makes you laugh. Carla read a **funny** story to me. ▲ **funnier, funniest.**

fur

Fur is the hair that covers an animal's body. In the winter, the **fur** of most animals grows thicker. Our dog's **fur** is white and black. ▲ **furs.**

furnace

A **furnace** is like a big stove. **Furnaces** are used to heat houses and buildings. Our **furnace** keeps us warm in the winter. ▲ **furnaces.**

furniture

Tables and chairs and beds are different kinds of **furniture.** When we moved, all of our **furniture** was put into a truck.

future

1. **Future** means the time that is to come. At the fair we saw a model of the car of the **future.**
2. **Future** also means happening in the time that is to come. My **future** plan is to become a writer.

Lori is putting **furniture** in her house.

Gg

Geese with Glasses

gallop
Gallop means to run fast. When horses run as fast as they can, they are **galloping**. ▲ **galloped, galloping.**

game
A **game** is something you play. Each **game** has its own rules. Baseball, checkers, chess, and tag are all **games.** ▲ **games.**

garage
A **garage** is a building where cars are kept. Some people also use a **garage** to store things like bicycles and tools. ▲ **garages.**

garbage
Food and other things that are thrown away are called **garbage.** After the picnic, we put our **garbage** in the **garbage can.**

garden
A **garden** is a place where people grow flowers or vegetables. When our cousins visit, they always bring us fresh tomatoes from their **garden.** ▲ **gardens.**

gas
1. A **gas** is something that weighs very little. The air is made of many kinds of **gases.** Usually you cannot see a **gas,** but sometimes you can smell it. One kind of **gas** is used in stoves and furnaces. This kind of **gas** is burned to cook food and to keep houses warm.
2. **Gas** is also a liquid that is put into cars and trucks to make them run. This kind of **gas** is called **gasoline.** ▲ **gases.**

gate

A **gate** is a door in a fence or wall. Josh closed the **gate** to keep the dog from running out of the yard. ▲ **gates.**

Each of us **gathered** wood to make a fire at camp.

gather

Gather means to bring together. The children **gathered** their books and left for school. We all **gathered** in the park to watch fireworks. ▲ **gathered, gathering.**

gave

Gave comes from the word **give.** Marina **gave** her grandfather a big hug. Mother **gave** Willis vegetable soup and a peanut butter sandwich for lunch.

geese

Geese means more than one **goose.** There is a family of **geese** in the pond.

Miranda is **gentle** when she touches Enrique.

It's time to **get** down from the tree.

genius

A **genius** is a person who has a great mind and can think in a very special way. That scientist was a **genius**. ▲ **geniuses.**

gentle

When you are **gentle,** you are very careful not to hurt someone or something. When you do something in a **gentle** way, you do it **gently.** Trisha put the eggs down **gently** on the counter.

geography

When you study **geography,** you learn about different parts of the earth. **Geography** tells you where places are and what they are like. People called **geographers** create maps to show some of this information.

germ

A **germ** is a very tiny living thing that can make you sick. **Germs** are so small that you cannot see them without a microscope. I cover my mouth and nose when I sneeze so I won't get **germs** on anyone. ▲ **germs.**

get

1. **Get** means to have something new or to earn something. Gerry hopes to **get** a watch for his birthday. Ana **got** a dollar for feeding her neighbor's dog.
2. When you arrive somewhere, you **get** there. When did you **get** home? I **got** home at 4 o'clock. ▲ **got, getting.**

ghost

A **ghost** is a kind of make-believe person. Some people believe that a dead person may come back as a **ghost**. The children dressed up as **ghosts** for Halloween. ▲ **ghosts.**

giant

1. A **giant** is a huge make-believe person. The **giant** in the story could hold three people in one hand. ▲ **giants.**

2. Giant also means very big. Many of the dinosaurs that lived millions of years ago were **giant** animals. We saw a **giant** rocket when we visited the space museum.

gift

A **gift** is something special that one person gives to another person. These books were birthday **gifts** from my cousins. Another word for **gift** is **present.** ▲ **gifts.**

giggle

1. When people **giggle**, they laugh in a silly way. We **giggled** when my little brother put his socks on his ears. ▲ **giggled, giggling.**

2. Giggle also means a short, silly laugh. When the clown slipped and fell, there were lots of **giggles** from the children in the audience. ▲ **giggles.**

giraffe

A **giraffe** is the tallest animal on earth. It has a very long neck and long, thin legs. **Giraffes** eat leaves from the tops of trees and other plants. ▲ **giraffes.**

girl

A **girl** is a child who will grow up to be a woman. **Girls** are female children, and boys are male children. ▲ **girls.**

Some **giraffes** grow to be 19 feet tall.

give

Give means to let someone have something to keep. When her clothes get too small, Suzy **gives** them to her little sister. Our class **gave** toys to poor children at Christmas. ▲ **gave, giving.**

glad

When you feel **glad,** it means you are happy. We are **glad** that Grandma and Grandpa are coming to visit. I'm **glad** you are feeling better today. ▲ **gladder, gladdest.**

glass

1. **Glass** is a hard material that you can see through. Windows are made of **glass. Glass** is easy to break if you are not careful.
2. A **glass** is a container that is used for drinking. It is usually made of **glass** or plastic. The baby is learning to drink from a **glass.** There are six **glasses** and six plates on the table.
3. Some people wear **glasses** in front of their eyes to help them see better. Dad wears his **glasses** to read the newspaper. ▲ **glasses.**

It is Laura and Keisha's turn to feed the hamsters and clean the **glass** cage.

globe

A **globe** is a ball with a map of the world on it. For our geography lesson we studied where the United States and other countries are on the **globe.** ▲ **globes.**

Our teacher is showing us Africa on the **globe.**

glove

A **glove** is a piece of clothing to wear on your hand. **Gloves** cover each finger and protect your hands or keep them warm. These wool **gloves** will keep your hands from getting cold. A baseball **glove** is very thick and protects your hand when you catch a ball. ▲ **gloves.**

glue

1. Glue is a liquid that is used to make things stick together. Uncle Leroy fixed the crack in the sink with a special kind of **glue.** ▲ **glues.**

2. Glue also means to stick things together with **glue.** Mike **glued** the broken toy back together. ▲ **glued, gluing.**

go

1. Go means to move from one place to another. We **go** to the supermarket every Thursday. Marta **went** to the library.
2. Go also means to take a turn. You can **go** first in the game this time.
3. Go is also used to mean that something will happen. I am **going** to be a doctor when I grow up. ▲ **went, gone, going.**

goal

1. A **goal** is something that a person wants to have or tries to become. Juan's **goal** is to own a store. My **goal** is to be an actor.
2. A **goal** is a place in some games where the players try to put the ball. ▲ **goals.**

This **goat** likes to climb rocks in the mountains where it lives.

goat

A **goat** is an animal. Most **goats** have horns, and many **goats** have beards. Some **goats** are raised on farms for their milk. Others are wild animals and live in the mountains. ▲ **goats.**

goggles

Goggles are a kind of glasses that are worn over the eyes to protect them. Some people wear **goggles** at work to protect their eyes from dust and flying dirt. Some people wear **goggles** under the water to look at the fish and the rocks.

gold

1. Gold is a yellow metal that is found in the ground or in streams. People make jewelry and coins from **gold.**
2. Gold is also the color of the metal. In fall, the leaves turn red and **gold.**

goldfish

Goldfish are orange or gold fish. Small **goldfish** are sometimes kept in an aquarium at home. Some **goldfish** grow to be big and live outdoors in lakes and ponds.

gone

Gone comes from the word **go.** Marvin got to the playground so late that all his friends had already **gone** home.

good

When something is **good,** it pleases you or other people. This peach tastes **good.** Josie is reading a **good** book about whales. My dog is **good** and doesn't jump on the furniture.
▲ **better, best.**

good-bye

Good-bye is what you say when you are going away. After school, I said **good-bye** to my teacher.

Kathy wears **goggles** when she uses electric tools.

Art and Naomi are waving **good-bye** to their cousin.

goose

A **goose** is a bird that can fly and swim. A **goose** is like a duck, but is much larger. ▲ **geese.**

gorilla

A **gorilla** is a large, very strong animal. It is a kind of ape with short legs and long arms. **Gorillas** are shy animals that eat fruits and vegetables. ▲ **gorillas.**

Gorillas live on the ground, not in trees as some other apes do.

got

Got comes from the word **get.** The band **got** a new drummer. My mother **got** home from work at 6 o'clock.

government

The **government** is a group of people who rule a country, state, or city. The **government** makes laws and makes sure that everyone obeys the laws. In the United States, the leader of the **government** is called the president. ▲ **governments.**

grab

Grab means to take hold of suddenly. The baby **grabbed** my hair. ▲ **grabbed, grabbing.**

grade

1. A **grade** is a year of work in school. Most children in the same **grade** are almost the same age. What **grade** are you in?
2. A **grade** is also a number or letter that shows how well a person does in school. Selma got a **grade** of 90 on her test. ▲ **grades.**

grandchild

You are the **grandchild** of your grandparents. A **grandchild** is either a **granddaughter** or **grandson.** ▲ **grandchildren.**

grandfather

Your **grandfather** is your father's father or your mother's father. Sometimes a **grandfather** is called **grandpa.** ▲ **grandfathers.**

grandmother

Your **grandmother** is your father's mother or your mother's mother. Sometimes a **grandmother** is called **grandma** or **nana.** ▲ **grandmothers.**

grandparent

Your **grandparents** are the parents of your mother and the parents of your father. Your **grandfather** and **grandmother** are your **grandparents.** ▲ **grandparents.**

Shirley **grabbed** Tracy's arms to keep her from falling down.

Steve and Ann are helping their **grandparents** pick fresh tomatoes.

Angie and her dad are sharing a **grapefruit** for breakfast.

grape

A **grape** is a small green or purple fruit. **Grapes** grow in bunches. ▲ **grapes.**

grapefruit

A **grapefruit** is a round, yellow fruit. It is larger than an orange. Some **grapefruits** are pink inside. ▲ **grapefruits** or **grapefruit.**

grass

Grass is a green plant that grows in lawns and fields. Many animals eat **grass.**
▲ **grasses.**

grasshopper

A **grasshopper** is an insect. A **grasshopper** has long back legs that it uses for jumping. **Grasshoppers** also have wings, but most cannot fly. ▲ **grasshoppers.**

The **grasshopper** is resting on the stem of a plant.

gray

Gray is the color we get when we mix black and white. Some people have **gray** eyes or **gray** hair. Storm clouds are usually **gray.**

great

1. **Great** means large or a lot. A **great** number of people voted in the election.
2. **Great** also means excellent or very important. My sister wants to be a **great** singer when she grows up.

green

Green is the color of growing grass and of leaves in the spring and summer. **Green** vegetables are good to eat. You can make the color **green** by mixing blue and yellow together. Pine trees stay **green** all year long.

greenhouse

A **greenhouse** is a kind of building used for growing plants. A **greenhouse** has walls and a roof that are glass or plastic. It lets in light and heat from the sun. ▲ **greenhouses.**

Flowers and plants can grow in a **greenhouse** all year long.

grew

Grew comes from the word **grow.** The small plant **grew** quickly after I put it in the sun.

grocery

1. A **grocery** is a store that sells food and other things. We bought eggs, milk, bread, and soap at the **grocery** store.
2. **Groceries** are the foods and other things that can be bought in a **grocery** store. We bought three bags of **groceries** on Saturday morning. ▲ **groceries.**

ground

The **ground** is what we stand on when we are outdoors. In many places snow covers the **ground** in winter and grass covers it in summer. ▲ **grounds.**

group

A **group** is three or more people or things that are together. A **group** of children played ball at the park on Saturday. ▲ **groups.**

grow

1. Grow means to get larger. Helen watered her tomato plants to help them **grow**. Jackson has **grown** 2 inches since last year.
2. Grow also means to live. Cactuses **grow** in the desert. ▲ **grew, growing.**

growl

Growl means to make a deep, angry sound in the throat. The dogs **growled** when someone knocked on the door.
▲ **growled, growling.**

grown

Grown comes from the word **grow.** The grapefruit seed has **grown** into a big plant.

Look how much Paul has **grown** this year.

grown-up

A **grown-up** is a person who has finished growing. Your parents are **grown-ups**. Another word for **grown-up** is **adult**.
▲ **grown-ups.**

guard

1. Guard means to keep safe from danger or to watch something closely. Our dog **guards** the house when we go away on vacation.
▲ **guarded, guarding.**
2. A **guard** is also a person who **guards** someone or something. The museum **guard** told us not to touch the paintings. ▲ **guards.**

guess

Guess means to try to think of an answer. When people **guess,** they are not sure that their answer is correct. Ellen tried to **guess** who was behind her. ▲ **guessed, guessing.**

guest

A **guest** is someone who comes to visit. Mom's friend, Ms. Long, stayed for dinner yesterday. Ms. Long was our **guest.** ▲ **guests.**

guitar

A **guitar** is a musical instrument with six or more strings. A person plays the **guitar** by hitting or pulling the strings. ▲ **guitars.**

gun

A **gun** is a weapon that is used to shoot something. ▲ **guns.**

gym

A **gym** is a big room or a building where people play games or do exercises. We play basketball in the **gym.** ▲ **gyms.**

Mrs. Solerno is our school crossing **guard**.

Shelly is practicing her **guitar** to get ready for the concert next week.

Hh

Hippo Hiding

habit

A **habit** is something that we do so often that we do it without thinking. Some **habits** are good, and some are bad. Brushing your teeth twice a day is a good **habit.** It is a bad **habit** not to clean up after yourself. ▲ **habits.**

habitat

A **habitat** is the place where an animal or plant lives and grows. The desert is the **habitat** of the camel. ▲ **habitats.**

had

Had comes from the word **have.** We use **had** when we talk about something that has already happened or that already belongs to you. Linda **had** an exercise class yesterday. Bob **had** a blue backpack.

hair

Hair is what grows on your head. You also have tiny **hairs** on your arms and legs. Marc is having his **hair** cut for the first time. ▲ **hairs.**

half

When you divide something into two pieces of the same size, each part is called **half.** Mom ate **half** a grapefruit. Dad sawed the board in **half** to make a bench. ▲ **halves.**

hall

A **hall** is like a long, narrow room. It may have other rooms on each side of it or at its ends. We lined up in the **hall** before we went into the gym. Jake walked down the **hall** to Room 23. ▲ **halls.**

Halloween

Halloween is a holiday that is celebrated on October 31. Children dress up in costumes and masks and often collect treats and have parties.

halves

Halves is the plural of **half.** Julie will eat both **halves** of the potato. A basketball game is divided into two **halves.**

hamburger

A **hamburger** is made from tiny pieces of meat put together in a round, flat shape. **Hamburgers** are cooked before they are eaten. Milton likes a **hamburger** on a roll with lettuce and tomato. ▲ **hamburgers.**

hammer

1. A **hammer** is a tool that is used for hitting nails. It has a heavy piece of metal at the top of a long handle. A **hammer** is also used to pull nails out of things. Please put the **hammer** back in the tool chest when you are finished with it. ▲ **hammers.**

2. Hammer also means to hit something with a **hammer.** The carpenter put two boards together and **hammered** a nail into each corner.

▲ **hammered, hammering.**

It's Jack's turn again to **hammer** nails into the house for the birds.

hamster

A **hamster** is an animal that looks like a mouse. **Hamsters** have fat bodies and short tails. They are often kept as pets. We keep our **hamster** in a cage. ▲ **hamsters.**

Henry is learning to use his **hands** so that he can "talk" to people who cannot hear.

hand

1. Your **hand** is the part of your arm from the wrist down. We use our **hands** to pick up things and hold them.
2. A **hand** is also an arrow that points to a number on a clock, meter, or dial. The **hands** of the clock pointed to 1 o'clock. ▲ **hands.**
3. When you **hand** something to someone, you give it to that person. Please **hand** me the margarine. ▲ **handed, handing.**

handle

A **handle** is the part of something that you hold when you lift that thing. Steven picked up the suitcase by the **handle.** ▲ **handles.**

hang

Hang means to be attached from above. Martin **hung** his new calendar on the wall. ▲ **hung, hanging.**

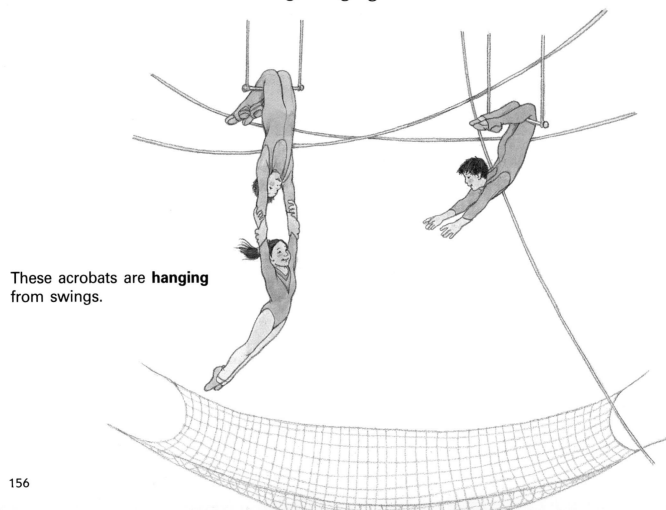

These acrobats are **hanging** from swings.

hanger

You hang clothes on a **hanger**. **Hangers** are often made of plastic or wood. There are a few empty **hangers** in my closet. ▲ **hangers**.

Hanukkah

Hanukkah is a Jewish holiday celebrated in December. It lasts for eight days. People light a candle each night of **Hanukkah** until all the candles are lit. **Hanukkah** is sometimes spelled **Chanukah**.

happen

Happen means to take place. If you listen to the story, you will hear what **happens** next. What **happened** in school today? ▲ **happened, happening**.

happy

When you are **happy**, you feel good about something. Our team was **happy** because we won the game. I will be **happy** to play with you today. ▲ **happier, happiest**.

harbor

A **harbor** is a safe place for boats near the shore. **Harbors** are on lakes, rivers, or oceans. We watched the fishing boats come into the **harbor**. ▲ **harbors**.

The **harbor** is filled with many sailboats.

hard

1. **Hard** means not soft. Rocks are **hard** and pillows are soft.
2. When something is **hard**, it needs a lot of work. This puzzle is very **hard** to do.
▲ **harder, hardest**.

157

harvest

1. The time of the year when corn, wheat, fruits, and other plants are picked and gathered is called **harvest.** Many people work during the **harvest.** ▲ **harvests.**

2. Harvest means to pick and gather corn, wheat, fruits, and other plants. The farmers used special machines to **harvest** the corn. ▲ **harvested, harvesting.**

has

Has comes from the word **have.** Betty **has** a new book. A tiger **has** sharp teeth.

hat

A **hat** is a piece of clothing that you wear on your head. A cap is one kind of **hat.** ▲ **hats.**

The baby turtles are **hatching** from their shells.

hatch

Hatch means to come from an egg. When a chicken is born, we say that it **hatches.** ▲ **hatched, hatching.**

hate

Hate means to have very strong feelings against someone or something. Barry **hates** scary movies. ▲ **hated, hating.**

have

When you **have** something, you own it or you feel it. David and Danny **have** new toy trucks. Molly and her friends **had** a good time at the party.
▲ **had, having.**

hay

Hay is made from grass or other plants. The plants are cut and dried as food for animals. Cows and horses eat **hay.**

The boys are **having** fun writing stories.

he

1. He is a word for a boy or a man or a male animal. Thomas said that **he** wants to go for a ride.
2. He'd means "he had" or "he would." **He'd** never been to the circus before. **He'd** do it if **he** could.
3. He'll means "he will." Jim says that **he'll** come to the picnic.
4. He's means "he is" or "he has." Bobby lives near me. **He's** my neighbor. **He's** been my friend for two months.

head

1. The **head** is the part of the body above the neck. Eyes, ears, nose, and mouth are all parts of the **head.** The brain is inside the **head.** Carolyn is a **head** taller than Billy Joe.
2. Head also means the front part of something. Migdalia is at the **head** of the line. ▲ **heads.**

heal

Heal means to become well again. When a cut or a broken bone gets better, it **heals.** The cut on my arm **healed** quickly.
▲ **healed, healing.**

Linda is good at standing on her **head.**

Elsie thinks you can **hear** the ocean when you listen to some shells.

healthy

When a person feels good and is not sick, that person is **healthy. Healthy** people eat good foods and get the right amount of exercise. ▲ **healthier, healthiest.**

hear

When you **hear,** sounds come through your ears. We **heard** thunder before it started to rain. ▲ **heard, hearing.**

hearing aid

A **hearing aid** is something worn in the ear to help someone hear better. I think my **hearing aid** needs a new battery. ▲ **hearing aids.**

heart

1. The **heart** is a part of the body. It is in the chest and sends blood to all parts of the body.
2. A **heart** is also a shape that looks like this: ♥. **Hearts** are often red, and sometimes they mean "I love you." ▲ **hearts.**

heat

1. **Heat** means being warm or hot. The **heat** in an oven will bake bread.
2. When you **heat** something, it becomes warm or hot. We lit the fire to **heat** the room. Jill **heated** the milk before giving it to the baby. ▲ **heated, heating.**

heavy

1. When something is **heavy,** it is hard to lift. The bag of groceries was too **heavy** for Derek to lift. This large suitcase is **heavier** than that small one.
2. **Heavy** also means thick. The children used **heavy** paper to make covers for their books. ▲ **heavier, heaviest.**

heel

1. The **heel** is the back part of a foot.
2. A shoe also has a **heel.** It is on the bottom of the shoe under your own **heel.** ▲ **heels.**

height

Height is how far something is from the ground. Tab's **height** is 3 feet. ▲ **heights.**

held

Held comes from the word **hold.** Dad **held** the twins until they were asleep.

helicopter

A **helicopter** is a machine that can fly in the air. **Helicopters** can fly straight up and down and land in very small spaces. ▲ **helicopters.**

hello

We say **hello** when we see someone we know or when we answer the telephone.

Pedro is telling Mr. Todd that he needs new **heels** on his shoes.

These people are training with the **helicopter** so they'll be ready for an emergency.

helmet

A **helmet** is a hard hat that is worn to protect the head. Soldiers, astronauts, and football players wear **helmets.** ▲ **helmets.**

Each rider in the race must wear a **helmet.**

help

Help means to do something for someone else. We **helped** Dad clean the garage. A person or thing that does something for someone else is called a **helper.** My teacher asked for a **helper** to hold the cups while she poured the juice. ▲ **helped, helping.**

hen

A **hen** is a female chicken. A **hen** can lay eggs. ▲ **hens.**

her

Her is a word for a girl or a woman. Mae's friend came to visit **her.** My sister can swim all by **herself. Her** also means belonging to a girl or a woman. Sue left **her** umbrella in the hall. These are my sneakers, and those sneakers are **hers.**

herd

A **herd** is a group of animals that live or travel together. **Herds** of cattle ate the grass until the ground was almost bare. ▲ **herds.**

Zebras, like many other animals, live in **herds.**

here

Here means where you are right now. Please bring the cup **here.** I'm **here** in the kitchen.

hero

A **hero** is someone we think of as special because of the good or brave things that person has done. ▲ **heroes.**

Billy is **hiding** from his grandpa.

heroine

A **heroine** is a woman or girl we think of as special because of the good or brave things she has done. ▲ **heroines.**

hide

Hide means to put yourself or something else in a place where it cannot be seen. The new puppy has **hidden** my slippers. There are some great places to **hide** near the pond. ▲ **hid, hidden** or **hid, hiding.**

We are trying to measure how **high** the ball bounces.

high

1. High means far up from the ground. That fish can jump **high** out of the water. The eagle flew **higher** and **higher** into the clouds. That is one of the **highest** mountains in the United States.

2. High also means a large amount. I don't want to pay such a **high** price for a new car. ▲ **higher, highest.**

hill

A **hill** is a high area of land. A **hill** is not as high as a mountain. We walked our bicycles up the **hill.** ▲ **hills.**

him

Him is a word for a boy or a man. Mr. Robb asked me to help **him** train his dog. My brother walked home by **himself.**

hippopotamus

A **hippopotamus** is a huge animal with a very large mouth. It has short legs and thick skin with no hair on it. **Hippopotamuses** spend a lot of time in the water. **Hippo** is a short word for **hippopotamus.**
▲ **hippopotamuses.**

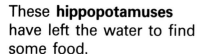

These **hippopotamuses** have left the water to find some food.

his

His means belonging to a boy or a man. This is my piece of pizza and that one is **his**. **John's** baseball glove has **his** name written on it.

history

History is the story of what has happened in the past. This year in school we are studying the **history** of our city. That old house has an interesting **history**. ▲ **histories.**

hit

Hit means to touch hard against something. Jack **hit** me on the back with his hand. Sandy **hit** the ball out of the park. ▲ **hit, hitting.**

hive

A **hive** is a box or house for bees to live in. ▲ **hives.**

hobby

A **hobby** is something that people do just for fun. The Smiths' **hobbies** are collecting stamps, making furniture, fishing, and swimming. Jeff's **hobby** is doing puzzles. ▲ **hobbies.**

At the carnival, Linda **hit** the bottles off the shelf and won a prize.

hockey

1. Hockey is a game played on ice. There are two teams, and each team has six players. The players wear ice skates and use long sticks to try to get a small rubber disk into the other team's goal.
2. Another kind of **hockey** is played on a large field. For this game, each team has 11 players. The players use shorter sticks and a ball instead of a rubber disk.

hog

A **hog** is a grown pig. **Hogs** are raised for their meat. **Hogs** have short legs but can run as fast as most people. ▲ **hogs.**

hold

1. **Hold** means to take something in your hands or arms. Scott asked Lois to **hold** his package while he opened the door. Ann **held** her mother's hand when crossing the street.
2. **Hold** also means to have space for something. The school bus **holds** 50 people. This suitcase is much too small to **hold** all of your toys and all of your clothes.
▲ **held, holding.**

hole

A **hole** is an empty or open place in something. Last fall the squirrels dug **holes** in the ground and put nuts in them. Robin has big **holes** in the knees of her pants.
▲ **holes.**

It is Sara's turn to try and hit the ball into the **hole.**

holiday

A **holiday** is a special day when we remember an important thing or a famous person. Thanksgiving, Christmas, and Hanukkah are **holidays.** ▲ **holidays.**

hollow

When something is **hollow,** it has an empty space inside. A drum is **hollow.** ▲ **hollower, hollowest.**

home

Home is the place where you live. The Jacksons' **home** is the red house on the corner. Aunt Barbara's **home** is an apartment in the city. The mice have their **home** under the fence. ▲ **homes.**

homework

Homework is work that a teacher asks students to do at home. Our teacher asked us to write a story for **homework.**

honest

When you are **honest,** you tell the truth. **Honest** people do not tell lies or take things that do not belong to them.

honey

Honey is a sweet liquid that is made by bees. It is yellow and thick. Lee likes to eat **honey** on toast.

hop

Hop means to make a short jump on one foot. You can also **hop** on both feet. Mercedes can **hop** for a long time. The rabbit **hopped** away. ▲ **hopped, hopping.**

Raccoons sometimes make homes in **hollow** logs.

April **hops** on one foot to play this game.

hope

Hope means to want something very much. We **hope** that tomorrow is a sunny day so that we can go to the beach.
▲ **hoped, hoping.**

horn

1. A **horn** is something you push, squeeze, or blow to make a sound. Some **horns** make music when you blow into them. Cars have **horns** that you push to make a loud noise. Ben squeezed the **horn** on his bicycle so everyone would know he was coming.
2. A **horn** is also a hard point that grows on the head of an animal. Some cows, goats, and deer have **horns.** ▲ **horns.**

Patti rides Duke, her favorite **horse,** almost every day.

horse

A **horse** is a large animal with four legs and a long tail. Before there were cars, people rode **horses** to get from one place to another. Now people ride **horses** for fun. Most **horses** are tame, but some are wild. ▲ **horses.**

hospital

A **hospital** is a place where people who are sick or hurt go to get better. Doctors and nurses work in **hospitals.** Many babies are born in **hospitals.** ▲ **hospitals.**

hot

Hot means very, very warm. When something is **hot,** it can burn you when you touch or taste it. Earl burned his hand when he touched the **hot** stove. ▲ **hotter, hottest.**

hot dog

A **hot dog** is meat that is rolled into a long, thin shape and cooked. There were **hot dogs** for sale at the baseball game. ▲ **hot dogs.**

hotel

A **hotel** is a building with many bedrooms. People pay to sleep in a **hotel** when they are away from home. There is a pool in our **hotel.** ▲ **hotels.**

hour

An **hour** is a part of a day. There are 24 **hours** in a day. An **hour** is the same as 60 minutes. ▲ **hours.**

house

A **house** is a building where people live. Usually only one or two families live in a **house.** There are many **houses** on our street. ▲ **houses.**

how

1. **How** is a word that you use to ask a question. **How** cold is it outside? **How** did you like the story?
2. We also use **how** when we talk about the way to do something. I don't know **how** to drive a car.

Hot soup tastes good on a snowy day.

Mary has learned **how** to ski very well.

Tim and his grandfather love to **hug** each other.

huddle

Huddle means to get close together into a small group. The baby chickens **huddled** under their mother's wing.
▲ **huddled, huddling.**

hug

1. **Hug** means to put your arms around someone and hold that person. People **hug** to show that they care very much about each other. When Rita's friend returned from vacation, Rita **hugged** her because she had missed her so much. ▲ **hugged, hugging.**
2. When you **hug** something, you give it a **hug.** I give my dog a big **hug** before I go to sleep at night. ▲ **hugs.**

huge

Huge means very, very big. An elephant is a **huge** animal. The balloons in the parade were **huge.** ▲ **huger, hugest.**

hum

When you **hum,** you make a sound with your lips closed and do not say words. When I don't know the words to a song, I **hum** the part I don't know. ▲ **hummed, humming.**

human

1. A **human** is a person. When we talk about **humans,** we call them **human beings.** Men, women, and children are **human beings.**
▲ **humans.**
2. **Human** also means anything having to do with a person. The **human** body has more than 200 bones.

hump

A **hump** is a round bump. Some camels have two **humps** on their backs and some have one. ▲ **humps.**

This camel has two **humps.**

hung

Hung comes from the word **hang.** The monkey **hung** by its tail.

hungry

When we are **hungry,** we want to eat. Fred was **hungry** all morning because he didn't eat breakfast. ▲ **hungrier, hungriest.**

hunt

Hunt means to chase something and try to catch it. Many animals **hunt** for food at night. Some people **hunt** also. A person who **hunts** is called a **hunter.** ▲ **hunted, hunting.**

hurricane

A **hurricane** is a storm with very strong winds and a large amount of rain. **Hurricanes** can cause huge waves in the ocean that flood the land. Some **hurricanes** are strong enough to make trees fall. ▲ **hurricanes.**

hurry

Hurry means to move fast. Let's **hurry** and clean up our room, so that we can go out and play. Matt **hurried** so that he wouldn't be late for school. ▲ **hurried, hurrying.**

Olive and her mother **hurried** to catch the bus.

hurt

When people **hurt,** they feel pain. My stomach **hurts.** Jim fell on the floor and **hurt** his arm. ▲ **hurt, hurting.**

husband

A **husband** is a man who is married. ▲ **husbands.**

Ii

I

1. When you talk about yourself, you use the word **I**. **I** am 6 years old today.
2. **I'd** means "I had" or "I would." They asked me if **I'd** seen the fireworks.
3. **I'll** means "I will." **I'll** play the piano if you'll sing.
4. **I'm** means "I am." **I'm** going to the aquarium with my sister on Saturday.
5. **I've** means "I have." **I've** got 50 cents in my pocket.

ice

Ice is water that is frozen. **Ice** is cold and hard.

iceberg

An **iceberg** is a huge piece of **ice** that floats in the ocean. ▲ **icebergs.**

ice cream

Ice cream is a sweet food that is frozen. It is made from cream and sugar.
▲ **ice creams.**

ice skate

1. An **ice skate** is a kind of boot with a long, sharp piece of metal on the bottom. ▲ **ice skates.**
2. When people **ice-skate,** they wear ice skates and move on ice. Al **ice-skates** backward. ▲ **ice-skated, ice-skating.**

idea

An **idea** is something that you think of. We all had different **ideas** about what to name our pet turtle. ▲ **ideas.**

if

If it rains, we will play inside. Ruth doesn't know **if** she can go to the park.

Insects on Ice

imagine

When you **imagine** something, you have a picture of it in your mind. We **imagined** what it would be like to live on the moon.
▲ **imagined, imagining.**

imitate

Imitate means to do the same thing that someone else is doing. When Tommy touched his nose, his baby sister Patty **imitated** him by touching her nose. ▲ **imitated, imitating.**

immediately

Immediately means now. If we leave **immediately,** we can get to the airport before our plane leaves.

important

When something is **important,** it means that you should pay attention to it. It is **important** for you to look both ways before you cross the street.

Sam **imitates** his older brother, and Shannon **imitates** her sister.

in

1. In means toward the middle. I put the bird **in** its cage. The hippopotamus is standing **in** the water. **In** is the opposite of **out.**
2. In can also mean during a time. The leaves change colors **in** the fall. I'll finish my homework **in** an hour.

incubator

An **incubator** is a special kind of box. It has heat and air to keep new babies warm. We saw the baby chickens hatch in the **incubator** at the farm. ▲ **incubators.**

independence

Independence means not to be ruled by another country. The United States celebrates its **independence** on the Fourth of July.

indoor

1. Indoor means inside a building. Our school has an **indoor** pool.
2. When you go into a building, you are **indoors**. The children went **indoors** when it began to rain.

information

Information is a group of facts that help you learn something. A dictionary gives you **information** on how words are spelled and what they mean.

insect

An **insect** is a very small animal that has six legs. Most **insects** have wings. Flies, grasshoppers, and ants are **insects**. ▲ **insects.**

inside

1. Inside means the side of something that is in. The **inside** of our car is green. ▲ **insides.**
2. Inside can also mean in or indoors. Sally looked **inside** the closet for her coat.

The **inside** of Alec's jacket is orange and red plaid.

instead

Instead means that something is done in place of something else. I think I'll wear my red sneakers today **instead** of my brown shoes.

instrument

1. An **instrument** is a tool that helps you do something. Pens are **instruments** for writing. Forks are **instruments** for eating.
2. Another kind of **instrument** can make music. A piano and a violin are musical **instruments**. ▲ **instruments.**

interesting

If something is **interesting** to you, you like to do it or pay attention to it. We thought the science museum was very **interesting.**

"Please come **into** the house," Janice said to her friend.

into

1. **Into** sometimes means inside. Martin reached **into** the bag to get some raisins.
2. We also use the word **into** to tell about something that changes. The caterpillar changed **into** a butterfly.

invention

An **invention** is something that is made or thought of for the first time. One of the earliest **inventions** was the wheel.
▲ **inventions.**

invisible

If something is **invisible,** it cannot be seen. In the story, nobody could see the good fairy because she was **invisible.**

invitation

When you ask people to go somewhere, you are giving them an **invitation. Invitations** are often written on cards. ▲ **invitations.**

Beth and Jasmine are excited about their **invitation** to Paul's party.

invite

Invite means to ask someone to go somewhere. Peter and his mom **invited** Sam to go to the circus with them. Jill is **inviting** Alan to play at her house. ▲ **invited, inviting.**

iron

1. Iron is a hard, strong metal. The bars of the fence were made of **iron.**
2. An **iron** is something you use to make your clothes smooth. It is flat on the bottom and gets hot. ▲ **irons.**

is

Is comes from the word **be.** Bill's coat **is** blue and Susan's **is** red. **Is** it going to rain?

island

An **island** is land that has water all around it. Some **islands** are tiny. Other **islands** are big enough to have people living on them. The state of Hawaii is made up of **islands.** ▲ **islands.**

The grocery store **isn't** open today because the owner is on vacation.

isn't
Isn't means "is not." That umbrella is mine. It **isn't** yours. It **isn't** sunny today.

it
It is a word for what you are talking about. My friend threw the ball and I caught **it.**

itch
When you **itch,** you feel that your skin is being tickled or stung and you want to scratch it. The mosquito bite on my arm **itches** a lot. ▲ **itched, itching.**

its
Its means that something belongs to the animal or thing you are talking about. The cat licked **its** paws.

it's
1. **It's** means "it is." **It's** very hot in here.
2. **It's** also means "it has." **It's** been three days since my baby sister came home.

Jj Kk

Juggling Kangaroo

jacket
A **jacket** is a short coat. Bob's **jacket** has buttons and thin blue stripes. Wilma's **jacket** has a zipper and is red and black. ▲ **jackets.**

jail
A **jail** is a place where people who do not obey laws have to stay. The police officer took the burglar to **jail**. ▲ **jails.**

jar
A **jar** is used to hold things. **Jars** are often made out of glass and have covers that fit tight. The teacher keeps our paints in **jars**. ▲ **jars.**

jealous
When you feel **jealous,** you are unhappy because someone has something that you do not have. Ray was **jealous** because his friend Charlie had a new baseball glove.

jeans
Jeans are pants made from a strong cotton cloth. When the children paint or play with clay, they wear old **jeans.**

jelly
Jelly is a sweet, soft food. It is usually made from fruit juice boiled with sugar. We ate peanut butter and **jelly** sandwiches for lunch today. ▲ **jellies.**

jewelry
Rings, bracelets, and necklaces are kinds of **jewelry.**

job

1. A **job** is something that needs to be done. Danny's **job** is to wash the dog. Sam has the **job** of setting the table for dinner.
2. A **job** is also something a person does to earn money. Mom's **job** is teaching. ▲ **jobs.**

These people have **joined** hands to make a long line.

join

1. **Join** means to put things together. I **joined** my toy railroad cars to make a train.
2. **Join** also means to become a part of something. Diana wants to **join** the swimming club. ▲ **joined, joining.**

joke

1. A **joke** is a story that makes people laugh. When my sister broke her leg, I told her **jokes** to make her feel more cheerful.
2. A **joke** is also a trick that you play on someone. We hid Dad's slippers as a **joke.** ▲ **jokes.**

journal

A **journal** is a book that you write in about things you have done or thought. ▲ **journals.**

Sylvia and her dad like to make fresh orange **juice**.

Eva **jumped** high to hit the ball with her head.

journey

A **journey** is a long trip. Carlos was very excited about his **journey** across the ocean. ▲ **journeys.**

joy

When you feel **joy,** you are very happy. Tara felt **joy** when she took her new puppy home from the pet store. ▲ **joys.**

juggle

Juggle means to throw two or more things into the air one after the other and catch them very quickly. When you **juggle,** you are throwing and catching things at the same time. I can **juggle** three balls at once without dropping any. ▲ **juggled, juggling.**

juice

Juice is a liquid that you get from fruits or vegetables. Claire likes tomato **juice.** Mike's favorite fruit **juice** is apple **juice.** ▲ **juices.**

jump

Jump means to go up into the air using your foot and leg muscles. Sasha had to **jump** to catch the ball. The deer **jumped** over the fence and ran into the woods. Molly **jumped** over the rope while the other children turned it. ▲ **jumped, jumping.**

jungle

A **jungle** is a place where many trees and plants grow. It is hot and rains a lot in a **jungle.** Monkeys, snakes, parrots, and mosquitoes live in the **jungle.** ▲ **jungles.**

just

1. When something is **just** right, it is perfect. These shoes are **just** my size.
2. **Just** also means a very short time ago. Roberto **just** fed the dog.

kangaroo

A **kangaroo** is a large animal that has strong legs in the back for jumping. It has small legs in the front. **Kangaroos** carry their babies in a pocket of skin on their stomachs. ▲ **kangaroos.**

keep

1. Keep means to have something. Wilbur's mother let him **keep** the kitten he found.
2. Keep also means to stay the same way. The rain **kept** everyone inside for the afternoon. Mr. Simon asked the children to **keep** quiet during the movie. ▲ **kept, keeping.**

ketchup

Ketchup is a thick, red liquid made from tomatoes. It is sometimes spelled **catsup.**

kettle

A **kettle** is a metal pot for boiling water. You can pour the water from a **kettle** without taking off the cover. Our **kettle** whistles when the water begins to boil. ▲ **kettles.**

The baby **kangaroo** is comfortable in its mother's pocket.

key

1. A **key** is something that is used to open or close a lock. Each lock has a special **key** that fits into it. This **key** opens the front door.
2. A **key** is also the part of a machine or musical instrument that is pressed down to make it work. A computer has **keys** for letters and numbers. A piano has black and white **keys.** ▲ **keys.**

keyboard

A **keyboard** is a set or row of keys. Pianos and computers have keyboards. ▲ **keyboards.**

Nathan needs two **keys** to open the door.

Susan is practicing how to **kick** a football.

kick

Kick means to hit something with your foot. Mike **kicked** the can. ▲ **kicked, kicking.**

kid

1. A **kid** is a baby goat.
2. A **kid** is also a child. Uncle Willy asked, "Do you **kids** want to play baseball?" ▲ **kids.**

kill

Kill means to make something die. The cat **killed** the mouse. ▲ **killed, killing.**

kind¹

A **kind** person thinks of others and is nice to them. The nurse in school is **kind** to all the children. ▲ **kinder, kindest.**

kind²

Kind also means a group of things that are alike in some way. Apples and oranges are **kinds** of fruit. ▲ **kinds.**

Many **kinds** of animals come to the river to drink.

kindergarten

Kindergarten is a grade in school. It comes before the first grade. In **kindergarten** we play games, build with blocks, use clay and paints, and listen to stories. We also sing and play instruments, care for pets, look at picture books, and make our own books.
▲ **kindergartens.**

king

A **king** is a man who rules a country. I like the story about a **king** and a queen who live in a castle. ▲ **kings.**

kingdom

A **kingdom** is a country that is ruled by a king or a queen. Mrs. Brown read the class a fairy tale about a magical **kingdom.**
▲ **kingdoms.**

kiss

Kiss means to touch with your lips. We **kiss** people to show we love them. Melba and Tony always **kiss** their parents before going to sleep each night. ▲ **kissed, kissing.**

kit

A **kit** is a group of things that are used for something special. This sewing **kit** has needles, pins, thread, and scissors in it. Maggie has a tool **kit** that she uses to fix her bicycle. Jimmy built his model airplane from a **kit.** ▲ **kits.**

kitchen

A **kitchen** is a room where people cook food and make meals. We have a stove, a refrigerator, a sink, and a table and chairs in our **kitchen.** Betty and Martin's family eats in the **kitchen.** ▲ **kitchens.**

Ed always gets a **kiss** from his mother before she leaves for work.

183

Amanda's **kite** looks like a flying fish.

kite

A **kite** is a toy that you fly in the air at the end of a long string. **Kites** are made of sticks that are covered with paper or plastic or cloth. They sometimes have pictures on them. ▲ **kites.**

kitten

A **kitten** is a baby cat. Our cat just had five black and white **kittens.** Sometimes a kitten is called a **kitty.** ▲ **kittens.**

knee

The **knee** is the part of the body where the leg bends. Your **knee** is in the middle of your leg. ▲ **knees.**

kneel

When you **kneel,** you get down on your knees with your legs and feet under you. You can also **kneel** on one knee. Mr. McGuire **kneels** when he works in the garden.
▲ **knelt** or **kneeled, kneeling.**

knew

Knew comes from the word **know.** When I lost my roller skates, my older sister **knew** where to find them.

knife

A **knife** is a tool that is used for cutting. A **knife** has a handle at one end and a sharp piece of metal at the other end. Mom took a **knife** from the drawer to cut the bread.
▲ **knives.**

knight

Long ago, a **knight** was a soldier for a king or queen. **Knights** were brave and honest and protected people who needed help. They wore armor and rode horses. ▲ **knights.**

knit

When you **knit,** you use long needles and wool to make scarves, sweaters, other clothes, and cloth. Carla **knitted** a red wool sweater for her doll. ▲ **knitted** or **knit, knitting.**

knob

A **knob** is a round handle for opening a door or a drawer. When Tara tried to open the drawer, the **knob** came off in her hand. A **knob** is also used on a radio, television, or other machine. If you turn that **knob** to the right, the radio will get louder.
▲ **knobs.**

knock

1. Knock means to hit something. When you **knock** on a door, you hit it with your fist to make a sound. On Halloween, we **knocked** on the doors of our neighbors to ask for treats. The branch of the tree was **knocking** against the window during the storm.
2. Knock also means to push and make something fall. The puppy **knocked** the lamp off the table. ▲ **knocked, knocking.**

knot

When you tie two pieces of string together, you make a **knot.** Ann made a mistake and tied her shoe with a **knot** instead of a bow. ▲ **knots.**

know

When you **know** something, it means that you are very sure about it. Inge **knows** everyone who lives on her street. By the end of the summer, all the children at camp **knew** how to swim. ▲ **knew, known, knowing.**

Seth and Glen are learning how to tie different **knots.**

L l

Lion Listening

ladder
A **ladder** is a set of steps that can be moved from one place to another. Mr. Fox used a **ladder** when he painted the top part of our house. ▲ **ladders.**

lady
A **lady** is a woman. There is a **lady** on the telephone who wants to speak with Mom. ▲ **ladies.**

laid
Laid comes from the word **lay.** The turtle **laid** its eggs in the sand.

lain
Lain comes from the word **lie.** Our cat, Toby, has **lain** by the fire all afternoon.

lake
A **lake** is water that has land all around it. The water in most **lakes** has no salt. We swim in the **lake** during the summer. ▲ **lakes.**

lamb
A **lamb** is a baby sheep. ▲ **lambs.**

lamp
A **lamp** is something that gives light. We turn on a **lamp** when it is dark. ▲ **lamps.**

land
1. **Land** is all of the earth that is not water. Fields and mountains are part of the **land.** Farmers grow corn on **land.** ▲ **lands.**
2. **Land** also means to go from the air onto the ground. The airplane **landed** at 5 o'clock. ▲ **landed, landing.**

language

The words we speak, read, and write are called **language.** English is the main **language** spoken in the United States. Some people also read and speak other **languages.**
▲ **languages.**

lap

Your **lap** is the top of your legs when you are sitting down. When you stand up, your **lap** disappears. Our cat likes to sit in my **lap.**
▲ **laps.**

large

Large means big. Things that are **large** take up a lot of space. Elephants and whales are **large** animals. ▲ **larger, largest.**

This clown's **large** red shoes and **large** orange nose make me laugh.

last¹

1. When something is **last,** it is at the end. What is the **last** word in this dictionary? Saturday is the **last** day of the week.
2. Last also means a time before the time now. I learned to ski **last** winter. **Last** night, Abby saw a movie.

last²

Last means to stay the way it is. The milk will **last** in the refrigerator for a few days. Snow on the mountain **lasted** until spring.
▲ **lasted, lasting.**

late

When you come **late,** you come after the time you were supposed to come. Nathaniel was **late** for school today. Barbara was **later** than Nathaniel. Cory came last. He was **latest** of all. ▲ **later, latest.**

laugh

1. **Laugh** means to make sounds with your voice that show you think something is funny. Willie's jokes always make me **laugh.**
▲ **laughed, laughing.**
2. A **laugh** is the sound of someone **laughing.** The **laughs** of the audience filled the theater. ▲ **laughs.**

launch

Launch means to start something and send it forward. ▲ **launched, launching.**

The rocket is being **launched** into space.

laundry

Things like clothes or towels that need to be washed or have just been washed are called **laundry.** We sorted and folded the **laundry** before putting it away.

law

A **law** is a rule made by the government of a city, state, or country. **Laws** help to keep people safe. ▲ **laws.**

lawn

A **lawn** is an area of grass around a house or building. Zachery cuts the **lawn** every other Saturday. ▲ **lawns.**

lay¹

1. **Lay** means to put something down. Please **lay** that book on the table.
2. **Lay** also means to make an egg. The hen **laid** two eggs. ▲ **laid, laying.**

lay²

Lay comes from the word **lie.** We **lay** on the grass watching the clouds.

lazy

Someone who is **lazy** will not work or do very much. When it is really hot outside, I often feel very **lazy.** ▲ **lazier, laziest.**

lead¹

When **lead** sounds like seed, **lead** means to show the way or to go first. The dog will **lead** the blind man across the street. Carol is **leading** in the race. The band **led** the parade. ▲ **led, leading.**

Hunter and Laura are doing their **laundry** today.

Our **lazy** cat sleeps all day by the window.

The birds have discovered that the bag **leaks.**

lead²
When **lead** sounds like bed, **lead** means the black part of a pencil that makes a mark. ▲ **leads.**

leader
A **leader** shows people the way or goes first. The **leader** of the United States is called the president. ▲ **leaders.**

leaf
A **leaf** is part of a plant. Many trees and flowers have green **leaves.** In the fall some **leaves** turn different colors. ▲ **leaves.**

leak
When something **leaks,** what is inside comes out slowly through a small hole or a crack. The air has been **leaking** out of the tire. ▲ **leaked, leaking.**

learn
When you **learn,** you get to know or understand something. We **learned** to read in the first grade. ▲ **learned, learning.**

Mrs. Abrams' class is visiting the museum to **learn** about art.

leash

A **leash** is a kind of rope or chain that you tie to a dog's collar. Tony tied the **leash** to a tree so that his dog wouldn't run away.
▲ **leashes.**

least

Least means the smallest amount. I grew 3 inches last year. My brother grew 4 inches, and my sister grew 2 inches. My brother grew the most in the past year, and my sister grew the **least.**

Samantha uses a **leash** when she walks her dog.

leather

Leather is a material made from the skins of animals. It is used to make shoes, gloves, and other things. Jill's sneakers are made of **leather.** ▲ **leathers.**

leave

1. Leave means to go away from a place. We **leave** home at 8 o'clock in the morning to go to school.
2. When you **leave** something, you don't take it with you. Remember not to **leave** your books at the playground. Pat forgot his homework and **left** it at home.
▲ **left, leaving.**

leaves

Leaves comes from the word **leaf.** The **leaves** of the tree turned bright red in the fall.

led

Led comes from the word **lead** that sounds like seed. In Martin's story, the dog **led** the children out of the forest.

left¹

Your body has a **left** side and a right side. When you look at the face of a clock, the 9 is on the **left** side. When you read, you start at the **left** side of the page. My sister writes with her **left** hand.

left²

Left comes from the word **leave.** We **left** our cat with a friend when our family went on vacation.

leg

A **leg** is a part of the body. People and animals stand and walk on their **legs.** People have two **legs.** Cows and cats have four **legs.** ▲ **legs.**

lemon

A **lemon** is a yellow fruit with a sour taste. Ethel likes the taste of **lemon** juice on fish. **Lemonade** is a drink that is made with **lemons,** sugar, and water. ▲ **lemons.**

length

The **length** of something is how long it is from one end to the other. The **length** of the swimming pool is 50 feet. The **length** of my bed is 6 feet. ▲ **lengths.**

leopard

A **leopard** is a large, wild animal. It is a kind of cat with dark yellow fur and black spots. ▲ **leopards.**

less

Less means not as much as something else. You have 7 cents, and I have 9 cents. You have **less** money than I do. If we take the bus, it will take **less** time than if we walk. This shirt is **less** expensive than that one.

In this race we run with our **legs** tied together.

lesson

A **lesson** is something you are supposed to learn. Sue takes dancing **lessons**. Karen helped her brother with his science **lesson**. ▲ **lessons.**

let

If you **let** someone do something, you say that the person can do it. Dad **let** us stay up later last night. ▲ **let, letting.**

let's

Let's means "let us." We say **let's** when we want someone to do something with us. **Let's** go to the zoo tomorrow.

Jess learns something new in each swimming **lesson**.

letter

1. A **letter** is part of the alphabet. **A, B,** and **C** are the first three **letters** of the alphabet. The word "jump" is spelled with four **letters**.
2. A **letter** is also a message that somebody writes on paper to send to somebody else. I got a **letter** in the mail today. ▲ **letters.**

lettuce

Lettuce is a vegetable that has large, green leaves. It is used in salads and sandwiches. ▲ **lettuces.**

liar

A **liar** is a person who does not tell the truth. ▲ **liars.**

librarian

A **librarian** is a person who works in a library. The **librarian** in our school helps us find the books we need. ▲ **librarians.**

The rabbit has discovered the **lettuce** patch.

Our **library** is always busy on Saturdays.

Arthur's dog always tries to **lick** his face.

library

A **library** is a room or a building where books are kept. People can use the books in the **library** or borrow them to read at home. ▲ **libraries.**

lick

Lick means to touch something with your tongue. The cat **licked** itself. Betty **licked** her ice-cream cone. ▲ **licked, licking.**

lie¹

When you tell something that you know is not true, you are telling a **lie.** Mom and Dad have taught us never to tell a **lie.** ▲ **lies.**

lie²

Lie means to be stretched out flat. When you **lie,** you are not sitting or standing. The dog likes to **lie** by the gate while the baby plays in the yard. ▲ **lay, lain, lying.**

life

1. When something is alive and able to grow, it has **life.** People and animals and plants have **life.**

2. The time that a person or an animal or a plant is alive is its **life.** The **life** of some large turtles may be as long as 100 years. ▲ **lives.**

lift

Lift means to pick something up. It was hard for Mike to **lift** the heavy bag. Jan **lifted** her arm and waved good-bye. ▲ **lifted, lifting.**

light¹

1. Light is energy that comes from the sun. When there is **light,** we are able to see things.

2. Something that gives **light** is called a **light.** Lamps and candles are **lights.** Betsy turned on the **light** in her bedroom to read her book. ▲ **lights.**

3. When you **light** something, you make it burn or give off **light.** Be careful when you **light** the candles. We are **lighting** our Christmas tree tonight. ▲ **lighted** or **lit, lighting.**

4. Light is also a way to describe color. Pink is a **light** color. ▲ **lighter, lightest.**

The crane is **lifting** the heavy container.

light²

When something is **light,** it is not heavy. The empty suitcase was **light.** ▲ **lighter, lightest.**

lighthouse

A **lighthouse** is a tower with a strong light on top. Lighthouses are built near dangerous places in the water to help ships pass by safely. We saw the **lighthouse** from our boat and were able to pass the rocks safely.

lightning

Lightning is a bright light sometimes seen in the sky during a storm. It is electricity between clouds or between a cloud and the ground. Thunder is the sound that comes after **lightning.**

like¹

When something is **like** something else, it looks, acts, feels, or seems the same in some way. Tad is dressed **like** a clown.

like²

If you **like** something, it means that it makes you happy. I **like** to read. ▲ **liked, liking.**

line

1. A **line** is a long, thin mark. Jan used a pencil to draw a **line** across the paper.
2. A **line** is also things in a row. We stood in line for the bus. ▲ **lines.**

lion

A **lion** is one kind of large, wild cat. **Lions** are yellow or brown. ▲ **lions.**

A male **lion** has a lot of fur around its neck.

lip

A **lip** is the part of your face around your mouth. People have two **lips**. ▲ **lips**.

liquid

A **liquid** is something that is wet when you touch it. A **liquid** can be poured. Water and milk are **liquids**. ▲ **liquids**.

list

A **list** is a number of things that are written down. Lauren made a **list** of the people she wanted at her party. ▲ **lists**.

listen

Listen means to try to hear in a careful way. The children **listened** to the story. Thelma likes to **listen** to music. I like **listening** to the sound of rain falling on the roof. ▲ **listened, listening**.

lit

Lit comes from the word **light**. We **lit** a candle to find our way down the dark hall. Uncle Dave **lit** the logs in the fireplace.

little

1. When something is **little**, it is small. My **little** sister can't walk yet. An ant is **little**. That is the **littlest** puppy that I have ever seen.
2. **Little** also means not very much. Jack drank only a **little** juice because he wasn't thirsty. Cally used a **little** red in her painting. We only spent a **little** time picking apples because it started to rain. ▲ **littler, littlest**.

Chris has a **list** of food to buy at the grocery store.

First we **listen** to Mrs. Henry play a song, and then we learn to sing it.

The **lizard** is resting on
top of a rock.

Lobsters live at the bottom
of the ocean.

live

1. **Live** means to be alive. No dinosaurs **live**
on earth now.
2. **Live** also means to have a home. Billy and
Elsie Jefferson **live** next door to us.
▲ **lived, living.**

lives

Lives comes from the word **life**. The **lives** of
the early explorers were filled with danger.
Vera likes to read stories about the **lives** of
heroes and heroines.

lizard

A **lizard** is an animal with four legs and a
long tail. Most **lizards** like to eat insects.
Lizards, snakes, turtles, and alligators are all
reptiles. ▲ **lizards.**

loaf

1. A **loaf** is bread that is baked in one long
piece. We bought two **loaves** of bread at the
bakery.
2. A **loaf** can also be another kind of food
that is shaped like a bread. Joe's favorite
dinner is meat **loaf** and salad. ▲ **loaves.**

lobster

A **lobster** is an animal that has a hard shell
and five pairs of legs. The two front pair of
legs end in large claws. Many people eat
lobsters. ▲ **lobsters.**

lock

1. A **lock** keeps something closed. There are
locks for doors, suitcases, bicycles, and other
things. You need a key to open some **locks.**
▲ **locks.**
2. **Lock** means to keep something closed with
a **lock**. Dad **locked** the garage door.
▲ **locked, locking.**

log

A **log** is a large round piece of wood from a tree. Eddie took a **log** from the pile. The cabin in the forest is made of **logs**. ▲ **logs**.

lonely

When you feel **lonely,** you feel unhappy about being alone. Gabe is **lonely** because all his friends are away for the summer. ▲ **lonelier, loneliest.**

long

1. Long means that one end of something is far away from the other end. There is a **long** hall between the first grade and second grade classrooms.
2. Long also means taking a lot of time. Jed was tired and took a **long** nap after lunch. An hour is **longer** than a minute. It is a **long** drive from where I live to the ocean. ▲ **longer, longest.**

These **logs** will be taken down the river to a place where they will be cut into lumber.

look

1. When you **look,** you use your eyes to see. Harry let me **look** at his new book. We **looked** out of the window at the deer. Katie and Robbie **looked** carefully before they crossed the street.
2. Look also means how people see you. Rita **looked** happy when she found her lost dog. ▲ **looked, looking.**

loose

When something is **loose,** it is not tight or fixed the way it should be. I need a belt because my pants are too **loose**. There is a **loose** button on my coat. ▲ **looser, loosest.**

A **lot** of children are climbing the ropes and playing here.

lose

1. When you **lose** something, it means that you cannot find it. Don't **lose** your new gloves. Jenny **lost** her pencil in the playground.
2. Lose also means not being able to keep something. Many trees **lost** their branches during the hurricane. Elizabeth **lost** her balance and slipped on the ice.
3. Lose also means to not win. Did Joe **lose** the race? ▲ **lost, losing.**

loss

A **loss** is something that is lost or has been lost. The **loss** of the game made our team unhappy. The fire caused great **losses.**
▲ **losses.**

lost

When something is **lost,** it is hard to find. We found the **lost** sock behind the dresser. When people or animals are **lost,** they cannot find their way home. Our cat was **lost** for two days.

lot

If there are a **lot** of things, it means that there are many of them. A leopard has a **lot** of spots. There was **lots** of food at the school picnic. ▲ **lots.**

loud

Something that is **loud** makes a lot of noise. A fire alarm is **loud** to tell people there is danger. The band played **loud** music as it marched in the parade. ▲ **louder, loudest.**

loudspeaker

A **loudspeaker** is something that makes sound louder. Radios have **loudspeakers.** Some telephones have **loudspeakers** too.
▲ **loudspeakers.**

love

Love means to care very much about someone or something. Eduardo and Elena **love** their grandparents and go to visit them often. My little brother hugs our dog to show that he **loves** it. ▲ **loved, loving.**

low

Low means close to the floor or ground. The fence was **low** enough to jump over without touching it. ▲ **lower, lowest.**

lucky

Lucky means that you have good things happen to you. Marc was **lucky** to find two quarters and a nickel lying in the middle of the sidewalk. ▲ **luckier, luckiest.**

lullaby

A **lullaby** is a song sung to a baby to help the baby go to sleep. ▲ **lullabies.**

lumber

Lumber means boards that have been cut from logs. Dad brought home some **lumber** to build me a new desk.

lunch

Lunch is the meal we eat in the middle of the day. Melba has **lunch** at school every day. ▲ **lunches.**

lunch box

A **lunch box** is a metal or plastic container with a handle. Some people carry their lunches to school or work in a **lunch box**. ▲ **lunch boxes.**

Johnny's chair and desk are much too **low** for his dad.

Sometimes Mom puts a surprise in my **lunch box**.

201

Mm

Mice Making Music

machine
A **machine** is something we use to do work. A **machine** may have parts that move to help it do its job. Airplanes are **machines** that fly. Cranes are **machines** that lift heavy things. ▲ **machines.**

mad
When someone is **mad,** it means that the person is angry about something. Jill was **mad** because we had to stop the game just when she was winning. ▲ **madder, maddest.**

made
Made comes from the word **make.** The clown **made** us laugh. The wall was **made** of stone.

magazine
A **magazine** has stories to read and pictures to look at. It has paper covers. Some **magazines** are published every week. Some are published once a month. Jed likes a **magazine** with jokes and word games. ▲ **magazines.**

magic
Magic is a special power to make unusual things happen. **Magic** seems to be real, but it is not. The tricks Brenda did at the party seemed to be done by **magic.** Something using **magic** or done by **magic** is **magical.** The witch in the story had **magical** powers.

magician
A **magician** is a person who uses magic to do tricks. The **magician** pulled a rabbit out of the hat. ▲ **magicians.**

magnet

A **magnet** is a piece of metal that sticks to other metals. Frank used his **magnet** to pick up the nails that spilled. ▲ **magnets.**

We can see the tiny parts of the grasshopper with the **magnifying glass.**

magnifying glass

A **magnifying glass** is a piece of glass that makes things look bigger than they are. When we looked at the shell through the **magnifying glass,** we could see its pattern of lines. ▲ **magnifying glasses.**

mail

1. The letters and cards that you get or send are **mail.** Mr. Thomas brings the **mail** to our house.
2. When you send someone a letter, you **mail** the letter. You need a stamp to **mail** a letter. Georgia **mailed** the birthday card to her grandfather. ▲ **mailed, mailing.**

main

Main means most important. The bank is on the **main** street in town. Dinner is the **main** meal in our house.

make

1. Make means to put something together. We helped Dad **make** a house for the dog.
2. Make also means to cause something to happen. When you tell funny stories, it always **makes** me laugh. ▲ **made, making.**

make-believe

When something is **make-believe,** it means that it is not real. Fairies are **make-believe.**

Fred and Linda are playing **make-believe** grown-ups who are going on a trip.

male

A **male** is a boy or a man. Fathers and uncles are **male** people. There are **male** animals, too. ▲ **males.**

man

A **man** is a grown-up male person. My uncle is a tall **man.** ▲ **men.**

manners

When you have good **manners,** you act in a polite way toward people. You show good **manners** when you say "please" and "thank you." You show bad **manners** when you chew with your mouth open.

mansion

A **mansion** is a very large house with many rooms. ▲ **mansions.**

This **mansion** was the home of the first president of the United States.

many

Many means a large number of things. This building has **many** floors. The train passed through **many** small towns on its way to the city. ▲ **more, most.**

map

A **map** is a drawing that shows where different places are. There are many kinds of **maps. Maps** can show countries, weather, oceans and rivers, mountains, and other things. Can you find your town on a **map?** When we study geography, we look at **maps.** ▲ **maps.**

We found the Lincoln Memorial on the **map** of Washington, D.C.

The band is **marching** down the street.

marble

1. Marble is a kind of hard, smooth stone. Artists carve statues from **marble**. **Marble** is often used on the walls and floors of buildings.

2. A **marble** is also a small, hard ball of glass used in games. Amy drew a big circle on the ground for a game of **marbles**. ▲ **marbles**.

march

When people **march** together, they all step the same way. On the Fourth of July, we **marched** in a parade. ▲ **marched, marching**.

margarine

Margarine is a soft, yellow food that is usually made from vegetable oil, milk or water, and salt. Many people use **margarine** instead of butter.

mark

1. Mark means to make a line or spot on something. Your dirty shoes **marked** the clean floor. ▲ **marked, marking**.

2. A **mark** is a line or spot you make. The baby made **marks** on the wall with a crayon.

3. A **mark** is also a letter or number that shows how good a person's work is. Another word for **mark** is **grade**. Roberto got better **marks** in art than in science. ▲ **marks**.

marry

Marry means to join with someone as husband or wife. My aunt and uncle have been **married** for five years.
▲ **married, marrying**.

mask

A **mask** is something you wear over your face to hide or protect it. Firefighters wear **masks** to protect them from smoke. ▲ **masks**.

Will the neighbors guess who is behind the **masks?**

206

match¹
Things **match** when they are the same.
Ted's socks don't **match** because one
is blue and the other is brown.
▲ **matched, matching.**

match²
A **match** is a short, thin piece of wood or
paper. When the tip is rubbed against
something, it makes a flame. **Matches** are
used to light a fire. ▲ **matches.**

material
Material is what something is made of.
Alice's winter coat is made of wool **material.**
Wood, stone, and glass are **materials** that
are used to make houses. ▲ **materials.**

mathematics
When you study **mathematics,** you learn
about numbers, amounts, shapes, and
measurements. When you add and subtract,
you are using **mathematics.**

mattress
A **mattress** is the thick, soft part of a bed.
Chris put a new cover on the **mattress.**
▲ **mattresses.**

may
1. You say **may** when you ask for something.
May I have some juice?
2. If you aren't sure something will happen but
there is a chance that it will, you say it **may**
happen. Since there are dark clouds in the
sky, it **may** rain this afternoon.

maybe
Maybe means that something might be. I
can't see who is knocking at the door.
Maybe it is John.

Tamara has bought a skirt
and blouse that **match.**

maze

A **maze** has many paths that are alike. It is hard to find your way through a **maze.** Andy got lost in the **maze** of halls in his new school. ▲ **mazes.**

Brownie's meal is at the end of the **maze.**

me

Me is a word you use when you speak about yourself. The bus takes **me** to school.

meal

A **meal** is the food you eat at one time. We eat three **meals** every day. They are called breakfast, lunch, and dinner. ▲ **meals.**

mean¹

1. **Mean** is a word you use to show that two things are the same. Huge **means** very big.
2. **Mean** is also a word you use to show what you are thinking. When Janet said "early," she **meant** "before breakfast." ▲ **meant, meaning.**

mean²

If you are **mean** to someone, you are not nice or friendly. It was **mean** of the children to hide the new student's books in the closet. ▲ **meaner, meanest.**

measure

Measure means to find out the size or amount of something. Julie helped her father **measure** the length of the new fence.
▲ **measured, measuring.**

measurement

The size or amount that is found by measuring something is called its **measurement.** The carpenter used a ruler to get the **measurements** of the shelf. ▲ **measurements.**

Angel is having his foot **measured** to learn what size shoe he will need.

meat

Meat is the part of an animal that we eat. Hamburgers are made from **meat.** ▲ **meats.**

medal

A **medal** is a piece of metal in the shape of a coin. **Medals** often hang from a ribbon or a chain. A **medal** is sometimes given as a reward to someone who has done something brave or important. Kay was given a **medal** for helping to save the boy who fell in the water. ▲ **medals.**

medicine

Medicine is something we take when we are sick to help us get well. When Jane had the flu, her mother gave her **medicine** twice a day. ▲ **medicines.**

Whitney is giving her sick bird its **medicine.**

meet

Meet means to come together with someone. I am happy to **meet** you. Dad and I are **meeting** Aunt Sue at a restaurant tonight.
▲ **met, meeting.**

melt

When something is **melted** by the heat, it changes from being hard or solid into being soft or liquid. The ice-cream cone **melted** in the sun and started dripping down my hand. When ice **melts,** it becomes water.
▲ **melted, melting.**

memory

1. **Memory** is being able to remember things. Aunt Mimi has a good **memory** for dates and never forgets anyone's birthday.
2. A **memory** is also a person or thing that is remembered. My summer in camp is one of my happiest **memories.** ▲ **memories.**

men

Men means more than one **man.** Two **men** carried the couch off the truck.

mess

Something is a **mess** when a lot of things are not where they belong. The kitchen was a **mess** after we made a cake. When a place is a **mess,** we say it is **messy.** ▲ **messes.**

Mom says that I must clean up the **mess** in my room this afternoon.

message

When you want to tell someone something, but the person is away, you can leave a **message**. I got a **message** from Mom for me to call her when I got home. ▲ **messages.**

met

Met comes from the word **meet.** Freda and Dave **met** in the park when they were walking their dogs.

metal

Metal is a shiny material that is found in the earth. Gold is a kind of **metal.** A dime, a ring, and a car are all made of **metal.** ▲ **metals.**

Aunt Ruth let me put the coins in the **meter.**

meter

A **meter** is something that measures. There are **meters** in buildings that show how much electricity, water, or gas has been used. ▲ **meters.**

mice

Mice means more than one mouse. The **mice** ate all the cheese. Raymond, Albert, and George dressed up as three **mice** for the Halloween party.

microscope

A **microscope** is a tool that makes very small things look much larger. When Tess put a drop of water under a **microscope,** she saw many things in it that she couldn't see with her eyes alone. ▲ **microscopes.**

The string looks different through a **microscope.**

Sonia, Kim, and José jump in the **middle** as Felipe and Maria turn the rope.

middle

The **middle** is the part in the center between the ends. Noon is in the **middle** of the day. We swam to the raft in the **middle** of the lake. ▲ **middles.**

midnight

Midnight is 12 o'clock at night. Everyone in our house is asleep at **midnight.**

might

Might comes from the word **may.** Terri said we **might** be late if we don't hurry.

milk

Milk is a white liquid that we drink. **Milk** comes from cows and goats. I like **milk** on my cereal. Cheese is made from **milk.**

mind

Your **mind** is the part of you that thinks, knows, feels, and dreams. You use your **mind** to learn and to remember things. ▲ **minds.**

mine

When something is **mine,** it means that it belongs to me. That skateboard is yours, but this one is **mine.** The jacket with the patch on the sleeve is **mine.**

minus

We use the word **minus** when we subtract one number from another: 5 **minus** 3 is 2. Another way of writing 5 **minus** 3 is 5 − 3.

minute

A **minute** is part of an hour. There are 60 **minutes** in 1 hour. Don finished washing the dishes in 10 **minutes.** ▲ **minutes.**

mirror

A **mirror** is a smooth piece of glass that we can see ourselves in. Some **mirrors** hang on the wall and some can be held in your hand. The dentist uses a tiny **mirror** to see into the back of my mouth. ▲ **mirrors.**

Carrie looks in the **mirror** and draws herself.

miss

1. Miss means not to do something that you plan to do. If we don't hurry, we will **miss** the beginning of the movie. Jack swung the bat at the ball, but he **missed** it.
2. Miss also means to be sorry that you don't have something, or that someone you like isn't with you. I **miss** my sister when she goes to camp in the summer.
3. Miss also means to be without something. My old jacket is **missing** a button. Your blue and green crayons are **missing.**
▲ **missed, missing.**

Miss

Miss is often used before the name of a girl or the name of a woman who is not married. My piano teacher is **Miss** Brown.

Sam is **missing** some of his front teeth.

Dad and I are building a **model** of a sailboat.

mistake

A **mistake** is something that is wrong. I made only one **mistake** on the spelling test. It was a **mistake** to wear a heavy sweater on such a warm day. ▲ **mistakes.**

mitten

A **mitten** is something you wear on your hand to keep it warm. A glove has parts for each finger, but a **mitten** doesn't. I lost my **mittens** at school. ▲ **mittens.**

mix

Mix means to put different things together. My friends and I are **mixing** lemon juice, water, and sugar to make lemonade. We **mixed** red paint and white paint to make pink. ▲ **mixed, mixing.**

model

A **model** is a small copy of something. Paul is painting his airplane **model** to make the wood look like metal. ▲ **models.**

mom

Mom is a name for your mother. Some children also call their mother **mommy.** ▲ **moms.**

money

Money is something we use to buy things. A dollar is **money** usually made of paper. Nickels, dimes, and other coins are **money** made of metal. I am trying to save my **money** so I can buy a skateboard.

monkey

A **monkey** is an animal with long arms and legs, fur all over its body, and a long tail. Some **monkeys** live in trees and some live on the ground. ▲ **monkeys.**

The **monkey** is sitting on top of some branches.

monster

A **monster** is a big, scary animal that is not real. I read a story about a red **monster** with two heads and six legs. ▲ **monsters.**

month

A **month** is part of a year. There are 12 **months** in a year. The **months** are January, February, March, April, May, June, July, August, September, October, November, and December. ▲ **months.**

moon

The **moon** moves around the earth. At night the **moon** shines in the sky. Sometimes you can see all of the **moon,** and sometimes you can see only a part of it. It takes one month for the **moon** to move around the earth. ▲ **moons.**

This astronaut is going for a ride on the **moon.**

more

More means a larger number or a larger amount. Four is **more** than three. There is **more** juice in my glass than in yours.

morning

Morning is the part of the day before noon. I like to wake up early in the **morning** when the sun shines through my window.
▲ **mornings**.

mosquito

A **mosquito** is a small insect that flies. When a **mosquito** bites me, it makes me want to scratch. ▲ **mosquitoes**.

most

Most means the largest number or part of something. **Most** of the children got to school on time. Micki spelled **most** of the words right. I like **most** foods.

Most of the babies are still sleeping.

mother

A **mother** is a woman who has one or more children. **Mothers** and fathers are parents. ▲ **mothers.**

motor

A **motor** is a machine that makes other machines work. This clock has an electric **motor** to move the hands. The **motor** of a car makes the car go. ▲ **motors.**

motorcycle

A **motorcycle** looks like a bicycle with an engine, but it is bigger and heavier. Police officers often use **motorcycles** instead of cars because it is easier to move them through traffic. ▲ **motorcycles.**

This high **mountain** has snow on it even in the middle of the summer.

mountain

A **mountain** is a very high area of land. **Mountains** are much higher than hills. Some people go skiing in the **mountains** for a vacation. ▲ **mountains.**

mouse

A **mouse** is a very small animal with a long, thin tail. Usually **mice** are gray. The cat chased the **mouse** across the room and into a hole in the wall. ▲ **mice.**

mouth

You use your **mouth** to speak and eat. You also use your **mouth** to smile or frown. Your teeth and tongue are in your **mouth.** The children wiped their **mouths** with their napkins after they finished eating. ▲ **mouths.**

move

Move means to go from one place to another. Eddie **moved** the box from the floor to the table. Zelda and her family **moved** to the country last year. ▲ **moved, moving.**

We are packing the truck to **move** to a new house.

movie

A **movie** is made of pictures that move. You can see a **movie** in a theater, or you can watch a **movie** on television. ▲ **movies.**

Mr.

Mr. is used before a man's name. **Mr.** Walker is my teacher this year.

Mrs.

Mrs. is often used before a married woman's name. **Mrs.** Kelly is Richard's mother.

Ms.

Ms. is often used before a woman's name. **Ms.** Rodriguez, I'd like you to meet my brother and sister.

much

Much means a lot of something. Dad had so **much** work that he had to stay late at the office. After the storm, the sun came out and melted **most** of the snow. ▲ **more, most.**

mud

Mud is wet dirt. Chuck fell in the **mud** chasing the ball. When something has **mud** on it, it is **muddy.**

The three baby pigs are playing in the **mud.**

muffin

A **muffin** is a food like bread in the shape of a cup. When our friends came to our house for breakfast, we had **muffins,** fruit, and milk. ▲ **muffins.**

mug

A **mug** is a large cup with a handle. You can drink milk or eat soup from a **mug.** My friend gave me a clay **mug** that she made in art class. ▲ **mugs.**

multiply

Multiply means to add a number to itself once, twice, or even many times. If you **multiply** 2 times 3, it is the same thing as 2 plus 2 plus 2. ▲ **multiplied, multiplying.**

muscle

A **muscle** is what we use to move parts of the body. Our **muscles** help us lift and carry things. A dancer has strong leg **muscles.** ▲ **muscles.**

Aunt Esther just baked some corn **muffins.**

219

Let's see if we can find these **mushrooms** in the book we brought with us.

museum

A **museum** is a place that collects and keeps things for people to see and learn about. Some **museums** show art. Some show things from long ago. My class visited a science **museum** that had dinosaur bones and old rocks. ▲ **museums.**

mushroom

A **mushroom** looks like a plant that is shaped like a small umbrella. **Mushrooms** do not have flowers or leaves, and they grow very quickly. Some **mushrooms** can be eaten, but many are dangerous to eat. ▲ **mushrooms.**

music

The sounds made by a piano or violin are **music.** When you sing, you are making **music.** Birds make **music** when they sing. **Musical** means having to do with **music.** The piano is a **musical** instrument.

musician

A **musician** is someone who plays a musical instrument or sings. A group of **musicians** played music at Uncle Peter's wedding. ▲ **musicians.**

The **musicians** are practicing for the concert they will play on Saturday.

must

If you **must** do something, it means that you should do it. We **must** wear seatbelts when we ride in a car.

mustache

A **mustache** is the hair that grows above a man's lip. My daddy's **mustache** tickles me when I kiss him. ▲ **mustaches.**

mustard

Mustard is a thick, yellow liquid that you put on food to add flavor. It is made from the seeds of a plant. Mom likes to put **mustard** on her hamburger, but my brother and I like ketchup better.

my

My means that something belongs to me. Alan is **my** brother. That is **my** pencil. If I am talking about **myself,** I am talking about me. I wrote this story by **myself** and drew the pictures for it.

mysterious

When something is **mysterious,** it is very hard to explain or understand. We heard some **mysterious** sounds coming from the empty house.

The heat from **my** body makes a picture of me on the wall.

mystery

A **mystery** is a story, play, or movie in which there is a puzzle about a crime. When my father watches a **mystery,** he likes to guess who did the crime before there are many clues. Katherine likes to read **mysteries** and often borrows them from the library. ▲ **mysteries.**

Nn

Necklace of Nuts

nail

1. A **nail** is the hard part on the ends of your fingers and toes. The **nails** on your fingers are called **fingernails.** What do you think the **nails** on your toes are called?

2. A **nail** is also a thin piece of metal that has a point at one end and a flat part at the other end. You hammer a **nail** into two things to keep them together. ▲ **nails.**

3. Nail means to attach something with a **nail.** We **nailed** a picture to the wall. ▲ **nailed, nailing.**

name

1. A **name** is a word that you call something by. Banana and orange are **names** of two kinds of fruit.

2. A **name** is also what you call a person or place or animal. My **name** is Toby Smith. What is your **name?** Mississippi is the **name** of a state and a river. ▲ **names.**

3. When you choose a **name** for something, you **name** it. We **named** the kitten Boots. ▲ **named, naming.**

nap

When you sleep for a short time, you take a **nap.** We take a **nap** after lunch every day. Our new baby takes lots of **naps.** ▲ **naps.**

napkin

A **napkin** is a piece of cloth or paper that you use to cover your lap while you are eating. You also use a **napkin** to wipe your mouth and hands. We took paper **napkins** to the picnic. ▲ **napkins.**

narrow

Something that is **narrow** is not wide. The deer jumped across the **narrow** stream. We walked in a line along the **narrow** path. ▲ **narrower, narrowest.**

nature

Nature is everything that is not made by people. Mountains, trees, rivers, and stars are all part of **nature.** People and animals are part of **nature** too. Buildings and telephones are not part of **nature.**

near

Near means close to or not far from someone or something. My cousins live in a house **near** ours. The **nearest** grocery store is four blocks from here. ▲ **nearer, nearest.**

neat

When something is **neat,** it looks clean and everything is in its place. My brother's room is **neat,** but mine is a mess. Pat has the **neatest** closet I have ever seen. ▲ **neater, neatest.**

neck

1. Your **neck** is the part of your body just below your head. I pull my jacket zipper up to my **neck** when it is cold outside. A giraffe has a long, thin **neck.** Margie wears a scarf around her **neck.**
2. A **neck** is also a narrow part that is like a **neck** in shape. The **neck** of a violin is made of a special kind of wood. ▲ **necks.**

necklace

A **necklace** is jewelry that is worn around the neck. We gave Mom a silver **necklace** for her birthday. ▲ **necklaces.**

The space between these rocks is very **narrow.**

Waldo is telling us that he **needs** to go out.

need

When you **need** something, you have to have it. The dog **needs** food and water every day. You will **need** a sweater when you go outdoors today. ▲ **needed, needing.**

needle

1. A **needle** is a thin piece of metal that you use when you sew or knit. A sewing **needle** has a hole at one end for thread and a point at the other end. The leaves of some plants are called **needles** because of their shape.
2. Another kind of **needle** holds the medicine a doctor or a nurse gives you. Doctor Alvarez used a **needle** to give me medicine for the flu. ▲ **needles.**

neighbor

A **neighbor** is someone who lives near you. Our **neighbor** cared for Sinbad, our dog, when we went on vacation. ▲ **neighbors.**

neighborhood

A **neighborhood** is an area of a city or town where people live. Most of the children in my **neighborhood** go to the same school. ▲ **neighborhoods.**

In our **neighborhood,** sometimes we play football after school.

neither

Neither means not one and not the other. **Neither** one of the two children wanted to go into the water. **Neither** Tyrone nor Ralph won the race. **Neither** team played very well today.

nest

A **nest** is a bird's home. Birds build their **nests** with leaves, sticks, mud, and other things. Most birds lay their eggs in **nests**. ▲ **nests**.

Stephanie has found a **nest** of blue eggs.

net

A **net** is a kind of material that has holes in it. **Nets** are often made of string or rope. We need a new basketball **net** because the one we have now is torn in four places. One of the acrobats fell from the swing, but he landed in the **net** below. Some fishermen go out into the ocean and put large **nets** into the water to catch fish. ▲ **nets**.

never

You say **never** when you mean not at any time. We were surprised when Mike said he had **never** been to the circus. I have **never** seen a flower as beautiful as this one.

new

1. Something that is **new** has never been used before. We bought a **new** television after our old one broke. Jerry's skateboard is **newer** than mine, but Freddy's is the **newest** of all.
2. We also say that something is **new** if it is just starting or beginning. We started a **new** game. Pam is the **newest** pupil in my class. ▲ **newer, newest**.

Mr. Owens uses a small **net** to catch the fish that Thelma has chosen.

In our art class, we make things from **newspapers**.

news

News is the story of something that has just happened. We hear **news** on the radio and on television. We read **news** in newspapers and magazines. Did you read the **news** about the fire at the factory?

newspaper

A **newspaper** tells you the news about your neighborhood and other places. **Newspapers** are printed on paper. You can read about sports and books in a **newspaper.** Many **newspapers** have advertisements in them, and some have comics. ▲ **newspapers.**

next

1. **Next** means coming after someone or something. Bill is the **next** person in line to pay for groceries. **Next** Friday is the last day of school until September.
2. **Next** also means beside or near something. The baby deer stayed **next** to its mother.

nice

When something is **nice,** it makes you feel good. The sun was shining, and it was a **nice** day. It was **nice** of Julie to let us ride her new bicycle. Luis is the **nicest** person I know. ▲ **nicer, nicest.**

nickname

A **nickname** is a name that you use instead of a real name. Dot is a **nickname** for Dorothy. Rob's **nickname** is Red because of the color of his hair. ▲ **nicknames.**

Rob's **nickname** is on the front of his shirt.

night

Night is the part of the day when it is dark outside. **Night** begins at sunset. You can see the moon and stars at **night.** There are some animals that hunt at **night.** ▲ **nights.**

nightmare

A **nightmare** is a very bad dream. A **nightmare** can scare the person who dreams it. Last night I had a **nightmare** about being lost in a dark forest. ▲ **nightmares.**

no

1. **No** is the opposite of **yes.** **No,** I don't know Al's cousin. Mom said **no** when I asked if I could stay up late again.
2. **No** also means not any. I know there is **no** juice or milk in the refrigerator.

nobody

Nobody means not one person. I knocked, but **nobody** came to the door. **Nobody** went to the beach on Saturday because it rained.

noise

A **noise** is a sound, often a loud sound. At the airport there is always a lot of **noise.** When we make **noise,** we are **noisy.** The crowd at the game was **noisy.** ▲ **noises.**

none

None means not one or not any. Dave wanted an apple, but there was **none** left in the basket. **None** of us can jump as high as Jill can.

nonfiction

Nonfiction means anything that is written about real people and real things. **Nonfiction** is the opposite of **fiction.** A story in the newspaper is one kind of **nonfiction.** The story of a person's life is also **nonfiction.**

In her **nightmare,** Kara is running from a monster.

noodle

A **noodle** is food in the shape of a long, flat strip. **Noodles** are made of flour, water, and eggs. **Noodles** and hamburgers are my favorite foods. Peter wanted **noodles** in his soup instead of rice. ▲ **noodles.**

Mrs. Thomas uses a machine to make **noodles.**

noon

Noon is 12 o'clock in the day. We eat our lunch at **noon.**

nor

Nor is a word we use with **neither.** Neither Sarah **nor** Paul likes to play football.

north

When you look at a map, the direction toward the top is **north**. If you look toward the sun when it comes up in the morning, **north** is on your left. The opposite of **north** is **south.**

nose

Your **nose** is in the center of your face. You breathe and smell things through your **nose.** ▲ **noses.**

not

You use **not** to say no about something. Ronnie is **not** home.

nothing

Nothing means no thing. The dinner was so good, there was **nothing** left on anyone's plate. The opposite of **nothing** is **something**.

notice

1. When you **notice** something, you see it or pay attention to it. In the fall, Erin **noticed** that the days were getting shorter. ▲ **noticed, noticing.**
2. A **notice** also means a printed message to make something known. Benji got a **notice** that the circus was coming. ▲ **notices.**

The **numbers** tell whose turn is next.

now

Now means at this minute. Do you really have to leave **now?** It is snowing **now.**

number

1. A **number** tells you how many there are of something. Both 2 and 50 are **numbers.**
2. A **number** is also used to tell one thing from another. Do you know your telephone **number?** ▲ **numbers.**

nurse

A **nurse** is a person who takes care of sick people. Some **nurses** work in hospitals, and others visit people in their homes. ▲ **nurses.**

nut

A **nut** grows on a tree. **Nuts** usually have hard shells. Most **nuts** can be eaten. ▲ **nuts.**

The squirrel is storing **nuts** for the winter.

Oo

Octopus at the Office

oak

An **oak** is a tree that has acorns. The wood from **oak** trees is very strong and is used in making furniture and boats. Mom and Dad bought a kitchen table made of **oak.** ▲ **oaks.**

obey

When you **obey** someone, you do what that person tells you to do. Lynn **obeys** her parents and gets home from school by 4 o'clock. When Andy told his dog to sit, it **obeyed** him immediately. ▲ **obeyed, obeying.**

ocean

The **ocean** is made of salt water and covers large areas of the earth. Fish and whales live in the **ocean.** Ships sail on the **ocean.** ▲ **oceans.**

o'clock

We use the word **o'clock** when we say what time it is. We go to school at 8 **o'clock** in the morning.

octopus

An **octopus** is an animal that lives in the ocean. It has a soft body and eight arms. The **octopus** uses its arms to move and to catch food. ▲ **octopuses.**

odd

1. Odd means strange or different. Our car is making an **odd** noise and needs to be fixed. ▲ **odder, oddest.**
2. Some numbers are **odd** numbers, and some are even numbers. The numbers 1, 3, 5, 7, and 9 are **odd** numbers. The numbers 2, 4, 6, 8, and 10 are even numbers.

of

Of sounds like glove. Would you like a glass **of** milk? My desk is made **of** wood. **B** is the first letter **of** Barbara's name. Most **of** the children went on the trip. **Z** is the last letter **of** the alphabet.

off

1. We use **off** when we mean away from something or from the top of something. The kitten pushed the ball **off** the table.
2. Off also means not on. When Grandfather comes home, he takes **off** his shoes and puts on his slippers. Please turn **off** the water.

Dale loves to jump **off** the diving board.

office

An **office** is a place where people work. Some buildings have many offices in them. The principal's **office** is at the end of the hall. Dad took me to the doctor's **office** when I was feeling sick. ▲ **offices.**

officer

1. An **officer** is a person in an army who leads others and tells them what to do.
2. An **officer** is also a man or woman who works for the police. The police **officer** helped the lost child find her mother and father. ▲ **officers.**

often

If you do something **often,** you do it many times. We go to the park **often** when the weather is warm. Timmy **often** builds car models.

Luis's mother is putting **oil** on the door so it will open more easily.

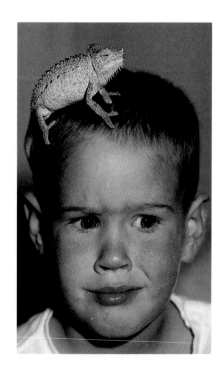

Scott isn't sure he likes his pet lizard **on** his head.

oil

1. Oil is a liquid that comes from vegetables and animals. It is used in cooking. We got out the pan and corn **oil** to make popcorn.
2. Another kind of **oil** comes from the ground. This **oil** is burned for heat and to make machines run. Our furnace burned a lot of **oil** last week because it was so cold outside. ▲ **oils.**

okay

Okay means that something is fine. Sally thought the radio was broken, but it was **okay.** This word is also spelled **OK.** Is it **OK** if I borrow your skateboard?

old

1. A person who has lived many years is **old.** Grandfather is **old,** but Toni is young.
2. Things are called **old** when they have been used for a long time. We gave away our **old** clothes to people who needed them.
3. We also use the word **old** when we talk about someone's age. I am 7 years **old.** Are you **older** than I am? ▲ **older, oldest.**

on

1. On means touching at the top of something. The bird is sitting **on** the fence.
2. On also means during a time. We went to the circus **on** Saturday.
3. When you put clothes **on,** you are wearing them. Eleanor put her jacket **on.**
4. On sometimes means that something is working. Do you still want the radio **on?**

once

1. If you do something **once,** you do it only one time. We buy groceries **once** a week.
2. Once also means as soon as. **Once** it stops raining, we can go outside.

one

1. One is the smallest number. The number **one** is written **1.** There is **one** sandwich left on the plate.
2. We say **one** when we talk about a person or thing. **One** of my sisters will take us to the concert. ▲ **ones.**

onion

An **onion** is the round or oval bulb of a plant that is also called an **onion. Onions** have a strong taste and smell and are eaten as a vegetable. When Mom cuts an **onion,** it makes tears come to her eyes. ▲ **onions.**

only

Only means that there is just one and no others. This is the **only** sweater I brought with me.

open

1. Open means not shut or closed. If a jar is **open,** there is no cover on it. The door was **open,** so I walked in.
2. Open also means to make something **open.** Please **open** the window.
3. Open also means to begin. The new play **opened** last Saturday night. ▲ **opened, opening.**

opening

An **opening** is an empty space. The rabbit pushed through an **opening** in the fence. ▲ **openings.**

opossum

An **opossum** is a small animal with gray fur. **Opossums** carry their babies in a pocket on their stomachs as kangaroos do. ▲ **opossums.**

Cheryl is **opening** her birthday present.

233

The man and the woman are going in **opposite** directions.

opposite

1. When something is **opposite** you, it is across from you. Karl and Elizabeth sat **opposite** each other at the table.
2. We also use **opposite** when we talk about two things that are different in every way. The **opposite** of **on** is **off**. The **opposite** of **day** is **night**. ▲ **opposites.**

or

The word **or** helps us when we are talking about two different things **or** people. Which do you like better, apples **or** pears? When I get home from school, I'll either play baseball **or** read.

orange

1. An **orange** is a small, round fruit. Oranges grow on trees. Would you like an **orange** with your breakfast? ▲ **oranges.**
2. **Orange** is also a color. Pumpkins are **orange.** I have an **orange** scarf.

orchestra

An **orchestra** is a group of people who play musical instruments together. Some of the instruments that are played in an **orchestra** are violins, horns, and drums. ▲ **orchestras.**

order

When things are in **order,** they are in the right place. Adam can say the letters of the alphabet in **order** from A to Z. Inge knows numbers in **order** from 1 to 25.

ostrich

An **ostrich** is a very large bird that has long legs and a long neck. The **ostrich** can run faster than any other bird. ▲ **ostriches.**

An **ostrich** cannot fly, but it can run very fast.

other

We use **other** when we mean something else or something that is different. I have decided to wear my **other** sweater to Annie's birthday party. Have you brought any **other** toys with you today?

our

Our means that something belongs to us. **Our** house is near the school. That brown dog is **ours.** If we are talking about **ourselves,** we are talking about us. We set the table all by **ourselves.**

out

1. **Out** means away from the inside. Tom took the toy train **out** of the box.
2. **Out** also means outdoors. Let's go **out** and play in the backyard.
3. **Out** can also mean through. We looked **out** the window to see if it was raining.

Darryl is taking the milk **out** of the refrigerator.

235

Ted has **outgrown** his jacket and it is too small.

outdoor

1. **Outdoor** means outside a building instead of inside. We went to an **outdoor** concert.
2. When you are **outdoors,** you are out under the sky. On warm evenings, we like to have our dinner **outdoors.**

outer space

Outer space is far away from the earth. The moon, the planets, and the stars are in **outer space.** Astronauts explore **outer space** in a spaceship.

outgrow

When you **outgrow** something, you get too big for it. The baby **outgrows** his clothes every few months. Anne **outgrew** her sneakers and had to buy some new ones.
▲ **outgrew, outgrown, outgrowing.**

outside

1. **Outside** means the part of something that is out. The **outside** of our house is painted white. ▲ **outsides.**
2. **Outside** also means outdoors or not inside. I was **outside** of the school when I heard the bell. The boys went **outside** to play in the yard.

oval

When something is **oval,** it is shaped like an egg. The turkey is on a big **oval** plate.

oven

An **oven** is the inside of a stove where you put things to heat or cook. Franny and her sister baked some bread in the **oven.** We watched the man put our pizza in the **oven** to cook. A **microwave oven** is a special kind of **oven** that can cook food very fast.
▲ **ovens.**

The mirror on Fran's table is **oval.**

over

1. Over means above or to the other side. Please move, Phil. I can't see **over** your head. Jill hit the ball **over** the fence.

2. Over also means on top of or covering. Aunt Becky put the blanket **over** the baby.

3. We say something is **over** when it has ended. School is **over** for the summer. Let's walk home when the game is **over.**

4. Over sometimes means again. We practiced the song **over** and **over** until we got it right.

5. You can also use **over** to mean turned on its side. The storm knocked the trees **over.**

Jackie jumped **over** the big puddle.

owe

Owe means to have to pay. Amy **owed** Marc some money for the crayons he helped her buy. ▲ **owed, owing.**

owl

An **owl** is a bird with large eyes. Most **owls** hunt and fly at night. ▲ **owls.**

own

1. When you **own** something, it belongs to you. I **own** a bicycle. My cousins **owned** four cats before they gave one away. ▲ **owned, owning.**

2. You also say **own** when you talk about something that belongs only to you. We each brought our **own** lunch to the picnic. A person who **owns** something is called the **owner.** The **owner** of the pet store showed me the new puppies.

This white and brown **owl** lives in the woods behind our house.

Pp
Qq

Penguin with a Pillow and a Quilt

pack
1. Pack means to put things together so you can carry them. We **packed** my toys in a box when we moved.
2. You also say that you **pack** something when you put things in it. Dad is **packing** his suitcase with clothes for his trip. ▲ **packed, packing.**

package
A **package** is a box with something in it. We sent a **package** of treats to my sister at camp. Will you help me tie the ribbon on these **packages?** ▲ **packages.**

pad
A **pad** is made up of pieces of paper that are glued together at one edge. The pages of a **pad** are empty so that you can write or draw on them. We leave a **pad** and pencil near the phone to write messages. Margo drew pictures on the pages of her **pad**. ▲ **pads.**

page
A **page** is one side of a piece of paper in a book, magazine, or newspaper. Nancy wrote her name on the first **page** of her book. The word "pair" is on **page** 239 in this book. Please don't tear any **pages** out of the magazine. ▲ **pages.**

paid
Paid comes from the word **pay.** I **paid** for the ice cream for all of us.

pail
A **pail** is round and open like a large can. It has a handle and might be made of metal, plastic, or wood. Jim filled the **pail** with water. ▲ **pails.**

pain

A **pain** is what you feel when something hurts. Jack felt a **pain** when he hit his leg against the table. The dentist asked me if I felt **pain** in my tooth. When something causes **pain**, it is **painful**. A bee can give a **painful** sting. ▲ **pains.**

paint

1. Paint is a liquid used to put color on things. **Paint** is wet when you put it on something. This **paint** will dry very fast. ▲ **paints.**
2. Paint also means to put **paint** on something. Paul **painted** a picture of a farm. A person who **paints** is called a **painter**. ▲ **painted, painting.**

painting

A **painting** is a picture that you **paint.** My **painting** of a dinosaur is in the art show. ▲ **paintings.**

pair

1. A **pair** is what we call two things that go together. A **pair** of birds sat on the branch.
2. Something that has two legs or two parts to it is also called a **pair.** Tim's old **pair** of pants has holes in the knees. I need a new **pair** of glasses. ▲ **pairs.**

pajamas

Pajamas are a shirt and a pair of pants that you wear when you go to bed. Jessica's favorite **pajamas** have red polka dots.

Pat and Sue did a good job of **painting** their dog's house.

Grandmother knitted me a new **pair** of mittens.

239

Alberta is cooking breakfast in a **pan**.

palace

A **palace** is a very large and beautiful house where a king, queen, or other ruler lives. The **palace** has many gardens around it. Sonia and Dale visited a **palace** with 50 rooms and marble floors. ▲ **palaces.**

pan

A **pan** is a flat metal dish used for cooking. Many **pans** have long handles. We cooked the fish in a large **pan.** ▲ **pans.**

pants

Pants are clothes that you wear on the bottom half of your body. **Pants** have two legs. Jamie wore new **pants** to the party.

paper

1. **Paper** is a material you write on or use for other things. **Paper** is made from trees or other plants. The pages of books and magazines are made of **paper.** We wrap presents in **paper.**
2. **Paper** is also another word for **newspaper.** Did you read about our school play in the **paper?** ▲ **papers.**

We cut and pasted **paper** to make our designs.

parachute

A **parachute** is used to drop people or things slowly and safely from an airplane. **Parachutes** look like big umbrellas. ▲ **parachutes.**

parade

A **parade** is a group of people or animals walking together in a line. Bands play music in some **parades.** ▲ **parades.**

Mary and the **parakeet** are good friends.

parakeet

A **parakeet** is a small bird with a long, pointed tail. **Parakeets** have blue, green, and yellow feathers. ▲ **parakeets.**

parent

A **parent** is a mother or a father. Jane's **parents** took us skating. ▲ **parents.**

park

1. A **park** is an area of land where people can play or rest. Most **parks** have trees and grass and benches. ▲ **parks.**
2. **Park** also means to put something in a place where it can stay for a while. Bob **parked** the car in the garage. ▲ **parked, parking.**

parking lot

A **parking lot** is a place where people can leave their cars for a short time. We left the car in the **parking lot** when we went shopping. ▲ **parking lots.**

Friends meet in the **park** to relax together.

241

parrot

A **parrot** is a kind of bird. **Parrots** may have blue, green, red, or yellow feathers. Some **parrots** can learn to talk. I got a **parrot** for my birthday. ▲ **parrots.**

part

A **part** is a piece of something. Your head is a **part** of your body. A television has many **parts.** ▲ **parts.**

party

A **party** is a lot of people who are having a good time together. We wore costumes to the Halloween **party.** ▲ **parties.**

pass

1. Pass means to go by. We **pass** your house on the way to school.
2. Pass also means to move something from one person to another. Please **pass** the cereal to me.
3. Pass also means to know something well enough so that you do not have to learn it again. I hope I **pass** the spelling test tomorrow. ▲ **passed, passing.**

Passover

Passover is a Jewish holiday celebrated in the spring. Families and friends gather together for a special meal on **Passover** and tell the story of the holiday.

past

1. When something is **past,** it has already happened or is over. It rained the **past** two days, but the sun is out now. Vacation is **past,** and it is time for school to begin.
2. Past also means that something or someone has gone by. Sarah threw the ball **past** Eddie, and it rolled to the fence.

Adrian put **parts** together to make a dinosaur.

242

Tess and Chris are **pasting** pieces of paper together to make pictures.

paste

1. Paste is something you use to make things stick together. Remember to put the top back on the **paste** jar, or the **paste** will dry up.
▲ **pastes.**
2. Paste also means to stick things together with **paste.** Charles **pasted** the photographs on all of the pages of his book.
▲ **pasted, pasting.**

pat

Pat means to touch gently with your hand. My horse likes it when I **pat** him on the head. Robert **patted** the baby on the back. ▲ **patted, patting.**

patch

1. A **patch** is a small piece of material that you sew onto your clothes to cover a hole. My pants have **patches** on the knees.
2. A **patch** is also an area of ground. Tess planted tomatoes and corn in the vegetable **patch.**
▲ **patches.**

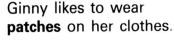

Ginny likes to wear **patches** on her clothes.

243

path

A **path** is a narrow place that you walk on. When we got to the camp, we took the **path** to the lake. We shoveled a **path** through the snow from the front door of our house to the street. ▲ **paths.**

The **patterns** in the two pieces of cloth are very different from each other.

pattern

A **pattern** is how colors or lines or marks are placed and look on something. There is a **pattern** of pink flowers on Julie's shirt. This butterfly's wing has a **pattern** of green and black dots on it. ▲ **patterns.**

paw

A **paw** is what we call a foot on some kinds of animals. **Paws** have claws or nails on them. Dogs, cats, lions, and foxes have **paws.** ▲ **paws.**

pay

Pay means to give money for something. I'll **pay** for the popcorn. Dad **paid** the person who fixed our car. ▲ **paid, paying.**

Sherry is **paying** for the toy with her own money.

pea

A **pea** is a small, round, green vegetable. Dad made **pea** soup last night. ▲ **peas.**

peace

Peace means a time when there is no fighting. When the world is at **peace,** there are no wars. Our country is at **peace.**

peach

A **peach** is a round, sweet fruit. It has a yellow and red skin. We had **peaches** for dessert. ▲ **peaches.**

peak

A **peak** is the point at the top of a mountain. We took a picture of the **peaks** covered with snow. ▲ **peaks.**

peanut

A **peanut** is something to eat. **Peanuts** have brown shells and grow under the ground. We always get a bag of **peanuts** at the baseball game. ▲ **peanuts.**

peanut butter

Peanut butter is a soft food that is made from peanuts. Bernice likes to eat **peanut butter** on crackers.

Tim is making himself a **peanut butter** sandwich.

pear

A **pear** is a sweet fruit. It has a yellow, brown, or red skin. **Pears** are bigger around the bottom than they are around the top. We had **pears** and cheese for dessert. ▲ **pears.**

pebble

A **pebble** is a small stone. There wasn't much sand at the beach, but there were lots of **pebbles.** I found a **pebble** in my shoe. ▲ **pebbles.**

Akeem is **peeking** at his birthday cake and presents.

peek
Peek means to look at something quickly or without anyone knowing. The squirrel **peeked** out from behind the tree.
▲ **peeked, peeking.**

peel
Peel means to take off the skin or outside part of some fruits and vegetables. Jean **peeled** the orange for her younger sister.
▲ **peeled, peeling.**

pen¹
A **pen** is a tool to write with. **Pens** are usually made of plastic or metal. He wrote his name with a blue **pen.** ▲ **pens.**

pen²
A **pen** is an area with a fence to keep animals in. The pigs live in a **pen.** ▲ **pens.**

pencil
A **pencil** is a tool to write with. It is often a long stick of wood with lead in it. Most **pencils** have an eraser on one end. Sue broke the point on her **pencil.** ▲ **pencils.**

penguin

A **penguin** is a black and white bird. **Penguins** live where it is very cold. They cannot fly, but they use their wings for swimming. ▲ **penguins.**

people

Men, women, and children are **people.** There were 20 **people** at Barbara's party.

pepper

1. **Pepper** is something we use on food to make it spicy. **Pepper** is usually black, but sometimes it is red or white.
2. A **pepper** is also a vegetable. **Peppers** can be red, green, or yellow. They are eaten raw or cooked. Do you like green **peppers** in salad? ▲ **peppers.**

Most **penguins** live in large groups.

perfect

When something is **perfect,** it means that nothing is wrong with it. Jane's math test was **perfect.** She made no mistakes.

perhaps

Perhaps means that something may happen. It is supposed to rain this afternoon, but **perhaps** the sun will shine instead.

period

1. A **period** is the small dot at the end of a sentence. This sentence ends with a **period.** But do you see that this one ends with a question mark?
2. A **period** is also an amount of time. They were on vacation for a **period** of six weeks. ▲ **periods.**

Too much **pepper** made Dad sneeze.

permit

Permit means to allow someone to do something. My parents will not **permit** my sister and me to play outside after it is dark. ▲ **permitted, permitting.**

person

A **person** is a man, woman, or child. Fifty people can ride on the bus, but only one **person** can drive it. ▲ **persons.**

The veterinarian will see many kinds of **pets** today.

pet

A **pet** is an animal that people care for in their homes. Dogs and cats are **pets.** Helen has two parakeets as **pets.** ▲ **pets.**

petal

A **petal** is a part of a flower. The **petals** of a daisy are narrow and white or yellow. ▲ **petals.**

pharmacy

A **pharmacy** is a store where drugs and medicines are sold. Another name for **pharmacy** is **drugstore.** ▲ **pharmacies.**

phone

1. Phone is a short word for **telephone.** The Colemans have three **phones** in their house. ▲ **phones.**

2. Phone means to use a telephone. We **phoned** my aunt tonight to sing "Happy Birthday" to her. ▲ **phoned, phoning.**

photograph

A **photograph** is a picture that you take with a camera. Polly took a **photograph** of our class. ▲ **photographs.**

piano

A **piano** is something that makes music. **Pianos** have black and white keys that you play with your fingers. Ian practices the **piano** every day for his concert. ▲ **pianos.**

pick

1. Pick means to take something in your hand. We're going to **pick** some flowers for Dad's birthday. The children **picked** up their toys and put them away.

2. Pick also means to choose something. Mom helped me **pick** a dress to wear to the party. ▲ **picked, picking.**

picnic

When you go on a **picnic,** you take food with you to eat outdoors. We brought sandwiches and fruit for a **picnic.** ▲ **picnics.**

picture

A **picture** is something that you draw or paint. You can also take **pictures** with a camera. I have a **picture** of a boat on my wall. ▲ **pictures.**

Renee is practicing a new song on the **piano**.

Kim and Angela are **picking** flowers for their new neighbor.

249

The **pig** wants to get out of the pen.

pie

A **pie** is something to eat. **Pies** are usually round. **Pies** can be filled with fruit, meat, eggs, or other things. ▲ **pies.**

piece

1. A **piece** is one part of a whole thing. We each had a **piece** of pumpkin pie after lunch.
2. A **piece** is also one out of many things. Please put all the **pieces** of the puzzle in this box. ▲ **pieces.**

pig

A **pig** is an animal with a fat body, short legs, and a short, curly tail. ▲ **pigs.**

pile

1. A **pile** is a lot of things lying on top of each other. We put all our old newspapers in a **pile** by the door. ▲ **piles.**
2. When we put things on top of each other, we **pile** them. Dad **piled** the logs next to the garage. ▲ **piled, piling.**

It is fun to jump into a big **pile** of leaves.

pill

A **pill** is a small, hard kind of medicine that people take when they are sick. The nurse gave me a **pill** to take with a glass of water. ▲ **pills.**

pillow

You use a **pillow** under your head when you rest or sleep. **Pillows** are usually soft. Most **pillows** are made of feathers or a kind of rubber. ▲ **pillows.**

pilot

A **pilot** is someone who flies an airplane. The **pilot** told us to wear our seatbelts. ▲ **pilots.**

pin

1. A **pin** is a thin piece of metal with a point at one end. A **pin** is used to hold things together. I used a **pin** to hold my skirt together when the button came off. ▲ **pins.**
2. When you use a **pin** to hold things together, you **pin** them. Toshi **pinned** a flower to her new coat. ▲ **pinned, pinning.**

These **pilots** are flying the airplane.

pine

A **pine** is a tree that has leaves that look like needles and stay on the tree all year. The wood of the **pine** is used to make furniture. ▲ **pines.**

pink

Pink is a light red color. When we mix white and red, we get **pink.** Our cheeks were **pink** when we were outside in the cold.

pipe

A **pipe** is a long piece of metal or plastic that liquids or gases can go through. The water in your house or apartment gets to your sink through **pipes**. ▲ **pipes**.

pirate

A **pirate** is a person on a ship who steals from other ships at sea. The **pirates** buried the treasure on an island. ▲ **pirates**.

We went to a play about **pirates**.

pitch

When you **pitch** a ball in a game, you throw it to a player who tries to hit it with a bat. Bob **pitched** for our baseball team. The person who is **pitching** is called the **pitcher**. Gail was the **pitcher** for the other team. ▲ **pitched, pitching**.

pizza

Pizza is a food that is usually flat and round. The bottom is made of a kind of bread. **Pizzas** have cheese and tomatoes on top. Sometimes **pizza** also has vegetables or meat on top of it. ▲ **pizzas**.

place

1. A **place** is where something is. A **place** is also where something happens. We had to look for **places** to hang our coats. Our town is a nice **place** to live.
2. A **place** is also a space or seat for a person. There weren't enough **places** for everyone at the table.
▲ **places.**

plaid

A **plaid** is a kind of pattern that has lines of different colors going across each other. Helen wore a **plaid** skirt with a red sweater. ▲ **plaids.**

The children saved a **place** for Karyn on the bus.

plain

When something is **plain**, it is easy to see, hear, or understand. As the airplane started to land, the people and houses on the ground were in **plain** sight. My friends made it **plain** that they did not agree with me.
▲ **plainer, plainest.**

plan

1. **Plan** means to think out a way to do something before you do it. The team **planned** how they were going to win the game. ▲ **planned, planning.**
2. A **plan** is the way you think of doing something. We are making **plans** for our summer vacation. ▲ **plans.**

plane

Plane is a short word for **airplane**. Serena likes to make model **planes**. ▲ **planes.**

Kevin and Phil are wearing different **plaid** shirts.

planet

A **planet** moves around the sun. There are nine **planets** that travel around the sun. The earth is one of the **planets.** ▲ **planets.**

plant

1. A **plant** is a living thing that grows and stays in one place. A **plant** also makes its own food. Trees, flowers, and grass are **plants.** ▲ **plants.**
2. When you put a **plant** in the ground so that it can grow, you **plant** it. My aunt **planted** a tree in the backyard. ▲ **planted, planting.**

plastic

Plastic is a material that many things are made from. It can be hard or soft. Some bottles are made of **plastic.** ▲ **plastics.**

plate

A **plate** is a dish. It is usually round and flat, and you put food on it. Johnny put the **plates** on the table for dinner. ▲ **plates.**

play

1. Play means to do something for fun. We're going to **play** a game of baseball.
2. Play also means to make music. Jeff **played** the piano at school yesterday.
3. Play can also mean to act in a play, movie, or other show. The actor who **played** the pirate was funny. ▲ **played, playing.**
4. A **play** is a story that you act out. Our class is putting on a **play**. ▲ **plays.**

player

A **player** is a person who plays sports, games, musical instruments, or other things. Vicki is a **player** on our hockey team. ▲ **players.**

playground

A **playground** is a place where you can play outdoors. ▲ **playgrounds.**

please

Please is a word that we use when we ask for something in a polite way. **Please** pass the peanuts.

There are many things to do at the **playground.**

plenty

Plenty means that there is more than enough of something. There was **plenty** of corn for everybody at the picnic.

plow

A **plow** is a large tool that farmers use to dig up the earth. **Plows** are usually pulled by tractors or animals. ▲ **plows.**

plural

Plural means more than one. We use the **plural** when we want to say more than one person or thing. The **plural** of **child** is **children.** The **plural** of **book** is **books.** ▲ **plurals.**

plus

We use the word **plus** when we add numbers or other things together: 2 **plus** 2 is 4. Another way of writing 2 **plus** 2 is 2 + 2.

David has filled his **pockets** with many things.

pocket

A **pocket** is a place that holds things. Barbara put her gloves in one **pocket** and her keys in another pocket. ▲ **pockets.**

poem

A **poem** is a special kind of writing. Some **poems** have words that rhyme. Another word for **poems** is **poetry.** A person who writes **poems** is called a **poet.** ▲ **poems.**

Lila **points** to her answer.

point

1. A **point** is the sharp or thin end of something. Needles, pins, pencils, and pens have **points**. Sally used the **point** of a stick to write in the dirt. Matt drew a star with five **points**. ▲ **points**.

2. Point also means to use a finger or another thing to show where something is. The police officer **pointed** to where we could safely cross the road. Mr. Samuels asked Kenneth to **point** to the right answer on the chalkboard. ▲ **pointed, pointing**.

pole

A **pole** is a long piece of wood or metal. The flag flies from a **pole** in front of our school. Franny got a new fishing **pole** for her birthday. The firefighters slide down the **pole** when they hear the alarm. ▲ **poles**.

police

The **police** are a group of people who work to keep us safe. They also make sure that everyone obeys the laws. The **police** caught the person who stole the money. Hank's aunt is a **police** officer.

Travis is sliding down the metal **pole** in the park.

polite

Polite people are kind and think of others. People who are **polite** have good manners. Jorge is a **polite** boy who tries to help people. ▲ **politer, politest.**

polka dot

A **polka dot** is one of many round dots that make a pattern on cloth or other material. Evie's grandma bought her a scarf with red **polka dots** on it. ▲ **polka dots.**

This part of the beach is **polluted** with trash.

pollute

Pollute means to make something in nature dirty. ▲ **polluted, polluting.**

pollution

Pollution means that something in nature has been made dirty. **Pollution** in the river is killing the fish. **Pollution** in the air can make it hard to breathe.

pond

A **pond** is water with land all around it. A **pond** is smaller than a lake. The **pond** in back of my house has fish and frogs in it. ▲ **ponds.**

pony

A **pony** is a small kind of horse. I rode a **pony** at the fair. ▲ **ponies.**

pool

A **pool** is filled with water to swim in. Our school has an indoor **pool**. We go swimming in the **pool** at the park during the summer. ▲ **pools.**

The **ponies** are running through the field.

poor

When people are **poor**, they have very little money. The money from the concert will be used to help **poor** people. ▲ **poorer, poorest.**

pop

Pop means to make a short, loud noise. When a balloon breaks, we say that it **pops**. Daryl is sad because his balloon **popped**. ▲ **popped, popping.**

popcorn

Popcorn is a kind of corn that pops open when you cook it. Tiffany and Jake shared some **popcorn** at the movie.

porch

A **porch** is a part of a house that is outdoors. Sometimes a **porch** has a roof. We sit on our **porch** in the summer because it is cool there. ▲ **porches.**

This house has two **porches.**

post office

A **post office** is a place where you mail letters and packages. You also buy stamps there. Some people pick up their mail at the **post office**. ▲ **post offices.**

Nathan is **pouring** the juice into another container.

pot

A **pot** is a deep, round container used for cooking. We make stew in a big **pot.** ▲ **pots.**

potato

A **potato** is a vegetable that grows under the ground. We baked **potatoes** for dinner. ▲ **potatoes.**

pour

1. **Pour** means to make a liquid go from one thing to another. Dad **poured** soup from the pot into our mugs.
2. When it rains very hard, we say that it is **pouring.** During our vacation, it **poured** for two days. ▲ **poured, pouring.**

powder

Powder is something made of many very small, dry pieces. When my feet itched, Mom put some **powder** on them. ▲ **powders.**

power

When you have **power,** you are able to do something or make something happen. ▲ **powers.**

practice

You **practice** by doing something over and over again until you do it well. We **practiced** spelling new words. ▲ **practiced, practicing.**

pray

When you **pray,** you speak to God. ▲ **prayed, praying.**

present

A **present** is something you give for a special reason. Each of the children brought a **present** to the party. Another word for **present** is **gift.** ▲ **presents.**

Rebecca **practices** her writing at school.

president

A **president** is the leader of a group of people. The election to choose a **president** for the United States is held every four years in November. George Washington and Abraham Lincoln were famous **presidents.** We are going to have an election to choose the **president** of our class next week. ▲ **presidents.**

press

1. **Press** means to push something. Murray **pressed** the button and the elevator came.
2. **Press** also means to use an iron. I **pressed** my favorite shirt so that I could wear it to the party. Priscilla has to **press** her costume for the play. ▲ **pressed, pressing.**

pretend

Pretend means to make believe. Tomás and Janie **pretended** to be robots. Eddie played a trick on me by **pretending** to be asleep. ▲ **pretended, pretending.**

pretty

When something is **pretty,** it is nice to see or hear. That is a **pretty** dress you are wearing. We listened to some **pretty** music at our school's concert last night. I think this dress is **prettier** than that one. That was the **prettiest** sunset that I have ever seen. ▲ **prettier, prettiest.**

pretzel

A **pretzel** is a food baked in the shape of a knot or stick. It has salt on the outside. Jon and Elaine like to share a bag of **pretzels** after school. We buy hot **pretzels** when we go to football games. ▲ **pretzels.**

Anita and Roger are **pretending** to be pirates on a ship.

What is the **price** of Yolanda's lemonade?

price

The **price** of something is how much money you pay for it. The **price** of these sneakers is $30. ▲ **prices.**

prince

A **prince** is the son of a king or queen. ▲ **princes.**

princess

A **princess** is the daughter of a king or queen. ▲ **princesses.**

principal

A **principal** is the leader of a school. Our **principal** is Mrs. Fernandez. ▲ **principals.**

print

1. **Print** means to write using letters like the letters in a book. The teacher **printed** his name on the chalkboard.
2. **Print** also means to use machines to make letters and pictures on paper. On our class trip, we saw machines **printing** books. ▲ **printed, printing.**

The boys decided to **print** a sign for their new business.

printer

A **printer** is a machine that is used with a computer. A **printer** takes the words stored in the computer and prints them on paper. ▲ **printers.**

prison

A **prison** is a place where someone who has not obeyed the law has to stay. **Prison** is another word for **jail.** ▲ **prisons.**

privacy

When people want to be alone, we say that they want **privacy**. Vanessa went to her room because she wanted **privacy** to think.

prize

When you do something very well, you may win a **prize** for it. Janice won first **prize** in the art show for her painting of a lion. ▲ **prizes.**

probably

You say **probably** when you think something is true, but you are not sure. We will **probably** go to the mountains on Saturday, but we haven't decided yet.

problem

1. A **problem** is a question that has not been answered. There are 10 **problems** on our mathematics test today.
2. A **problem** is also something that you have to think about. We had a **problem** finding Tony's house because we had lost his address. ▲ **problems.**

We have a **problem** with our kite.

program

A **program** is a show that you watch on television or hear on the radio. My favorite **program** comes on at 6 o'clock. ▲ **programs.**

promise

Promise means to say that you will be sure to do something. Lionel **promised** not to tell my secret to anyone. ▲ **promised, promising.**

Sarah **protects** her head, her elbows, and her knees when she roller-skates.

protect

Protect means to keep from danger. The mother bear **protected** her cubs from the other animals. Seatbelts help to **protect** people in automobile accidents.
▲ **protected, protecting.**

proud

When you are **proud,** you feel good about something you or someone else has done. Ron was very **proud** of the card he made for his mother's birthday. Jeff's parents were **proud** of him when he won the prize.
▲ **prouder, proudest.**

prove

Prove means to show that something is true. I can **prove** that this book is mine because it has my name on it.
▲ **proved, proving.**

public

If something is **public,** it means that it is for all people. Most of the children in our town go to **public** school. A **public** beach is for anybody to use. Our **public** library is open every day except Sunday.

Everyone may use the **public** library.

publish

Publish means to print a newspaper, magazine, book, or other written thing and try to sell it. My grandmother wrote a book of poems that was **published** a long time ago. Margaret's uncle **publishes** a magazine about horses. ▲ **published, publishing.**

Mercedes and Billy are making **pudding** for dessert.

pudding

Pudding is a soft, sweet dessert. Vicky's favorite dessert is chocolate **pudding.**
▲ **puddings.**

puddle

A **puddle** is a small area of water that is made when it rains or when snow melts. I like to step in **puddles** and make the water splash. There were **puddles** in the road after the rain.
▲ **puddles.**

pull

When you **pull** something, you move it toward you. The dogs **pulled** the sled across the snow. The dentist **pulled** out my loose tooth. ▲ **pulled, pulling.**

265

We chose the biggest **pumpkin** we could find.

pumpkin

A **pumpkin** is a big, round, orange fruit that grows on the ground. We cut a face in a **pumpkin** for Halloween. ▲ **pumpkins.**

punch

Punch means to hit something hard with your fist. Al **punched** Ned on the arm when they had a fight. ▲ **punched, punching.**

punish

A person is **punished** when a person has done something wrong. My parents said I would be **punished** for not doing my homework. To **punish** me, they won't let me watch television for a week. ▲ **punished, punishing.**

pupil

The **pupils** are using headphones to listen to a story.

A **pupil** is someone who goes to school. There are 25 **pupils** in our class. Another word for **pupil** is **student.** ▲ **pupils.**

puppet

A **puppet** is a doll that you put over your hand and move with your fingers. Another kind of **puppet** has strings that you pull to make it move. In school, we put on a show using **puppets**. ▲ **puppets**.

puppy

A **puppy** is a baby dog. The **puppies** slept close to their mother. ▲ **puppies**.

purchase

Purchase means to get something by paying money. We **purchased** our train tickets at the railroad station. ▲ **purchased, purchasing**.

pure

When something is **pure**, it is not mixed with anything else. My scarf is made of **pure** wool. ▲ **purer, purest**.

purple

Purple is a color. When we mix red and blue, we get **purple**.

purpose

When you do something on **purpose,** it means that you have a reason for what you do. Debbie dropped the books on **purpose** to make a loud noise and scare us.

purr

Purr means to make a soft, quiet sound. Cats **purr** when they are happy. My cat always **purrs** when I scratch her back. ▲ **purred, purring**.

purse

A **purse** is a bag for carrying money and other small things. **Purses** are made of cloth, plastic, or other soft material. Annette put her keys in her **purse**. ▲ **purses**.

The **puppet's** arms move when you pull on the strings.

267

Gil is **pushing** the chair closer to the television.

push

When you **push** something, you move it in front of you. Georgia **pushed** the shopping cart for her mother. ▲ **pushed, pushing.**

put

When you **put** something in a place, you make it be there. I **put** the plates on the shelf. ▲ **put, putting.**

puzzle

1. A **puzzle** is any problem that is confusing. Amy tried many times to find the answer to the **puzzle.**
2. A **puzzle** is a game with many little pieces that you must work with or think about before they fit together. When all the pieces of the **puzzle** are put together, they show a picture of an airplane. ▲ **puzzles.**

queen

A **queen** is a woman who rules a country. The **queen** waved to the people as she rode in the carriage. ▲ **queens.**

question

When you ask a **question,** you are trying to find out something. I asked a **question** about how birds build their nests. Beth knew the answer to the **question.** ▲ **questions.**

question mark

A **question mark** comes at the end of a sentence that is a question. Does this sentence end with a **question mark** or a period? ▲ **question marks.**

Maggie and her father are putting the **puzzle** together piece by piece.

quick

When something is **quick,** it means that it moves fast or happens in a short time. We ate a **quick** lunch. When you do something fast, you do it **quickly.** When the traffic light changed to green, Irv **quickly** crossed the street. ▲ **quicker, quickest.**

quiet

1. When something is **quiet,** it makes little or no noise. The class was **quiet** when our teacher read us a story. When you do something in a **quiet** way, you do it **quietly.** We talked **quietly** while the baby slept.
2. Quiet also means that there isn't any sound in a certain place. The house was so **quiet** you could hear the wind outside. ▲ **quieter, quietest.**

quilt

A **quilt** is like a blanket. It is made of two pieces of cloth that are filled with soft material. I sleep under a soft, warm **quilt** during the winter. ▲ **quilts.**

quite

Quite means very or a lot. It is **quite** warm today. There was **quite** a crowd of people at the new store when it opened. **Not quite** means almost. It is **not quite** time for dinner. My little brother could **not quite** reach the top of the table.

Margot and her aunt made this **quilt** by sewing many small pieces of cloth together.

quiz

A **quiz** is a short test. We had a spelling **quiz** today on the new words we learned yesterday. ▲ **quizzes.**

Rr

Robots Reading

rabbit
A **rabbit** is a small animal with long ears, soft fur, and a short tail. **Rabbits** have strong legs in the back and can hop very fast. ▲ **rabbits.**

raccoon
A **raccoon** is a small, furry animal. It has black marks on its face that look like a mask and black rings on its tail. We saw two **raccoons** in the woods yesterday. ▲ **raccoons.**

race
1. A **race** is a contest to find out who or what can go the fastest. Don won the **race** by 10 feet. ▲ **races.**
2. Race also means to move very fast. The dogs **raced** around the house to the backyard. ▲ **raced, racing.**

radar
Radar is an instrument used to find and follow things like airplanes, automobiles, and storms. **Radar** helps pilots land their airplanes safely.

radio
A **radio** is a machine that you can turn on to listen to music, news, or other programs. Some evenings we listen to music on our **radio.** ▲ **radios.**

raft
A **raft** is a kind of flat boat made of logs or boards that have been joined together. Some **rafts** are made of rubber or plastic and are filled with air. Floating on a **raft** in the middle of a lake is a perfect way to spend a hot afternoon. ▲ **rafts.**

rag

A **rag** is a small piece of cloth. It is usually made of torn material. Dorothy and Fred used **rags** to wash the car. ▲ **rags.**

railing

A **railing** is a fence that protects you from falling over or into something. We put a **railing** around our pool. ▲ **railings.**

The only way to get through some of these mountains is by **railroad.**

railroad

A **railroad** is a way of traveling by train. If you follow the **railroad** tracks, you will get to the train station. ▲ **railroads.**

rain

1. **Rain** is water that falls in drops from clouds to the ground. Ted went out in the **rain** without his boots. When there is a lot of **rain,** we say it is **rainy.** ▲ **rains.**
2. **Rain** also means to fall in drops of water. It **rained** yesterday. ▲ **rained, raining.**

The **rainbow** appeared after the rain stopped.

rainbow

The colors that you sometimes see in the sky after it rains are called a **rainbow. Rainbows** have the shape of a curve. They happen when light from the sun shines through tiny drops of water in the air. ▲ **rainbows.**

Lisa's **raincoat** is the same color as her boots and her umbrella.

raincoat

A **raincoat** is a coat that you wear to keep dry in the rain. We put on our **raincoats,** boots, and hats to go outside when it was raining. ▲ **raincoats.**

raise

1. When you **raise** something, you lift it up. Karl and Alice helped the teacher **raise** the flag to the top of the flagpole. Faye **raised** her hand because she knew the answer to the teacher's question.
2. Raise also means to help something to grow. One farmer in our town is **raising** corn, and another is **raising** chickens.
▲ **raised, raising.**

rake

1. A **rake** is a tool for gathering leaves or other things together. A **rake** has teeth like a comb and a long handle. ▲ **rakes.**

2. Rake can also mean to gather things together with a **rake.** Barbara and Jim **raked** all the leaves into a big pile. ▲ **raked, raking.**

ramp

A **ramp** is a kind of road or sidewalk that goes up from one place to another. A **ramp** does not have steps. There are **ramps** at our school for people who can't use the stairs. Maggie pushed the cart up the **ramp.** ▲ **ramps.**

ran

Ran comes from the word **run.** The fox **ran** back into the woods when it saw us coming toward it. Patricia **ran** home from school.

ranch

A **ranch** is a kind of farm that has cattle, sheep, or horses on it. My aunt and uncle live on a **ranch** and raise cattle. ▲ **ranches.**

rang

Rang comes from the word **ring.** Jennifer **rang** the bell, and Mr. Brown opened the door. When the fire alarm **rang,** we rushed out of the building.

ranger

A **ranger** is a person whose work is to protect forests, parks, and other areas. The **ranger** showed us where the picnic area was. ▲ **rangers.**

Jake is using the big **rake** to **rake** the leaves.

273

Matt has to **reach** high to hand his aunt the bulb.

Timothy has found an unusual place to **read**.

rat

A **rat** is an animal that looks like a big mouse. **Rats** have long noses and long, thin tails. ▲ **rats.**

raw

Raw means not cooked. Gabe likes to eat a salad made of **raw** carrots, tomatoes, and lettuce. ▲ **rawer, rawest.**

reach

1. When you **reach** for something, you put out your hand to touch it. Joe can't **reach** the top shelf unless he stands on his toes. Ingrid **reached** up to get the kitten out of the tree.
2. **Reach** also means to get to a place. When the bus **reached** our street, we asked the driver to stop. ▲ **reached, reaching.**

read

When you know how to **read,** you can understand the words you see. Can you **read** that sign? Molly is **reading** a book about lions. When **read** rhymes with bed, we are talking about something that has already happened. I **read** three books while I was on vacation. Luke's sister **read** a story to him before he went to bed. ▲ **read, reading.**

ready

If you are **ready,** it means that when there is something to do, you can do it. Once I pack my clothes, I will be **ready** to go on the trip. Everyone is **ready** to start the race.
▲ **readier, readiest.**

real

When something is **real,** you know it is true. Is that a **real** bug, or is it made of plastic? The giant in the fairy tale was not **real.** It was make-believe.

reality

Reality means something that is **real.** The things that happen every day are **reality.** When you write about the things you do, you are writing about **reality.** The opposite of **reality** is **fantasy.** ▲ **realities.**

really

1. **Really** comes from the word **real.** We use **really** when we are very sure about something. I **really** want to be a doctor.
2. **Really** also means very. We had a **really** good time at the carnival.

reason

A **reason** tells you why something happened. The **reason** Ellen gave for being late for the concert was that there was a lot of traffic. ▲ **reasons.**

recess

A **recess** is a short time when you stop working. We played outside the school during **recess.** ▲ **recesses.**

recipe

A **recipe** tells you how to make something to eat or drink. Read the **recipe** before you start to make the soup. ▲ **recipes.**

record

A **record** is a round, flat disk made of plastic. It has music or other sounds on it. At the party, we listened to **records** and sang along. ▲ **records.**

rectangle

A **rectangle** is a shape with four sides and four corners. The cover of this book is in the shape of a **rectangle.** ▲ **rectangles.**

Lottie is using **rectangles** and other shapes to draw a picture on her computer.

Brandie is looking for her other **red** sock.

recycle

When we **recycle** something, we make it so that it can be used again. Our town **recycles** cans, bottles, and newspapers.
▲ **recycled, recycling.**

red

Red is the color of blood. Most fire engines are painted **red.**

reflection

A **reflection** is what you see when you look in a mirror or in still water. You can also see your **reflection** in very shiny things. I see my **reflection** in the pond. ▲ **reflections.**

refrigerator

A **refrigerator** is a large machine that keeps food cold. We put milk in the **refrigerator** to keep it fresh. ▲ **refrigerators.**

You can see the **reflection** of the building in the water.

relative

A **relative** is someone who is part of your family. Your parents, sisters and brothers, and grandparents are your **relatives.** So are your aunts, uncles, and cousins. ▲ **relatives.**

relax

If you are tired from working or playing too much, you need to **relax.** Reading, watching television, or taking a walk are some ways to **relax.** Madeline likes to **relax** by reading mystery stories. ▲ **relaxed, relaxing.**

Our **relatives** get together every year for a picnic.

remember

When we **remember** something, we think of it again, or we do not forget it. I will always **remember** when I got my puppy. Joey **remembered** to close the door when he went outdoors. ▲ **remembered, remembering.**

remind

Remind means to make someone remember. My sister **reminded** me to feed the cat before I left for school. ▲ **reminded, reminding.**

rent

Rent is money that you pay to use something. My parents pay **rent** every month for our apartment. ▲ **rents.**

repeat

If you **repeat** something, you do it or say it again. The teacher asked me to **repeat** my answer because he could not hear me.
▲ **repeated, repeating.**

Can you name any of the **reptiles** in this picture?

reptile

A **reptile** is a kind of animal that crawls on its stomach or walks on very short legs. Snakes, turtles, and lizards are all **reptiles.** Most **reptiles** lay eggs. An alligator is a kind of **reptile.** ▲ **reptiles.**

responsibility

When you have a **responsibility,** you have a job or something that you are supposed to do. Julie has the **responsibility** of caring for her pet. ▲ **responsibilities.**

rest¹

1. When you **rest,** you stop what you are doing for a while because you are tired. The children need to **rest** after lunch before they go out to play again. ▲ **rested, resting.**
2. A **rest** is the time you are **resting.** After the long hike, we all took a **rest.** ▲ **rests.**

rest²

Rest means what is left after everything else is gone. After my birthday party, I took the **rest** of the cake to my neighbors.

restaurant

A **restaurant** is a place to eat. In a **restaurant,** you sit at a table or a counter. Someone brings you your food, and you pay for it.
▲ **restaurants.**

return

1. **Return** means to come back or to go back. My cousin **returned** to France after visiting us last week.
2. When you **return** something, you give it back. Flora **returned** the records to the library. ▲ **returned, returning.**

Roberta is **returning** the books to the library.

reward

If you lose something important, you may give a **reward** to someone for finding it. Mrs. Brown gave Ted a $5 **reward** for finding her lost dog. ▲ **rewards.**

rhinoceros

A **rhinoceros** is an animal with one or two big horns on its nose. **Rhinoceroses** have very thick, heavy skin and short legs.
▲ **rhinoceroses.**

The **rhinoceros** is one of the largest animals in the world.

rhyme

Words **rhyme** when they sound alike at the end. Bread, red, and bed **rhyme**. School **rhymes** with pool. ▲ **rhymed, rhyming.**

ribbon

A **ribbon** is a long, thin piece of cloth used to make something look nice. Sue put a red **ribbon** on the birthday gift. ▲ **ribbons.**

rice

Rice is a food that comes from the small white seeds of a plant. We had **rice** and beans for lunch. Dad put **rice** in the soup.

Rice plants need lots of water to grow.

rich

People who are **rich** have a lot of money or land. ▲ **richer, richest.**

riddle

A **riddle** is a question or problem that is hard to answer or understand. Here is a **riddle:** What has two hands but no fingers? Answer: A clock. ▲ **riddles.**

ride

1. When we **ride** something, we are on it or in it while it moves. We **rode** on the train during our vacation. Elizabeth learned how to **ride** a horse at camp. ▲ **rode, riding.**
2. A **ride** is also a short trip in or on something. We took a **ride** around the block on our bicycles. ▲ **rides.**

right

1. Your body has a **right** side and a left side. **Right** is the opposite of **left.** In the United States, people drive cars on the **right** side of the road.
2. Right also means not having a mistake. **Right** is the same as correct. Nancy knew the **right** answers to all the questions on the test.
3. Right also means immediately. Let's leave **right** after lunch.

Tess is giving Josie and her toys a **ride.**

ring¹

A **ring** is something in the shape of a circle. We all sat in a **ring** around Ms. Hughes as she told us the story. A **ring** may be a piece of jewelry that you wear on your finger. Cynthia has a **ring** made of gold. ▲ **rings.**

ring²

Ring means to make a sound with a bell. At camp, they **ring** a bell when dinner is ready. Do you hear the telephone **ringing?** ▲ **rang** or **rung, ringing.**

rink

A **rink** is a place where people ice-skate or roller-skate. ▲ **rinks.**

In this game, you try to knock the marbles out of the chalk **ring.**

Trisha **ripped** her pants climbing over the fence.

The yellow bananas are **ripe,** but the green ones are not.

rip

Rip means to tear something like paper or cloth. Don't let the baby **rip** the pages out of the book. ▲ **ripped, ripping.**

ripe

When something is **ripe**, it has finished growing and is ready to be eaten. When bananas turn yellow, they are **ripe.** Those are the **ripest** tomatoes that I have ever seen. ▲ **riper, ripest.**

river

A **river** is water that is always moving from high ground to low ground. **Rivers** end when they come to another **river,** a lake, a sea, or an ocean. ▲ **rivers.**

road

A **road** is a wide path that cars travel on. Before there were cars, horses and wagons traveled on **roads.** Yesterday we watched the workers fill the hole in the **road.** ▲ **roads.**

roar

Roar means to make a loud, deep sound. Bears, lions, and tigers can **roar.** When the airplane was landing, we could hear the engine **roar.** ▲ **roared, roaring.**

roast

Roast means to cook in an oven or over a fire. Grandma **roasted** a chicken for dinner tonight. ▲ **roasted, roasting.**

rob

Rob means to take something that does not belong to you. It is wrong to **rob** things. **Rob** means the same as steal. The man who **robbed** the bank has been sent to jail. ▲ **robbed, robbing.**

robin

A **robin** is a bird with a red chest and a black or gray back. We see **robins** in the spring and summer. ▲ **robins.**

robot

A **robot** is a machine. It can do some of the same work that people do. Some **robots** do work that is dangerous for people to do. ▲ **robots.**

rock¹

A **rock** is a big stone. Bill and Jeannie climbed over the **rocks** at the park. ▲ **rocks.**

rock²

When you **rock,** you gently move backward and forward or from side to side. I **rocked** the baby in my arms. ▲ **rocked, rocking.**

rocket

A **rocket** is a machine that can fly up into the air very quickly. People travel into outer space in very large **rockets.** ▲ **rockets.**

rocking chair

A **rocking chair** is a chair that rests on two long pieces of wood in the shape of a curve. When you sit in a **rocking chair** and lean forward and backward, the chair rocks. ▲ **rocking chairs.**

rode

Rode comes from the word **ride.** We **rode** horses on the beach. Mom and Dad sat in front, and we **rode** in the back seat.

rodeo

A **rodeo** is a show with contests in which cowboys and cowgirls ride horses and do tricks. ▲ **rodeos.**

This **robot** looks a little like a person, but it is still a machine.

283

roll

1. Roll means to move by turning over and over. **Roll** the ball to me and I will kick it back to you.

2. Roll also means to move on wheels. Micki and her friends **rolled** down the street on their skateboards. ▲ **rolled, rolling.**

We can't wait to use our new **roller skates.**

roller skate

1. A **roller skate** is a skate with wheels on the bottom. ▲ **roller skates.**

2. When you **roller-skate,** you move on **roller skates.** We went to the park on Saturday morning to **roller-skate.**
▲ **roller-skated, roller-skating.**

roof

A **roof** is the top part of a building. In the city, many houses have flat **roofs.** There is a chimney on top of our **roof.** ▲ **roofs.**

room

1. A **room** is a part of a house or other building. The **room** you sleep in is your **bedroom**.
2. Room can also mean space. There is plenty of **room** in the car for six people. I ate so much dinner that I had no **room** for dessert. ▲ **rooms.**

rooster

A **rooster** is a male chicken. **Roosters** make a loud noise early in the morning when the sun comes up. ▲ **roosters.**

root

A **root** is the part of a plant that grows under the ground. **Roots** take water and food from the ground to feed the plant. ▲ **roots.**

rope

A **rope** is a very strong, thick string for pulling, lifting, or hanging things. **Rope** is also used to hold something in place. We used **rope** to tie all the boxes together. ▲ **ropes.**

rose

A **rose** is a flower that grows on a bush. **Roses** are red, white, yellow, or other colors. Dave has a garden of **roses.** ▲ **roses.**

rough

1. Something that feels **rough** is full of bumps. The bark of a tree feels **rough**.
2. Rough also means not gentle. The children were too **rough** playing football, and Wally hurt his hand. The ocean was **rough** during the storm. ▲ **rougher, roughest.**

The **rooster** is standing on the fence.

Bev likes the sweet smell of **roses.**

The children climbed up to make three **rows** across.

round

When something is **round,** it has the shape of a ball or a globe. A circle is **round.** The earth is **round.** ▲ **rounder, roundest.**

row

A **row** is a line of people or things. My desk is in the last **row** in our classroom. Jenny planted a **row** of flowers along the wall. ▲ **rows.**

rub

When you **rub** something, you move your hand or something else over it. The cat **rubbed** against Tom's leg. ▲ **rubbed, rubbing.**

rubber

Rubber is a material that you can pull and it won't break. Tires are made of **rubber.** **Rubber** also keeps out water. Some boots are made of **rubber.** Sal wears **rubber** boots when it rains.

rude

When you are **rude,** you are not being polite to someone. It was **rude** of Ellen to yell at Tom when he asked to borrow her book. ▲ **ruder, rudest.**

rug

A **rug** is made of very strong cloth and is used to cover a floor. I have a **rug** in my bedroom. ▲ **rugs.**

rule

1. A **rule** tells you what you can do and what you cannot do. One of the **rules** at school is that you cannot run in the halls. Sara never wants to follow the **rules** when we play games. ▲ **rules.**
2. **Rule** also means to lead. The queen **ruled** her country well. ▲ **ruled, ruling.**

ruler

1. A **ruler** is a tool for measuring how long something is. **Rulers** are long and straight. You can also use a **ruler** to draw a straight line. I measured my drawing with a **ruler.**
2. A **ruler** is also someone who is the leader of a country. The king and queen were fair **rulers.**
▲ **rulers.**

rumble

Rumble means to make a deep sound. Diego heard thunder **rumbling** just after he saw the lightning. The old truck **rumbled** over the bumps in the road.
▲ **rumbled, rumbling.**

run

1. Run means to move with your legs as fast as you can. Elsie had to **run** to catch the bus. My parents exercise by **running** every day. A **runner** is someone who **runs.** All the **runners** were ready for the big race.
2. Run also means to work without any problems. When our car was broken, it wouldn't **run.** After we got it fixed, it **ran** again. ▲ **ran, run, running.**

rung

Rung comes from the word **ring.** When the bell is **rung,** we can go out to the playground for recess.

rush

Rush means to move, go, or come quickly. We have to **rush** or we'll be late for school. The police **rushed** the sick person to the hospital. ▲ **rushed, rushing.**

Miranda and Gerald are using **rulers** to draw straight lines.

Tim likes to **run** beside his friend Bobby.

287

Ss

Skunk on a Skateboard

sad

When you are **sad,** you feel very unhappy. Sometimes you cry when you are **sad.** Louise was **sad** when her cat ran away. ▲ **sadder, saddest.**

safe

Safe means to be protected from danger. When people are **safe,** nothing bad can happen to them. It is not **safe** to skate on thin ice. When you do something **safely,** you do it in a **safe** way or are careful when you do it. My parents always drive **safely.**
▲ **safer, safest.**

said

Said comes from the word **say.** He **said,** "I know where your baseball glove is."

sail

1. A **sail** is a large piece of cloth on a boat. When the wind blows on the **sail,** it makes the boat move forward.
▲ **sails.**
2. Sail also means to move over water. The children **sailed** their toy boats on the pond. ▲ **sailed, sailing.**

sailboat

A **sailboat** is a boat that uses a sail to make it move on the water. ▲ **sailboats.**

salad

A **salad** is a cold food that is made with different vegetables, fruits, or meats. Some **salads** are made with lettuce and tomatoes. Some **salads** have chicken or fish or noodles in them.
▲ **salads.**

sale

When there is a **sale,** things are sold for less than they usually cost. The store is having a **sale** on jeans. ▲ **sales.**

salt

Salt is found in the ocean and in the ground. Some people put **salt** in their food to make it taste better. It is white.

same

If something is the **same,** it is just like something else, or it has not changed. All the fish in the bowl are the **same** color. I have the **same** teacher as last year.

sand

Sand is a kind of earth that is made of tiny pieces of rock. There is **sand** on beaches and in deserts.

sandwich

A **sandwich** is food that is made of two pieces of bread with something between them. I had soup and a peanut butter **sandwich** for lunch. ▲ **sandwiches.**

The shirts we are wearing are the **same.**

We bought a giant **sandwich** for our party.

sang

Sang comes from the word **sing.** At the party we **sang** "Happy Birthday" to Peggy.

sank

Sank comes from the word **sink.** My feet **sank** into the sand.

sat

Sat comes from the word **sit.** The bird **sat** on the fence.

Carlin is putting the money he **saved** into the bank.

save

1. **Save** means to keep someone or something **safe.** The firefighters **saved** the family from the burning building.
2. **Save** also means to keep something to have or use later. Mom and Dad **saved** all my baby pictures. I am going to **save** my money to buy a game. ▲ **saved, saving.**

saw

Saw comes from the word **see.** We **saw** elephants at the zoo.

say

When you **say** something, you are speaking words. My baby sister has learned to **say** a few words. On the radio, they **said** it was going to snow today. ▲ **said, saying.**

scale

1. A **scale** is a machine that tells how heavy something is. There are different kinds of **scales** for weighing people, vegetables, and trucks. We put two more tomatoes on the **scale.**
2. **Scales** are also hard little pieces of skin that cover fish, snakes, and some other kinds of animals. ▲ **scales.**

Diego is using the **scale** to weigh his pet.

scare

If something **scares** you, it makes you feel afraid. Loud noises always **scare** the puppy. When something **scares** you, we say it is **scary.** It was **scary** when the lights went out during the storm. ▲ **scared, scaring.**

scarecrow

A **scarecrow** is put in a field to keep the birds away. A **scarecrow** looks like a person who is dressed in old clothes. ▲ **scarecrows.**

scarf

A **scarf** is a piece of cloth that you wear around your head or your neck. ▲ **scarves.**

This movie **scares** Alexia and Blake every time they watch it.

school

School is a place where people go to learn things from a teacher. We are learning to read at **school.** ▲ **schools.**

science

Science is something you study in school. **Science** can teach you about animals and plants. You can also learn about the earth and the stars from **science.**

scientist

A **scientist** is a person who works in a special part of science. Some **scientists** study the weather. ▲ **scientists.**

scissors

Scissors are a tool that you use for cutting paper and other things. **Scissors** have two sharp parts that are held together in the middle.

scratch

Scratch means to rub something sharp against something else. You can also **scratch** something to stop it from itching. The puppy **scratched** its ear with its paw. ▲ **scratched, scratching.**

It feels good to **scratch** your back when it itches.

scream

Scream means to shout or call in a loud voice. People **scream** when they are frightened or angry or excited. The children **screamed** as they played in the big waves at the ocean. ▲ **screamed, screaming.**

screen

You put a **screen** over a window to keep the bugs out and to let the air in. A **screen** is made of many tiny wires, and you can see through it. ▲ **screens.**

scrub

Scrub means to wash or clean by rubbing. After we played with clay, we had to **scrub** our hands to get them clean.
▲ **scrubbed, scrubbing.**

sea

The **sea** is made of salt water and covers large parts of the earth. Another word for **sea** is **ocean.**
▲ **seas.**

These **seals** can often be seen resting on this rock.

seal¹

A **seal** is an animal that lives in the ocean most of the time and swims very well. **Seals** have thick, smooth fur and a long body. They make a sound like a dog barking. ▲ **seals.**

seal²

Seal means to close something so that it cannot come open. Before we mailed our valentines, we checked to be sure that we had **sealed** all the envelopes.
▲ **sealed, sealing.**

season

A **season** is a time of year. There are four **seasons** in a year. They are spring, summer, fall, and winter. What's your favorite season? ▲ **seasons.**

seat

A **seat** is a place to sit. We sat in the back **seat** of the car. There were not enough chairs, so we found **seats** on the floor. ▲ **seats.**

Seth is **sealing** the box with strong tape before he mails it.

The first thing I do when I get into the car is put on my **seatbelt**.

seatbelt

A **seatbelt** is a kind of belt that goes around you when you ride in a car or an airplane. A **seatbelt** keeps you from falling out of your seat if there is a bump or an accident. ▲ **seatbelts.**

second¹

Second means next after the first one. Ginny is the **second** person in line. My classroom is on the **second** floor of the school.

second²

A **second** is part of a minute. There are 60 **seconds** in a minute. ▲ **seconds.**

secret

A **secret** is something that not many people know. Sometimes only one person knows a **secret.** The present I'm giving Mother for her birthday is my **secret.** ▲ **secrets.**

secretary

A **secretary** is a person who writes letters and does work for another person or a group. Jan won the election for **secretary** of the stamp club. ▲ **secretaries.**

see

1. **See** means to look at something with your eyes. I could **see** Steve's kite up in the sky.
2. **See** also means to find out. Let's **see** if there is any more juice. ▲ **saw, seen, seeing.**

seed

A **seed** is a part of a plant. New plants grow from **seeds.** The **seeds** we planted in our vegetable garden grew into tomatoes and green peppers. We also planted some pumpkin **seeds.** ▲ **seeds.**

Roberta plants the **seeds** in a row.

seem

Seem means that something looks or feels a certain way. The children **seem** to be having a lot of fun in the snow. Gary was so tall that he **seemed** older than he was.
▲ **seemed, seeming.**

seen

Seen comes from the word **see.** Have you ever **seen** an elephant?

seesaw

A **seesaw** is a long board that two people sit on to make it go up and down. When one end of the **seesaw** is down, the other end is up. ▲ **seesaws.**

select

Select means to pick out. Mom said we could **select** the tape our family would watch tonight. Have you **selected** the baseball bat you want?
▲ **selected, selecting.**

selfish

If a person is **selfish,** that person does not like to share things. Frank was **selfish** when he wouldn't let his cousin Joe play with any of his toys.

sell

When you **sell** something, you give it to someone who gives you money for it. The furniture store **sells** tables, chairs, and beds. I **sold** my old bicycle and bought a new one. Janet is **selling** bracelets that she made from beads.
▲ **sold, selling.**

Clint and Myra **sell** tickets to make money for the basketball team.

send

Send means to make something go from one place to another. I'm going to **send** my friend a letter. We **sent** some flowers to our grandmother when she was sick.
▲ **sent, sending.**

sentence

A **sentence** is a group of words that makes a whole thought. The first word in a **sentence** begins with a capital letter. A **sentence** ends with a period. ▲ **sentences.**

serve

Serve means to bring food to the place where someone is going to eat it. We **served** lunch in the kitchen. ▲ **served, serving.**

set

1. Set means to put one thing on another. Rosa **set** her books on the table. I **set** the table for dinner. ▲ **set, setting.**
2. A **set** is a group of things that go together. Jerry got a new **set** of trains for his birthday. ▲ **sets.**

Dean and Rae are **setting** the table for a party.

sew

Sew means to put together with a needle and thread. I **sewed** a button on my shirt. Mom is **sewing** a patch over the hole in my jeans. ▲ **sewed, sewed** or **sewn, sewing.**

shade

1. **Shade** is a place that is protected from the sun. It was a hot day, so we sat in the **shade.** When a place is covered with **shade,** it is **shady.** It is too **shady** here to grow any flowers.

2. A **shade** is also something that keeps light out or makes light less bright. There is a **shade** on the window in my bedroom. The lamp has a new **shade** on it. ▲ **shades.**

shadow

A **shadow** is a dark area that is sometimes made when light shines on a person or thing. The **shadow** is the same shape as the person or thing. Mom can make a **shadow** with her hands that looks like a talking rabbit. ▲ **shadows.**

Do Tina and Janie know that their **shadows** are following them?

shake

Shake means to move up and down or from side to side. **Shake** the bottle of juice before you open it. Our dog **shook** water off its fur. ▲ **shook, shaken, shaking.**

shall

Shall means will. I **shall** be happy when school starts.

shape

The **shape** of something is the way it looks. The **shape** of a ball is round. Kim made the clay into the **shape** of a snake. ▲ **shapes.**

We always **shake** hands before a game.

The swing is big enough for two to **share.**

share

1. Share means to give some of what you have to someone else. Roberto said he would **share** his cookies with us.
2. Share also means to use something together. I **share** my toys with my sister and brother. ▲ **shared, sharing.**

shark

A **shark** is a fish that lives in the ocean. It has a large mouth with sharp teeth. **Sharks** eat other fish. ▲ **sharks.**

sharp

1. When something is **sharp,** it is easy to cut or tear things with it. Mom cut the apple with a **sharp** knife. Do you have a **sharp** pair of scissors I can borrow? Alligators have **sharp** teeth.
2. Some things are called **sharp** when they have a point at one end. My red pencil is **sharp,** but my blue pencil is **sharper.** My black pencil is **sharpest** of all.
▲ **sharper, sharpest.**

she

1. She is a word for a girl or a woman or a female animal. Bertha said **she** is coming to my house for dinner.
2. She'd means "she had" or "she would." **She'd** always wanted to ride in a helicopter. **She'd** like to go to the game with us.
3. She'll means "she will." **She'll** be late if **she** doesn't hurry.
4. She's means "she is." **She's** going to the library with me.

sheep

A **sheep** is an animal with curly hair. Wool is made from the hair of **sheep.** Baby **sheep** are called **lambs.** ▲ **sheep.**

How many **sheep** do you see in the picture?

shelf

A **shelf** is a place to put things. It can be made of wood, metal, or plastic. In my room, I have **shelves** on the wall to hold my books and toys. ▲ **shelves.**

shell

A **shell** is a hard part that covers something. Eggs and nuts have **shells.** Some animals, like turtles, have shells. The **shells** that you find at the beach used to have animals living in them. ▲ **shells.**

shine

1. Shine means to give out light or to be bright. The sun **shines** during the day. When something **shines,** it is **shiny.** I have two **shiny** new pennies.
2. Shine also means to make something bright. Uncle Fred **shined** his shoes before he left for work this morning. ▲ **shone** or **shined, shining.**

ship

1. A **ship** is a big boat that travels in the ocean or on big lakes or rivers. It carries people and things over the water. **Ships** use sails and engines to make them run. There are **ships** in the harbor. ▲ **ships.**
2. Ship also means to send something to another place. When we move to a new town, we will **ship** our furniture there on a truck. ▲ **shipped, shipping.**

Dave takes a lot of time to clean and **shine** his car.

shirt

A **shirt** is a piece of clothing that covers the top part of your body. You wear a **shirt** with pants or a skirt. ▲ **shirts.**

Marco likes to **shop** for paper in this store.

shoe

A **shoe** is something that you wear on your foot. **Shoes** may be worn over socks. ▲ **shoes.**

shone

Shone comes from the word **shine.** The moon **shone** in my window.

shook

Shook comes from the word **shake.** The wet bear **shook** all over to get dry.

shoot

1. **Shoot** means to send something forward from a weapon. The older children at camp can learn how to **shoot** arrows. The police officer **shot** the gun.
2. **Shoot** also means to come out. The bean plants are **shooting** up from the ground. ▲ **shot, shooting.**

shop

1. A **shop** is a place where you can buy things. Alice went to the pet **shop** to buy food for her fish. ▲ **shops.**
2. **Shop** also means to buy things. We went **shopping** for groceries on Saturday morning. ▲ **shopped, shopping.**

shore

The **shore** is the land along the edge of an ocean, a lake, or a river. We found pretty shells as we walked along the **shore.** It is important to keep the **shore** clean. ▲ **shores.**

short

Short means not far from one end to another. If something is **short,** it is not long or tall. My dog has **short** legs. Daria has **short,** red hair. Terry took a **short** nap after lunch. ▲ **shorter, shortest.**

Jonathan is **short,** so he has to stand on his toes to reach his cup.

should

Should means that it is important to do something. You **should** eat breakfast.

shoulder

Your **shoulder** is the top part of your arm where it joins your body. My backpack fits over my **shoulders**. ▲ **shoulders**.

shouldn't

Shouldn't means "should not." You **shouldn't** run into the street.

shout

To **shout** means to speak in a very loud voice. Sometimes we **shout** when we are excited or angry. ▲ **shouted, shouting.**

shovel

1. A **shovel** is a tool with a long handle. It is used for digging. ▲ **shovels.**
2. Shovel also means to use a **shovel**. Let's **shovel** the snow. ▲ **shoveled, shoveling.**

The whole family works together to **shovel** the snow off the sidewalk.

Mr. Vega **shut** the door on his coat.

show

1. Show means to let someone see something or to explain something. I want to **show** my friends my new bicycle. Sarah **showed** me how to use the new computer program. Has Carl **shown** you the map he drew? ▲ **showed, shown, showing.**
2. A **show** is also something that you see on television or in a theater. We saw a **show** about dogs on television last night. We are going to a puppet **show** today. ▲ **shows.**

shower

1. When you take a **shower,** you wash yourself in water that is coming down on you. Susie took a **shower** instead of a bath.
2. A **shower** is also a short period of rain. We brought our umbrellas because we expected **showers** today. ▲ **showers.**

shut

Shut means to close something. Please **shut** the window. When Lenny **shut** his eyes, his friends ran and hid. ▲ **shut, shutting.**

shy

When you are **shy**, you feel a little scared when there are people around. The **shy** little boy hid behind his mother when the guests came. ▲ **shyer, shyest.**

sick

When you are **sick,** you do not feel well. When Akiko was **sick,** she coughed a lot and took medicine. ▲ **sicker, sickest.**

side

A **side** is one part of something. The box has four **sides.** I live on one **side** of the street, and my friend lives on the other **side.** Which **side** won the baseball game? ▲ **sides.**

sidewalk

A **sidewalk** is a place to walk that is next to the street. I like to roller-skate on the **sidewalk** in front of our house. ▲ **sidewalks.**

sight

1. Sight is how you see. Jeremy's **sight** got better when he started wearing glasses.
2. Sight is also the distance you can see. The plane flew out of **sight.**

Dean **signs** his name on my arm.

sign

1. A **sign** is words or pictures that tell you what to do or what something is. There was an arrow on the road **sign** that showed us where to turn. ▲ **signs.**
2. Sign also means to write your name. I **signed** my name at the end of my letter. ▲ **signed, signing.**

The cars have to wait for a **signal** before they can drive through.

signal

A **signal** is a way of showing people what to do. **Signals** are used instead of words. A **signal** may be a light, a sign, a flag, a moving hand, or a sound. The red lights are a **signal** that a train will be coming very soon. ▲ **signals.**

silence

Silence means that there are no sounds. When there is **silence,** it is very, very quiet. Our teacher asked for **silence** during the spelling test. ▲ **silences.**

I love my **silly** slippers.

American Indians made these bracelets from **silver** and turquoise.

silly

When someone or something is **silly,** it makes us laugh. That **silly** clown did such funny things. The second clown stood on his head and did even **sillier** things than the first one. ▲ **sillier, silliest.**

silver

Silver is a shiny white metal that can be made into many shapes. It is used to make coins, jewelry, bowls, spoons, forks, and other things.

since

1. **Since** means from that time until now. Bill has been sick **since** Monday. We have lived in this house **since** I was a baby.
2. **Since** also means because. **Since** it's Saturday, we don't have to go to school.

sing

Sing means to make music with your voice. Let's **sing** the song together. The birds **sang** in the trees. A person who sings is called a **singer.** ▲ **sang, sung, singing.**

sink

1. A **sink** is something that you wash things in. **Sinks** have special parts to let water in and out. We washed the vegetables in the kitchen **sink**. ▲ **sinks.**

2. Sink also means to go down into water. I threw a rock into the pond and watched it **sink** to the bottom. The divers looked for treasure in the ship that had **sunk.**

▲ **sank** or **sunk, sunk** or **sunken, sinking.**

sip

When you **sip** something, you drink only a tiny amount at a time. The soup is hot, so please **sip** it slowly. ▲ **sipped, sipping.**

sister

Your **sister** is a girl who has the same mother and father as you do. My **sister** and I both have blue eyes. ▲ **sisters.**

sit

Sit means to rest the bottom part of your body on something. Harry **sat** on his dad's lap. My dog and I will **sit** on the floor.

▲ **sat, sitting.**

size

The **size** of something is how big or little it is. Can you guess the **size** of that tree? All of my shoes are the same **size.** ▲ **sizes.**

Is this hat the right **size** for Frankie?

skate

1. You put **skates** on your feet when you roller-skate or ice-skate. Some **skates** fit over your shoes, and other **skates** are like shoes.

▲ **skates.**

2. Skate also means to move on **skates.** We **skate** on the lake when it freezes. A person who **skates** is called a **skater.**

▲ **skated, skating.**

Kay and Terry learned how to do amazing things on their **skateboards.**

skateboard

A **skateboard** is a low, flat board with wheels on the bottom. You ride a **skateboard** by standing on it and pushing off with one foot. ▲ **skateboards.**

ski

1. A **ski** is one of a pair of long, narrow strips made of wood, metal, or plastic. **Skis** are worn with special boots and are used for moving quickly over snow or water. ▲ **skis.**
2. Ski also means to move on **skis.** We **skied** all morning. ▲ **skied, skiing.**

skin

Skin covers the outside of something. My **skin** gets little bumps all over it when I am cold. This apple has a red **skin.** ▲ **skins.**

skip

Skip means to move by hopping first on one foot and then on the other. Mary **skipped** down the street. ▲ **skipped, skipping.**

skirt

A **skirt** is a piece of clothing that girls and women wear. **Skirts** are worn on the bottom part of the body. ▲ **skirts.**

skunk

A **skunk** is an animal with a big tail. It is black with a white stripe on its back. When **skunks** are afraid or angry, they put out a very bad smell. ▲ **skunks.**

sky

The **sky** is what you see above you when you are outdoors. You can see the moon and the stars in the **sky** at night. ▲ **skies.**

Be careful of the **skunk.**

skyscraper

A **skyscraper** is a very tall building. New York City and Chicago are famous for their **skyscrapers.** ▲ **skyscrapers.**

sled

A **sled** is something you sit on to ride on the snow. A **sled** has long pieces of metal on the bottom that help it slide. Jennifer pulled her brother up the hill on the **sled.** ▲ **sleds.**

sleep

When you **sleep,** you rest with your eyes closed. My cat likes to **sleep** in the sun. I **slept** for 8 hours last night. When you need **sleep,** you are **sleepy.** My brother is very **sleepy** because he missed his nap today. ▲ **slept, sleeping.**

slide

1. **Slide** means to move easily on something. She **slid** the book across the table to me. ▲ **slid, slid** or **slidden, sliding.**
2. A **slide** is something that you play on by climbing up and then sliding down. ▲ **slides.**

Two of these **skyscrapers** are really tall.

slip

Slip means to slide and fall down. Be careful not to **slip** on the wet floor. The dish **slipped** out of my hand and broke on the floor. ▲ **slipped, slipping.**

slipper

A **slipper** is a soft, comfortable shoe that goes on your foot very easily. ▲ **slippers.**

slippery

When something is **slippery,** it means that you might slip or slide on it. Roads get **slippery** when they have water or ice on them. The cars slid on the **slippery** road.

slow

When something is **slow,** it does not go very fast. Chuck was so **slow** getting dressed that he was late for school. When you do something in a **slow** way, you do it **slowly.** When Lola hurt her foot, she walked **slowly.** ▲ **slower, slowest.**

small

Small means not big. A mouse is a **small** animal. It is much **smaller** than a cat. ▲ **smaller, smallest.**

Our pet show is only for **small** animals.

smell

1. When you **smell** something, you use your nose to find out about it. We could **smell** the turkey roasting in the oven. The bread **smelled** good as it baked.
▲ **smelled** or **smelt, smelling.**
2. When you are **smelling** something, you are getting to know its **smell**. The **smell** of the popcorn made me hungry. The rose had a sweet **smell**. ▲ **smells.**

smile

1. When you **smile,** the corners of your mouth turn up. You **smile** when you are happy. Everyone **smiled** when we had our picture taken. ▲ **smiled, smiling.**
2. When you **smile,** you have a **smile** on your face. The winning team had **smiles** on their faces. ▲ **smiles.**

smoke

Smoke is a dark cloud that comes from something that is burning. We saw **smoke** coming from the chimney. When a place has a lot of **smoke** in it, we say that place is **smoky**. The room was **smoky** because we were burning wet logs in the fireplace.

smooth

If something is **smooth,** you do not feel any bumps on it when you touch it. The skin of an apple is **smoother** than the skin of an orange.
▲ **smoother, smoothest.**

snake

A **snake** is a long, thin animal with no legs. **Snakes** move by sliding along on the ground.
▲ **snakes.**

Eugene has a good reason to **smile.**

The **snake** can bend its body into many curves.

Eric decided to wear his favorite pair of **sneakers**.

snap

Snap means to make a quick, sudden noise. I like to **snap** my fingers to the music. The dry twigs **snapped** when we stepped on them.
▲ **snapped, snapping.**

sneak

Sneak means to move or act in a secret way. The guests **sneaked** into Soshi's house for her surprise party. ▲ **sneaked** or **snuck, sneaking.**

sneaker

A **sneaker** is a soft, comfortable shoe with rubber on the bottom and cloth or other material on top. I put my **sneakers** on before I go out to play. ▲ **sneakers.**

sneeze

When you **sneeze,** you blow air out of your mouth and nose in a loud way. I always **sneeze** a lot when I have a cold.
▲ **sneezed, sneezing.**

sniffles

When you have the **sniffles,** you take short, quick breaths through your nose because you have a cold.

snow

1. **Snow** is rain that freezes in the sky. **Snow** comes down in little white pieces called **snowflakes.**
2. **Snow** also means to fall as **snow.** We like to take out our sleds when it **snows.** It **snowed** all day yesterday, and it is still **snowing** today.
▲ **snowed, snowing.**

snowman

Snow that has been made into the shape of a person is called a **snowman.** We made a **snowman** by putting three large balls of snow on top of each other. ▲ **snowmen.**

We put a hat on our **snowman** and used a carrot for its nose.

so

1. So means very. I am **so** glad that Sandy can come to the beach with us. It was **so** cold last night that the lake froze.
2. So also means too. I am going to the football game and **so** is Brian.

soap

People use **soap** to wash and clean things. We use blocks of **soap** to clean ourselves. Special kinds of **soap** are used to clean our clothes and our dishes.
▲ **soaps.**

soccer

Soccer is a game played by two teams on a long, wide field. Each team has 11 people. The players try to move a round ball into a goal by kicking it or hitting it with any part of the body except their hands or arms.

We practice **soccer** in the afternoon after school.

sock

A **sock** is a soft cover for your foot. **Socks** are worn inside shoes. ▲ **socks.**

soft

1. When something is **soft** it feels smooth. My kitten has **soft** fur.
2. When something is **soft,** it is also not hard. Ronnie likes to sleep with a **soft** pillow.
3. When something is **soft,** it is also gentle. The **soft** breeze felt warm.
▲ **softer, softest.**

sold

Sold comes from the word **sell.** At the school fair my class **sold** cookies.

The **soft** fur feels nice against Debby's cheek.

soldier

A **soldier** is someone who is in an army. In a game I have, the blue **soldiers** and the red **soldiers** fight each other to see who will win the castle. ▲ **soldiers.**

solid

When something is **solid,** it is hard and has a shape. Ice is water that has become **solid.**

some

Some means a part of a thing or group of things. I'd like **some** of that sandwich. **Some** of the puppies were black and white, and **some** were all black.

someone

Someone means a person, but you don't know which person. **Someone** left the door open. **Somebody** is another word for **someone.** I hear **somebody** knocking at the front door.

Each of us can now do a forward **somersault.**

somersault

When you do a **somersault,** you roll your body so that your feet go over your head. First the acrobat did a forward **somersault,** and then he did a backward one. ▲ **somersaults.**

something

Something means a thing, but you don't know what it is. Grant saw **something** jump in the pond. When **something** was wrong with our new radio, we took it back to the store.

sometimes

Sometimes means once in a while but not always. **Sometimes** my older sister lets me wear her clothes.

somewhere

Somewhere means some place, but you do not know where. I forgot my jacket at school or **somewhere** else.

son

A **son** is the male child of a mother and a father. A **son** can be a boy or a man. Your father is the **son** of your grandparents. ▲ **sons.**

song

A **song** is music that has words you sing. Jenna played the piano, and we sang a **song.** ▲ **songs.**

soon

Soon means in a very short time. This has been a long ride, but we will be there **soon.**

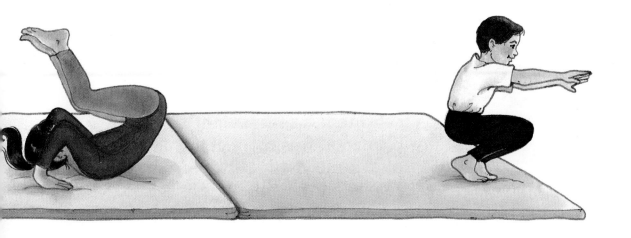

sore

If you feel **sore**, it means that a part of your body hurts. After I fell down the stairs, my back felt **sore**. ▲ **sorer, sorest.**

sorry

If you are **sorry,** it means that you feel sad about something. Jeff was **sorry** that he broke the glass. I'm **sorry** that you can't visit me today. ▲ **sorrier, sorriest.**

sort

Sort means to put things into groups. Harvey **sorted** his socks by putting the brown ones in one pile and the blue ones in another pile. ▲ **sorted, sorting.**

sound

1. A **sound** is something that you hear. Thunder makes a loud **sound.** I like the **sound** of the birds singing outside my window. A piano, a trumpet, and a drum are all musical instruments that make different **sounds.**

2. A **sound** is also the noise you make when you speak. The words "bat" and "cat" begin with different **sounds,** but they end with the same **sound.** ▲ **sounds.**

soup

Soup is a kind of food that you eat with a spoon. **Soup** is a liquid and is usually hot. Do you like tomato **soup** or chicken **soup** better? ▲ **soups.**

sour

Sour is a strong taste that might make the sides of your mouth come together. When a food is **sour,** it means that it does not taste sweet. Lemons and green apples are **sour.** ▲ **sourer, sourest.**

Kevin does not like the **sour** taste of lemons.

south

South is a direction. When you look at a map, the bottom part is **south.** If you face the sun when it goes down in the evening, **south** is on your left. The opposite of **south** is **north.**

space

1. Space is a place that has nothing in it. Mom found a **space** to park the car in. Write your name in the **space** at the top of the paper. ▲ **spaces.**
2. Space is also the place where all of the planets and stars are. The earth, moon, and sun are in **space.**

Jessie is pointing to the country that is **south** of the United States.

spaceship

A **spaceship** carries astronauts and their tools into outer space. The **spaceship** took the astronauts to the moon. A camera in the **spaceship** took pictures during the trip. Another word for **spaceship** is **spacecraft.**
▲ **spaceships.**

spaghetti

Spaghetti is a long, thin noodle that looks like string. I like to eat **spaghetti** with tomatoes and cheese on it.

speak

Speak means to say words. Cleo is going to **speak** to her Aunt Nancy on the telephone. Were you **speaking** to me or to someone else?
▲ **spoke, spoken, speaking.**

special

When something is **special,** it is important and not like anything else. Your birthday is a **special** day. Juan is a **special** friend of mine.

Carter is going to **speak** in front of a group.

spell

Spell means to put letters together so that they make a word. Can you **spell** your name? Ann **spelled** nine words right and one word wrong. ▲ **spelled** or **spelt, spelling.**

spelling

Spelling is the way words are spelled. Ketchup and catsup are two **spellings** of the same word. We study **spelling** in school every afternoon. ▲ **spellings.**

spend

Spend means that you pay money for something. How much did you **spend** for that book on astronauts? I **spent** 2 dollars. ▲ **spent, spending.**

spice

Spices come from the seeds or other parts of certain plants and are used to add flavor to food. Pepper is a **spice.** When food has a lot of **spice** in it, we say it is **spicy.** When I was very young, I didn't like **spicy** foods. ▲ **spices.**

spider

A **spider** is a kind of bug that has eight legs. **Spiders** do not have wings. ▲ **spiders.**

spill

When you **spill** something, it falls out of what it was in. I dropped the box of crayons, and most of them **spilled** all over the floor. ▲ **spilled** or **spilt, spilling.**

spin

Spin means to go around in a circle. Jennifer likes to **spin** the toy boat on the ice. Chuck's top has been **spinning** for at least 2 minutes. ▲ **spun, spinning.**

Ned was not quite fast enough to keep the grape juice from **spilling.**

splash

Splash means to throw water or some other liquid around. Stand back or the car will **splash** mud on you. The seal **splashed** into the cold ocean water. ▲ **splashed, splashing.**

spoke

Spoke comes from the word **speak.** I **spoke** to Jean on the phone.

spoken

Spoken comes from the word **speak.** Have you **spoken** to Ken lately?

spoon

A **spoon** is something that is used for eating. It has a handle with a small round bowl at the end. We eat both soup and cereal with a **spoon.** We also use **spoons** for stirring things. ▲ **spoons.**

sport

A **sport** is a kind of game that people play to exercise and have fun. Baseball, basketball, football, soccer, and tennis are kinds of **sports.** We play **sports** in the gym on Tuesdays and Thursdays. ▲ **sports.**

spot

A **spot** is a small mark that is different from the area around it. There's a **spot** on the rug where Jackie spilled the juice. When I was sick, I had red **spots** on my skin. ▲ **spots.**

We jumped off the raft and **splashed** into the water.

You can tell this is a leopard by its **spots.**

spring

Spring is a season of the year. **Spring** comes after winter and before summer. In the **spring** the trees grow leaves and flowers begin to grow. Tulips are flowers that bloom in the **spring.** ▲ **springs.**

spun

Spun comes from the word **spin.** The wheels of the car **spun** in the mud.

square

A **square** is a shape with four sides and four corners. The sides of a **square** are all the same size. ▲ **squares.**

squeeze

Squeeze means that you push hard on the sides of something. Gary **squeezed** juice from the oranges. ▲ **squeezed, squeezing.**

squirrel

A **squirrel** is a small animal with a big tail. It lives in trees. ▲ **squirrels.**

stage

A **stage** is a place where people act, dance, or sing while an audience watches them. The orchestra played a concert on the school **stage.** ▲ **stages.**

stairs

Stairs are a set of steps. You use **stairs** to go up or down. We walked up the **stairs** to the second floor.

stamp

A **stamp** is a small piece of paper that is put on a letter to mail it. You buy **stamps** at the post office. Sometimes people collect **stamps.** ▲ **stamps.**

Javier **squeezed** the tube too much.

stand

1. Stand means to be on your feet. Since there were no seats on the bus, we had to **stand**. It started to rain while we were **standing** in line at the movie theater.
2. Stand also means to be straight up and down. A ladder **stood** against the side of the barn. ▲ **stood, standing.**

We can see many **stars** in the sky tonight.

star

1. A **star** is a small, bright light that can be seen in the sky at night. **Stars** are very, very far away. Some groups of **stars** make shapes in the sky.
2. A **star** is also a shape that has five or more points. The American flag has 50 **stars** on it. My jacket has small **stars** on each pocket. ▲ **stars.**

stare

When you **stare** at something, you look at it very carefully for a long time. I **stared** at the monkeys at the zoo, and they **stared** back. ▲ **stared, staring.**

start

1. Start means to begin to do something. Linda's piano lesson will **start** at 4 o'clock. Our school **starts** in September.
2. Start also means to make something happen or go. We **started** a sewing club at school. Marco got in the boat and **started** the engine. ▲ **started, starting.**

state

A **state** is one part of a country. There are 50 **states** in the United **States**. Most of the **states** in the United **States** are near other **states**. Alaska and Hawaii are **states** that are far away from the other **states**. ▲ **states.**

The train is in the **station**.

station

A **station** is a place where something special is done. We get gas for a car at a gas **station**. Police officers work in police **stations**. People get on or off a train at a train **station**. ▲ **stations.**

statue

A **statue** is a copy of a person or animal that is made out of stone, clay, or some other solid material. ▲ **statues.**

stay

1. **Stay** means that you do not leave a place for a while. Karen **stayed** to help me put the books away.
2. **Stay** also means that something is the same and does not change. I hope we'll **stay** friends forever. ▲ **stayed, staying.**

steal

Steal means to take something that does not belong to you. Someone tried to **steal** money from the bank. ▲ **stole, stolen, stealing.**

steam

When water is boiled, it changes into **steam.** **Steam** is often used to heat buildings and to run engines. We turned off the stove when **steam** came out of the kettle.

stem

A **stem** is the part of a plant that holds the leaves and the flowers. Food and water travel up the **stem** from the ground to all parts of the plant. ▲ **stems.**

step

1. **Step** means to raise your foot from one place and put it down somewhere else. Be careful not to **step** in the puddle. ▲ **stepped, stepping.**
2. **Step** also means a place to put your foot when you are going up or down. Someone left a toy on the top **step.** We sat on the front **steps** of our house. ▲ **steps.**

This is a **statue** you can climb on.

The **step** is a little high.

Do you know what a
stethoscope is for?

stethoscope

A **stethoscope** is an instrument that a doctor or a nurse uses to listen to your heart.
▲ **stethoscopes.**

stew

Stew is meat or fish and vegetables cooked together in one pot. ▲ **stews.**

stick¹

A **stick** is a long, thin piece of wood. I threw a **stick,** and my dog ran after it. ▲ **sticks.**

stick²

1. **Stick** means to push something that is sharp into something else. If you **stick** a pin into a balloon, it will pop.
2. **Stick** also means to make something stay on something else. Bobbie **stuck** a stamp on the envelope. ▲ **stuck, sticking.**

still

1. If you are **still,** it means that you are not moving or making any noise. Mom told us to keep **still** while she took our picture.
▲ **stiller, stillest.**
2. If something is **still** happening, it means that it started to happen a while ago and it has not stopped. Is it **still** raining?

sting

1. A **sting** is a tiny cut made by an insect. The bee **sting** on my foot hurts. ▲ **stings.**
2. When an insect **stings** you, it makes a tiny cut in your skin. ▲ **stung, stinging.**

stir

Stir means to mix something by moving it around with a spoon or a stick. **Stir** the paint before you use it. I **stirred** milk into the soup. ▲ **stirred, stirring.**

stole

Stole comes from the word **steal.** The cat **stole** a piece of fish from the counter. **Stolen** also comes from the word **steal.** Some books were **stolen** from the library last year.

stomach

Your **stomach** is the place in your body where food goes after you swallow it.
▲ **stomachs.**

stone

Stone is a piece of rock. The building is made of **stone.** The artist made a statue out of **stone. Stones** are small pieces of rock. We threw **stones** across the pond. ▲ **stones.**

stood

Stood comes from the word **stand.** Everyone **stood** when the President walked into the room.

stool

A **stool** is a kind of seat. It does not have a place for your back or arms. That piano player is sitting on a **stool** instead of a bench.
▲ **stools.**

stop

Stop means not to do something any longer. Please **stop** making so much noise. The car **stopped** when it reached the traffic light.
▲ **stopped, stopping.**

stoplight

Stoplight is another word for **traffic light.**
▲ **stoplights.**

Stone can be carved into different shapes.

Mack **stopped** at the corner and waited until it was safe to cross the street.

Cam always reads me my favorite **stories**.

store

1. A **store** is a place where you buy things. We went to the shoe **store**, and I got a new pair of shoes. ▲ **stores.**

2. Store also means to put something away so that you can use it later. The squirrels **stored** food in autumn to eat during winter. ▲ **stored, storing.**

storm

During a **storm,** it rains or snows and the wind blows hard. Sometimes there is also thunder and lightning during a **storm.** ▲ **storms.**

story

When you tell a **story,** you tell about something that has happened. A **story** can be about something that is real, or it can be make-believe. Grandpa told us a **story** about a huge dog and a small cat. I like to write my own **stories.** ▲ **stories.**

stove

A **stove** is something that is used to cook food on. **Stoves** use electricity, gas, or wood to make them hot. ▲ **stoves.**

straight

If something is **straight,** it does not bend or turn to one side. Dad made sure that the picture on the wall was hung **straight.** Please try to sit up **straight** at your desk. Margaret's hair is much **straighter** than mine. ▲ **straighter, straightest.**

strange

Strange means very different from what you expect. The kitchen had a **strange** smell. Joseph drew a picture of a **strange** animal with red ears. ▲ **stranger, strangest.**

straw

1. A **straw** is a thin tube used for drinking things. It is made of paper or plastic. Les drinks his milk through a **straw**.
2. Straw is also the dry stems of some plants. Our pony sleeps on **straw** in the barn. Some brooms are made of **straw**.
▲ **straws.**

strawberry

A **strawberry** is a small, red fruit with little seeds on it. I like to eat **strawberry** jelly on my toast. ▲ **strawberries.**

stream

A **stream** is water that is moving. Everyone stared at the fish jumping and splashing in the **stream.** ▲ **streams.**

street

A **street** is a road in a town or city. **Streets** often have sidewalks and buildings on both sides. What **street** do you live on? ▲ **streets.**

stretch

When you **stretch** something, you make it as long as it can be. I like to **stretch** my arms when I wake up in the morning. The lazy lion **stretched** and then went back to sleep.
▲ **stretched, stretching.**

This scarecrow has **straw** hair and a **straw** body.

Elsa and Dorita are **stretching** their leg and back muscles.

We play this game with a long piece of **string.**

strike

Strike means to hit something. My toy plane **struck** a tree trunk, but it did not break.
▲ **struck, striking.**

string

1. A **string** is a thin piece of rope. I fly my kite on a very long **string.**
2. A **string** is also a thin piece of another material. The **strings** on a guitar and a violin are used to make music. ▲ **strings.**

strip

A **strip** is a long, narrow piece of something. They tore the paper into **strips** of different lengths. ▲ **strips.**

stripe

A **stripe** is a long line that is a different color from what is next to it. Tigers and zebras have **stripes.** Joanie's favorite shirt is white with red and blue **stripes.** ▲ **stripes.**

strong

If you are **strong,** it means that you have a lot of power. Bruce isn't **strong** enough to move the heavy desk. The wind was so **strong** that it blew down a big tree. My older sister is bigger and **stronger** than I am.
▲ **stronger, strongest.**

The dog is **strong** enough to pull Joannie.

struck

Struck comes from the word **strike.** Lightning **struck** the tree and hurt it.

stuck

Stuck comes from the word **stick.** Our car got **stuck** in the mud.

student

A **student** is someone who is learning things at a school. All the **students** in my class went to the fair. The fourth grade in Henry's school has 29 **students.** Another word for **student** is **pupil.** ▲ **students.**

study

When you **study,** you try hard to learn about something. Rosa **studies** ballet. Marco **studied** a book about whales, and then he wrote a story about them. Our class is **studying** the planets. ▲ **studied, studying.**

Howard is looking through a magnifying glass to **study** the flower on the cactus.

stuff

1. **Stuff** can be anything. I have some **stuff** in my closet that I haven't played with in a long time. The trunk in the basement is full of old **stuff** that needs to be thrown away.
2. **Stuff** also means to pack something very full. We **stuffed** all our clothes into one suitcase. Jenny **stuffed** her books and jacket into her backpack. ▲ **stuffed, stuffing.**

stung

Stung comes from the word **sting.** My arm hurt when the bee **stung** me. A bee has **stung** the pony.

The **submarine** is coming out of the water.

submarine

A **submarine** is a ship that can travel under water. ▲ **submarines.**

subtract

Subtract means to take one number away from another number. If you **subtract** 3 from 7, you get 4. When one number is **subtracted** from another number, it is called **subtraction.** ▲ **subtracted, subtracting.**

subway

A **subway** is a railroad in a city that goes under the ground. Many people ride to work on the **subway. Subways** run on electricity. ▲ **subways.**

such

Such means very much. We had **such** a nice time at the party!

sudden

When something is **sudden,** it means it happens very fast. There was a **sudden** storm. When something happens in a **sudden** way, it happens **suddenly.** It was sunny all morning, and **suddenly** it started to rain.

The **sudden** rain came as a big surprise.

sugar

Sugar is something that is put in food to make it sweet. **Sugar** can be white or brown. There is a lot of **sugar** in candy.

suit

A **suit** is a kind of clothing that has two parts. One part is a jacket. The other part is a pair of pants or a skirt. ▲ **suits.**

suitcase

People carry clothes in a **suitcase.** A **suitcase** looks like a flat box with a handle. We packed our **suitcases** for our trip. ▲ **suitcases.**

sum

The **sum** is the number you get when you add two numbers together. The **sum** of 2 and 3 is 5. Another way of writing this is $2 + 3 = 5$. ▲ **sums.**

Derek will not get all his things into one **suitcase.**

summer

Summer is a season of the year. **Summer** comes after spring and before fall. We go on vacation in the **summer.** ▲ **summers.**

sun

The **sun** is a star. We see it in the sky during the day. The **sun** gives us light and keeps us warm. When a lot of light is coming from the **sun,** we say it is **sunny.** ▲ **suns.**

sunburn

You have a **sunburn** when the light from the sun makes your skin hurt and become red. Beryl played in the shade so she wouldn't get a **sunburn.** ▲ **sunburns.**

sung

Sung comes from the word **sing.** The school chorus has **sung** many times at the music festival.

Most of us know the song by now because we have **sung** it many times.

sunk

Sunk comes from the word **sink.** The old ship **sunk** during the hurricane.

sunrise

The sun coming up in the morning is called **sunrise.** We were up at **sunrise** every morning of our camping trip. ▲ **sunrises.**

sunset

The sun going down in the evening is called **sunset.** We sat on the beach to watch a beautiful **sunset.** ▲ **sunsets.**

supermarket

A **supermarket** is a large store that sells food and other things like soap and paper towels. ▲ **supermarkets.**

suppose

1. If you **suppose** that something will happen, it means that you think it will happen. How do you **suppose** this book ends? I **suppose** I'll see you after the show.
2. If you are **supposed** to do something, it means that you should do it. I'm **supposed** to go home now. ▲ **supposed, supposing.**

sure

When you are **sure** about something, you know that what you are thinking is true. I am **sure** you can find information on reptiles in our school library. ▲ **surer, surest.**

surprise

1. A **surprise** is something that you don't know about before it happens. We baked a cake as a **surprise** for Mom's birthday. ▲ **surprises.**
2. When you **surprise** people, it means that you do something that they do not know is going to happen. We want to **surprise** Grandmother by bringing her some flowers. ▲ **surprised, surprising.**

swallow

After you chew food, you **swallow** it. The food goes down your throat and into your stomach. The tiger chewed the meat and then **swallowed** it. ▲ **swallowed, swallowing.**

Sometimes the sky looks red at **sunset.**

Wilson was **surprised** that the package was for him.

331

swam

Swam comes from the word **swim**. We **swam** in the pool all morning.

swamp

A **swamp** is land that is very wet. Special kinds of plants and animals live in **swamps**. ▲ **swamps.**

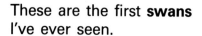

These are the first **swans** I've ever seen.

swan

A **swan** is a large bird that lives in the water. **Swans** have long necks. Many **swans** have white feathers. ▲ **swans.**

sweater

A **sweater** is a piece of clothing that you wear over the top part of your body. Some **sweaters** are put on over your head, and others have buttons. I wear a wool **sweater** on really cold days. ▲ **sweaters.**

sweep

When you **sweep** a floor, you brush it with a broom to get the dirt up. Mrs. Olsen **sweeps** the sidewalk in front of her store every day. ▲ **swept, sweeping.**

During the baseball game, the umpire **sweeps** the base to keep it clean.

sweet

If a food is **sweet,** it tastes as if there is sugar in it. Ice cream and candy are **sweet.**
▲ **sweeter, sweetest.**

swept

Swept comes from the word **sweep.** My brother **swept** the kitchen floor.

swim

Swim means to move in the water. People **swim** by using their arms and legs. We will **swim** in the lake this summer. The ducks **swam** in the pond.
▲ **swam, swum, swimming.**

swing

1. A **swing** is a thing that you sit on to move up and down in the air. There is a **swing** in our yard that hangs from a tree. ▲ **swings.**
2. When you **swing** something, you make it move back and forth through the air. Patricia likes to **swing** her arms when she walks.
▲ **swung, swinging.**

We got dressed up to have our picture taken on Grandmother's **swing.**

swum

Swum comes from the word **swim.** Have you ever **swum** all the way across the pool?

swung

Swung comes from the word **swing.** Nan **swung** at the ball with the bat.

synagogue

A **synagogue** is a building where Jewish people go to pray, sing, and learn.
▲ **synagogues.**

T t

Turtles Talking

table

A **table** is a piece of furniture with a flat top and four legs. Hector put his books on the **table.** ▲ **tables.**

tag

Tag is a game in which one of the players is "it." The person who is "it" chases the other players until he or she touches someone. Then the person who is touched becomes "it."

tail

A **tail** is the part of an animal's body at the end of the back. Cats and dogs and fish have **tails.** ▲ **tails.**

take

1. Take means to bring or carry with you. Dad will **take** us to the movies this afternoon. We are **taking** cheese sandwiches on the picnic.
2. Take also means to get hold of something. **Take** the book off the desk.
3. Take also means to get or use something. We **take** the bus to school.
4. Take also means to do or study something. Jan **took** a photograph of her friends at camp. Maria is **taking** computer lessons.
▲ **took, taken, taking.**

tale

A **tale** is a story. Joel likes to hear **tales** of life at sea. ▲ **tales.**

talk

Talk means to say words. The baby is learning to **talk.** Kara **talked** to her friend on the telephone.
▲ **talked, talking.**

tall

If something is **tall,** it goes up far from the ground. Jim is 5 feet **tall.** Alex is **taller** than Jim. Kate is the **tallest** of all. ▲ **taller, tallest.**

tame

An animal that is **tame** is not wild, afraid, or shy. It has been taught by people to obey and be gentle. The elephants that we saw at the circus were **tame.** The **tamest** animals at the farm were the little goats that let us feed and pat them. ▲ **tamer, tamest.**

tap

Tap means to hit something gently. The teacher **tapped** on the desk to get our attention. ▲ **tapped, tapping.**

tape

1. Tape is a long, thin piece of plastic, cloth, or metal. Some **tape** has glue on it and is used to make things stick together. Ann used **tape** to fix the torn page in her book. **2. Tape** is also a strip of plastic that has music or pictures on it. You listen to or watch this kind of **tape** on a machine. ▲ **tapes.**

Ted has just seen a movie on **tape.** Now Ellen is going to listen to music on **tape.**

taste

1. Taste tells you the flavor of food when you put it in your mouth. Lemons have a sour **taste.** Sugar has a sweet **taste.** ▲ **tastes.** **2. Taste** also means to put food in your mouth to see what it is like. May I **taste** your soup? Karen is **tasting** the pudding to see if it is ready. Danny **tasted** the fish that he and his father cooked. ▲ **tasted, tasting.**

Gerald's aunt is **teaching** him to ride his new bike.

Cary is **tearing** off a piece of paper towel.

taught

Taught comes from the word **teach**. My uncle Frank **taught** my cousin and me how to swim last summer.

taxi

A **taxi** is a car you pay to ride in. We took a **taxi** to the airport. Another word for **taxi** is cab. ▲ **taxis.**

teach

Teach means to help someone learn something. Our neighbor is going to **teach** me how to use my new camera. I am **teaching** our dog a new trick.
▲ **taught, teaching.**

teacher

A **teacher** is someone who helps people learn things. Ms. Green is a second grade **teacher.** Mr. Edwards is my piano **teacher.** ▲ **teachers.**

team

A **team** is a group of people who play a game together. There are 20 people on our football **team.** I hope you will play on my **team.** ▲ **teams.**

tear¹

Tear means to pull something apart. **Tear** sounds like hair. The art teacher told us to **tear** the piece of paper in half. Jerry was careless and **tore** his pants on a nail.
▲ **tore, torn, tearing.**

tear²

A **tear** is a drop of water that comes out of your eye when you cry. **Tear** sounds like hear. Ron wiped the **tears** from the baby's face. Faith laughed so much that **tears** came to her eyes. ▲ **tears.**

tease

When you **tease** people, you bother them or make fun of them. The players on the other team **teased** Andrea when she missed the ball. It was mean of them to **tease** her.
▲ **teased, teasing.**

teeth

Teeth comes from the word **tooth.** The baby has two new **teeth.** Keith is going to have braces put on his **teeth.**

telephone

A **telephone** is used to talk to someone who is far away. It has electric wires that carry the sound of your voice. I like to talk to my friends on the **telephone. Phone** is a short word for **telephone.** ▲ **telephones.**

The bear is showing its **teeth.**

telescope

A **telescope** is an instrument that makes things that are far away seem larger and nearer. When we looked through the **telescope,** we could see stars and planets that we couldn't see before. ▲ **telescopes.**

We could see the people on the ship when we looked through the **telescope.**

television

A **television** shows pictures with sound. People watch the news and other programs on **television**. **TV** is a short word for **television**. ▲ **televisions**.

tell

1. **Tell** means to say something in words. Grandfather promised to **tell** us the story about his first ride on a horse. The baby-sitter **told** us to get ready for bed.
2. **Tell** also means to know. Can you **tell** which twin is Dorothy and which one is Deborah? ▲ **told, telling**.

Mrs. Evans **tells** stories to the children.

temperature

The **temperature** of something tells you how hot or cold it is. The **temperature** outside was so cold that the puddles changed into ice. The doctor used a thermometer to take my **temperature** to see if I had a fever. ▲ **temperatures**.

temple

A **temple** is any building where people go to sing and pray. ▲ **temples**.

tennis

Tennis is a game played by two or four people. When people play **tennis,** they hit a ball to each other over a net. My sister plays on the **tennis** team at school.

tent

A **tent** is a place to live in that can be folded up and moved. It is made of cloth. We slept in a **tent** on our camping trip. The circus was in a big **tent.** ▲ **tents.**

tepee

A **tepee** is a tent that has a shape like a cone. **Tepees** are made from animal skins that have been stretched over poles. A long time ago, American Indians lived in **tepees.** ▲ **tepees.**

terrible

1. When something is **terrible,** it means that it makes you feel afraid. The thunder made a **terrible** noise.
2. Terrible also means very bad. We had **terrible** weather on our vacation. It rained every day. The food at that new restaurant was **terrible.**

test

A **test** shows how much a person knows about something. A **test** has questions to answer and problems to do. I spelled two words wrong on the spelling **test** today. ▲ **tests.**

than

We use **than** when we tell how things are different. The mother cat is bigger **than** her kittens. An hour is much longer **than** a minute. I am 2 inches taller **than** my brother.

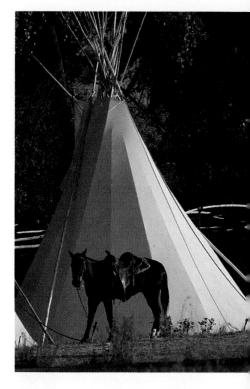

Tepees can be taken down and carried from one place to another.

A **terrible** wind storm knocked down branches and telephone poles.

339

thank

You **thank** someone who has been nice to you. When you **thank** people, you are happy about what they have done. Jenny called to **thank** us for the birthday present we sent her. **Thank** you for helping me carry my suitcase. ▲ **thanked, thanking.**

Our whole family has dinner together on **Thanksgiving.**

Thanksgiving

Thanksgiving is a holiday celebrated on the last Thursday in November. Many people eat turkey for dinner on **Thanksgiving** and give thanks for what they have.

that

This is my pencil, and **that** one is yours. Where did you get **those** books? This is a good song, but **that** one is my favorite. The shirt **that** I'm wearing is new. She said **that** she would come with us. I hope **that** she does. It was so cold **that** the pond froze. I'm not **that** hungry now. ▲ **those.**

the

We use **the** when we talk about one special person, thing, or group. **The** woman wearing a red dress is my mother. Please close **the** door. **The** sun is very bright.

theater

A **theater** is a place where you can go to see a movie or a play. My family enjoys seeing new plays at the **theater.** ▲ **theaters.**

their

Their means that something belongs to other people. **Their** dog is black, and ours is brown. Our car is outside, and **theirs** is in the garage.

them

We use **them** when we talk about more than one person or thing. My friends asked me if I wanted to play ball with **them.** They went to school by **themselves.**

then

1. You use **then** when you tell about something that happened after. The game ended and **then** we went home.
2. You also use **then** when you tell about something you can do instead. If you don't want your sandwich, **then** please give it to me.

Ray and Melvin are holding **their** lambs.

there

Please put the box over **there** in the corner. We went to the park, and we saw Jan **there. There** are 20 people in my class. **There** is no more pie.

Sam looks at the **thermometer** to find out the temperature outside.

thermometer

A **thermometer** is an instrument that tells how hot or cold something is. Some **thermometers** have a line of numbers and a liquid that goes up or down when something gets hotter or colder. ▲ **thermometers.**

these

These comes from the word **this. These** cars are mine, and those cars are yours. **These** are very pretty flowers.

they

1. We use **they** when we talk about more than one person or thing. Nan and Pete were late for school because **they** missed the bus.
2. They'd means "they had" or "they would." Sue and Bob said **they'd** seen the play before. I wish **they'd** come with us.
3. They'll means "they will." **They'll** be here in a few minutes.
4. They're means "they are." **They're** building a new house on our street.
5. They've means "they have." **They've** gone to the party already.

thick

1. When something is **thick,** there is much space from one side to the other. This is a **thick** book.
2. When a liquid is **thick,** it is hard to pour. It took a long time for Jodi to pour the **thick** glue into the jar. ▲ **thicker, thickest.**

thief

A **thief** is a person who steals. **Thieves** stole televisions from the store. ▲ **thieves.**

Kara can reach the table because she is sitting on a **thick** book.

thin

1. When something is **thin**, there is not much space between one side of it and the other. I would like a **thin** piece of cheese on my sandwich. The paper was so **thin** that we could see through it.
2. Thin also means not fat. A horse has a long, **thin** face. ▲ **thinner, thinnest.**

thing

Almost anything you can talk about, think of, or do can be called a **thing.** Please pick up the toys and other **things** on the floor. Helping me with my packages was a nice **thing** to do. ▲ **things.**

Malcolm didn't **think** his new boots would be so hard to put on.

think

1. Think means to use your mind to decide things. The teacher told us to **think** carefully before we answered the questions on the test.
2. Think also means to have an idea in your mind about a person or thing. Jack **thinks** Marion will win the race. What do you **think?** Tell me what you **think** of the story I wrote.
▲ **thought, thinking.**

third

Third means next after the second one. My sister is in the **third** grade. March is the **third** month of the year.

thirsty

When you are **thirsty,** you want something to drink. We were so **thirsty** that we each drank two large glasses of water. ▲ **thirstier, thirstiest.**

The **thirsty** dog is having a drink of water.

343

This hat is too small for **this** horse.

this

1. We use **this** when we talk about something that is closer than something else. **This** coat is mine, and that one is yours.
2. We also use **this** when we talk about something that is here. **This** morning it is sunny. **This** book is a dictionary. **This** is my cousin Angela. ▲ **these.**

those

Those comes from the word **that.** These gloves are mine, and **those** are Daniel's. I baked **those** cookies. I do not know who **those** people are.

though

I was late for school, **though** I got up early. The movie was funny, **though** it was not as funny as the one I saw last week. I enjoyed it, **though.**

thought

1. Thought comes from the word **think.** We took our umbrellas because we **thought** it might rain.
2. A **thought** is an idea. Martha wrote down her **thoughts** about the book she read.
▲ **thoughts.**

thread

Thread is thin string that is used for sewing. Victor knows how to use a needle and thread. ▲ **threads.**

threw

Threw comes from the word **throw.** Robert caught the ball and **threw** it back to Ana.

throat

The **throat** is the part of your body that is at the front of your neck. When I was sick, my **throat** felt sore. ▲ **throats.**

through

1. Through means from one side or end to the other. Carmen hammered the nail **through** the piece of wood. The children crawled **through** the tunnel in the playground.

2. Through also means finished. I will be **through** with my homework soon.

throw

1. Throw means to send something through the air. **Throw** the ball to the dog, and she will bring it back to you.

2. When you **throw** something away, you don't want it any longer. If the milk smells bad, you should **throw** it away. Jeff **threw** away some broken toys.
▲ **threw, thrown, throwing.**

thumb

The **thumb** is the short, thick finger at the side of your hand. Your **thumb** makes it easier to pick things up. ▲ **thumbs.**

Here comes our car **through** the car wash.

Mr. Henry **throws** the garbage into the truck.

345

thunder

Thunder is a loud sound in the sky that comes after lightning. We hear **thunder** during a storm.

ticket

A **ticket** is a piece of paper that shows you have paid for something. You need a **ticket** to ride on a train. We gave our **tickets** to the man at the door of the theater. ▲ **tickets.**

tickle

When you **tickle** people, you touch them gently in a way that makes them laugh. ▲ **tickled, tickling.**

Alan and Crystal are **tying** big pine cones together.

tie

Tie means to hold something together with a string or ribbon. Ann knows how to **tie** her shoes. ▲ **tied, tying.**

tiger

A **tiger** is a very big cat that has orange or yellow fur with black or brown stripes. A **tiger** is a wild animal. We saw **tigers** at the zoo. ▲ **tigers.**

Everyone is holding **tight.**

tight
1. When you hold something **tight,** you squeeze it. Joanne held on **tight** to the railing of the escalator.
2. When something is **tight,** it fits close to your body. Steve gave the pants to his little brother because they were too **tight** for him.
▲ **tighter, tightest.**

time
1. Time is when something happens. A clock or a watch tells us what **time** it is. It is almost **time** for my favorite TV program.
2. Time is also how long something takes. We don't have much **time** to finish the test.
3. Time can also be something you have done. We had a good **time** at the beach today. ▲ **times.**

times
When a number is multiplied by a number, we use the word **times:** 2 **times** 2 is 4. Another way of writing 2 **times** 2 is 2 × 2.

tiny
If something is **tiny,** it is very small. An ant is a **tiny** insect. ▲ **tinier, tiniest.**

Tim looks **tiny** next to the huge statue.

Only the **tip** of the iceberg is above the water.

tip

The **tip** of something is the end part of it. There are rubber **tips** on the legs of the chair. ▲ **tips.**

tire

A **tire** is a round piece of rubber that fits around a wheel. Cars, buses, bicycles, and trucks all have **tires.** Most **tires** are filled with air. I changed the **tire** because it was flat. ▲ **tires.**

tired

When you are **tired,** you want to rest or sleep. People get **tired** when they work or play a lot. We were **tired** when we finished cleaning the garage.

to

1. We use **to** when we tell where something is going. We are going **to** the zoo.
2. We also use **to** when we talk about things we do. Gary is learning **to** swim.
3. We also use **to** when we mean on. Dottie attached the sign **to** the wall.

toad

A **toad** is an animal that is like a frog. **Toads** have dry, rough skin, and they can jump very far. **Toads** like to live on dry land instead of in the water like frogs. ▲ **toads.**

toast

Toast is bread that has been made brown by heat. A **toaster** is a machine for making **toast.** I had **toast** with cheese for lunch.

today

Today is the day that it is now. **Today** is Marilyn's birthday. Do you want to go to the park **today?**

Myra was so **tired** that her daddy carried her to bed.

toe

A **toe** is a part of your foot. Each foot has five **toes.** My **toes** were cold, so I put on a pair of socks. ▲ **toes.**

together

When people or things are in the same place, they are **together.** Maria and Jane ride the bus to school **together.** Dad mixed the milk and eggs **together.** All the cows stood **together** in the middle of the field.

The police officer and Lynn cross the street **together.**

toilet

A **toilet** is a bowl that has water in it, and a seat that you sit on. When you use a **toilet,** food and water that your body can't use go into the **toilet.** Then you push the handle on the **toilet,** and it fills with clean water again. ▲ **toilets.**

told

Told comes from the word **tell.** Ms. Fulton **told** us about her trip to Alaska.

The toad uses its long **tongue** to catch insects.

tomato

A **tomato** is a soft, red fruit. Most **tomatoes** are full of juice. ▲ **tomatoes.**

tomorrow

Tomorrow is the day after today. If today is Monday, then **tomorrow** will be Tuesday.

tongue

The **tongue** is a part of your mouth. It is long and you can push it out of your mouth. Your **tongue** helps you to taste and swallow food and to speak. ▲ **tongues.**

tonight

Tonight is the night of the day it is now. We are going to the museum this morning, and **tonight** we're going to a hockey game.

too

1. We use **too** to mean also. George and Martha like to play baseball, and their little brother does **too.**
2. We also use **too** when we mean that something is more than enough. There were **too** many toys in the box, and it wouldn't close. It's **too** cold to swim in the ocean.

took

Took comes from the word **take.** Jim **took** his new book to school to show his friends.

tool

A **tool** is something you use to do a job. A hammer, a rake, and a ruler are different kinds of **tools.** ▲ **tools.**

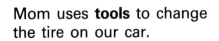

Mom uses **tools** to change the tire on our car.

tooth

1. A **tooth** is one of the hard, white parts in your mouth. **Teeth** are used for biting and chewing food. The dentist told me to brush my **teeth** twice a day.
2. A **tooth** may also be one of a row of points that are on a comb or rake. My comb is missing two **teeth**. ▲ **teeth.**

toothbrush

A **toothbrush** is a small brush with a long handle. It is used to clean the teeth.
▲ **toothbrushes.**

top¹

1. The **top** of something is the highest part. Gloria climbed to the **top** of the slide.
2. The **top** of something is also a part that covers it. Please put the **top** back on the box. ▲ **tops.**

top²

A **top** is a toy in the shape of a cone. A **top** spins on the end that has a point.
▲ **tops.**

Phyllis and Ramon are spinning **tops.**

tore

Tore comes from the word **tear.** Elizabeth **tore** her shirt on the fence. **Torn** also comes from the word **tear.** Her shirt was **torn** in two places.

tornado

A **tornado** is a fierce storm with very strong winds that blow around in a circle.
Tornadoes can pick up things and drop them many miles away. ▲ **tornadoes.**

toss

Toss means to throw gently. Please **toss** me a pair of socks. ▲ **tossed, tossing.**

touch

Touch means to put your hand on something. If you **touch** the kitten's fur, you will feel how soft it is. ▲ **touched, touching.**

tow

Tow means to pull or drag something behind you. When our car broke down, a truck **towed** it to the gas station. Yesterday I saw a truck **towing** a bus. ▲ **towed, towing.**

The small tugboat is **towing** the big barge up the river.

toward

Toward is used when we talk about going in the direction of something. All the puppies ran **toward** their mother. Another way to spell **toward** is **towards.** I started walking **towards** the playground to meet my friends.

towel

A **towel** is a piece of paper or cloth that is used for wiping or drying something. Ken wrapped himself in a **towel** after he took a shower. ▲ **towels.**

tower

A **tower** is a tall, narrow part on top of a building. The church on our street has a **tower** with bells in it. ▲ **towers.**

town

A **town** is a place where people live and work. A **town** has houses and other buildings in it. It is smaller than a city. Our **town** has a post office, a bank, a gas station, a theater, and a restaurant on the main street. ▲ **towns.**

tow truck

A **tow truck** is able to pull a car that cannot be driven. **Tow trucks** are used to move cars that have broken down or are stuck in mud or snow. A **tow truck** pulled our car to the garage after the accident. ▲ **tow trucks.**

toy

A **toy** is a thing to play with. People and animals play with **toys.** Dolls, kites, and balls are **toys.** Our cat likes to play with a **toy** mouse. ▲ **toys.**

trace

When you **trace** a picture, you put a thin piece of paper over it. Then you follow the lines of the picture with your pencil. When you finish, you have a copy of the picture on your paper. Toby **traced** a picture of a dinosaur. ▲ **traced, tracing.**

Louise is taking a picture of her friends in the **tower.**

After Billy **traces** a picture of the cat, he is going to color it.

We used lots of **tracks** when we made our model railroad.

track

1. A **track** is one of the long metal pieces that the wheels of a train go on.
2. A **track** is also the mark left by the foot of an animal. We saw deer **tracks** in the woods.
▲ **tracks.**

tractor

A **tractor** is a machine with a strong engine and heavy tires. **Tractors** are used to pull heavy things over rough ground. ▲ **tractors.**

trade

Trade means to give a person something of yours for something of his or hers. My friends and I like to **trade** toy cars.
▲ **traded, trading.**

traffic

Traffic is cars, trucks, and buses moving along a road at the same time. There is not much **traffic** on the road where I live.

Don and Ernie **trade** baseball cards.

traffic light

A **traffic light** is a big light at a street corner. **Traffic lights** change color to show cars and people what to do. A green light means to go, a yellow light means to be careful, and a red light means to stop. Even though the **traffic light** was green, we stopped to let a fire engine pass.
▲ **traffic lights.**

trail

1. A **trail** is a path through an area that is not lived in. The campers followed the **trail** through the woods.
2. A **trail** is also a mark, smell, or path made by a person or animal. The rabbit left a **trail** of footprints in the snow. ▲ **trails.**

trailer

A **trailer** is something that is pulled by a car or truck. A **trailer** has wheels, but it does not have a motor. Some **trailers** are used to carry things, and some are made for people to live in. ▲ **trailers.**

train

1. A **train** is a line of railroad cars that are joined together. **Trains** are used to carry people or things from one place to another. We took a **train** when we went to visit my grandfather. ▲ **trains.**
2. **Train** also means to teach a person or animal how to do something. My mother **trains** people to use computers. We **trained** our dog to bring back the ball when we throw it. ▲ **trained, training.**

The **traffic light** is being fixed so that we can cross the street safely.

355

The cats always get into the **trash.**

trap

1. A **trap** is something that is used to catch an animal or a person. **Traps** that look like cages are used to catch lobsters. ▲ **traps.**
2. **Trap** also means to catch in a **trap.** The spider **trapped** two insects in its web. ▲ **trapped, trapping.**

trash

Trash is stuff that you throw away. Most of our **trash** is paper, boxes, and old food.

travel

Travel means to go from one place to another. We **traveled** by car on our vacation. ▲ **traveled, traveling.**

treasure

A **treasure** is money, jewelry, or other things that are important. The king and queen hid their **treasure** in a special room. ▲ **treasures.**

treat

A **treat** is a nice, special thing. Going to the circus was a **treat** for us. ▲ **treats.**

tree

A **tree** is a tall plant that has a trunk. **Trees** have branches and leaves. ▲ **trees.**

triangle

1. A **triangle** is a shape that has three straight sides.
2. A **triangle** is also a musical instrument with three sides. It is made of metal and rings when you hit it with a metal stick. ▲ **triangles.**

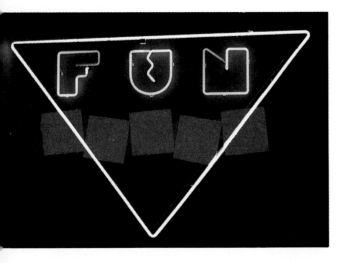

The white lines in this sign are in the shape of a **triangle.**

trick

1. A **trick** is something you do to make people think you have done something else. Jack shut the door with a bang as a **trick** to make us think he had left.

2. A **trick** also is something special that a person or animal has to practice to do well. Matt learned a new card **trick**. Jennifer gave her dog a reward after he did the **trick**. ▲ **tricks**.

tricycle

A **tricycle** has two wheels in the back and one wheel in the front. **Tricycles** are like bicycles, but they are easier to ride. Judy likes to ride her **tricycle** on a path through the park. ▲ **tricycles**.

tried

Tried comes from the word **try**. Marlo **tried** to lift the big suitcase, but it was too heavy for her. We **tried** to catch the train, but we were too late.

trip

1. When you go on a **trip,** you go from one place to another. We took a **trip** to the mountains. ▲ **trips**.

2. When you **trip,** you hit your foot on something and almost fall. Mark **tripped** over the box on the floor. ▲ **tripped, tripping**.

trophy

A **trophy** is a small statue or other prize. A **trophy** is given to someone who wins a contest or game or does something special. My brother won a **trophy** for being the best player on his school basketball team. ▲ **trophies**.

Dad **tried** to catch the cup, but it was too late.

Martha won a **trophy** in the spelling contest.

Peter will have **trouble** if he wants to put his model in there.

trouble

1. When you have **trouble,** something has caused a problem. **Trouble** means that something is hard to do or even dangerous. Pat had **trouble** putting on his boots. We had **trouble** driving in the storm.

2. Being in **trouble** also means that you have done something wrong and someone will be angry. Dee broke the lamp and is in **trouble.** ▲ **troubles.**

truck

A **truck** is like a large automobile. People use **trucks** to carry big, heavy things. We used a **truck** to move our furniture to our new house. ▲ **trucks.**

true

True means correct and not wrong. Is it **true** that Ted will be going to our school next year? It is **true** that an elephant has four legs. ▲ **truer, truest.**

trumpet

A **trumpet** is a musical instrument that is made of metal. You blow into one end of a **trumpet,** and the sound comes out the other end. ▲ **trumpets.**

Ted plays the **trumpet** in the school band.

trunk

1. A **trunk** is the main part of a tree. The **trunk** has bark on it, and branches grow out from it.
2. A **trunk** is also the long nose of an elephant. Elephants use their **trunks** to pick up things.
3. A **trunk** is also a large box that you keep things in. When spring comes, I put my winter clothes in my **trunk.** ▲ **trunks.**

trust

If you **trust** a person, you believe the person is honest. I told Bill my secret because I know I can **trust** him. ▲ **trusted, trusting.**

truth

If something you say is **true,** then you are telling the **truth**. He was telling the **truth** when he said he didn't know the answer. ▲ **truths.**

try

When you **try** to do something, you find out if you can do it. I **tried** to run up the hill, but I got too tired. ▲ **tried, trying.**

tub

1. A **tub** is a large open container that you use for taking a bath. Another word for **tub** is **bathtub.**
2. A **tub** also is a round container that is used to hold butter, honey, or other foods. ▲ **tubs.**

Kim is **trying** to carry the big pumpkin.

tube

A **tube** is a hollow piece of glass, rubber, plastic, or metal. It sometimes has the shape of a pipe. **Tubes** are used to carry or hold liquids and gases. ▲ **tubes.**

Mary's dog **tugs** at her towel as she tries to dry herself.

tug

Tug means to pull on something. My little sister is always **tugging** on Mom's skirt to get her attention. ▲ **tugged, tugging.**

tugboat

A **tugboat** is a boat that pulls or pushes other boats. The ship needed two **tugboats** to push it into the harbor. ▲ **tugboats.**

tulip

A **tulip** is a flower that has the shape of a cup. **Tulips** grow from bulbs. ▲ **tulips.**

tunnel

A **tunnel** is a road or path built under the ground or under water. There is a **tunnel** under the river. ▲ **tunnels.**

turkey

A **turkey** is a kind of bird. It is like a chicken, but it is bigger. Many people eat **turkey** for Thanksgiving dinner. ▲ **turkeys.**

turn

1. **Turn** means to move around in a circle or part of a circle. The wheels of a bicycle **turn** when you ride it. Dad **turned** to wave good-bye.
2. **Turn** also means to make something work or stop working. You **turn** on a radio or television. You also **turn** on a light. Please **turn** off the water. ▲ **turned, turning.**
3. A **turn** is a person's time to do something. It is Brigit's **turn** to hit the ball. ▲ **turns.**

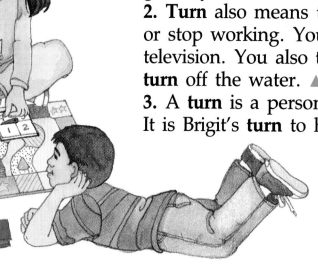

Richie waits for his **turn** to play the game.

turquoise

1. Turquoise is a color. You can make the color **turquoise** by mixing green and blue together.

2. Turquoise is also the name of a stone that is used to make jewelry.

turtle

A **turtle** is an animal with short legs and a hard shell covering its body. **Turtles** live on land and in water. When it is afraid, a **turtle** pulls its head and legs inside its shell. ▲ **turtles.**

twice

If you do something **twice,** you do it two times. Jane liked the book so much that she read it **twice.**

twig

A **twig** is a tiny branch of a tree. We used dry **twigs** to start a fire when we went camping in the woods. ▲ **twigs.**

twin

Twins are two children who are born at the same time to the same mother. Some **twins** look alike and other **twins** do not. ▲ **twins.**

Have you ever seen so many **twins** in one place?

two

Two is the number that is one more than one. You have **two** eyes and **two** ears. The number **two** is written **2.** ▲ **twos.**

tying

Tying comes from the word **tie.** Mitchell is **tying** the package with string.

U u V v

Unicorn on Vacation

ugly
When something is **ugly,** it is not pretty. Francine made an **ugly** face to try and scare me, but it made me laugh instead. ▲ **uglier, ugliest.**

umbrella
An **umbrella** is a big piece of cloth or plastic that folds up and down on a stick. You use an **umbrella** to protect yourself from the rain or the sun. Mom forgot her **umbrella** and got wet in the rain. The sun was so hot that we sat under an **umbrella** at the beach. ▲ **umbrellas.**

umpire
An **umpire** makes sure that the rules are followed in a baseball game. "Play ball!" the **umpire** shouted. ▲ **umpires.**

uncle
Your **uncle** is your father's brother or your mother's brother. Your aunt's husband is also your **uncle.** ▲ **uncles.**

under
Under means in a place that is lower than something else. The dog was hiding **under** the bed. My missing paper was **under** the book. Jack is wearing a sweater **under** his jacket.

understand
When you **understand** something, you know what it means. English is the only language that Carol **understands.** Andy **understands** both English and Spanish. Ginger **understood** the teacher's question.
▲ **understood, understanding.**

underwear

Underwear is the clothing you wear under your clothes. I fold and put away my **underwear** when the laundry is done.

undress

Undress means to take off clothes. My little brother is learning how to **undress** himself. Madeline likes to dress and **undress** her dolls when she plays with them.
▲ **undressed, undressing.**

unhappy

Unhappy means not happy. I was very **unhappy** when my sister broke my favorite toy truck.

unicorn

A **unicorn** is a make-believe animal that looks like a white horse with one long horn in the middle of its head. I like to read fairy tales about **unicorns.**
▲ **unicorns.**

Jim's mother is asking him why he is **unhappy.**

United States

The **United States** is a country. It is also called the **United States of America.** The capital of the **United States** is Washington, D.C. We live in the **United States.** Our teacher asked Helen to point to our state on the map of the **United States.**

unless

You can't borrow my bicycle **unless** you promise to take care of it. The baseball game will be played this afternoon **unless** it rains. **Unless** we hurry, we will be late for the concert.

Sally enjoys hanging **upside down.**

until

Until means up to the time of. We can play outside **until** it gets dark.

unusual

When something is **unusual,** it is not the way we expect it to be. Snow in July would be very **unusual** weather.

up

1. **Up** means to go from a lower place to a higher place. Sharon went **up** the steps and into the building. Jamie looked **up** from his book when Geoff came into the room.
2. **Up** also means out of bed. I didn't get **up** until 9 o'clock this morning. Kim and Martha aren't **up** yet.

upside down

When something is **upside down,** the top becomes the bottom. I turned a pail of sand **upside down** and made a sand castle.

upstairs

When you go **upstairs,** you go to a higher floor. My bedroom is **upstairs.**

us

We use the word **us** when we are talking about ourselves. Uncle Ben took **us** to the zoo yesterday.

use

When you **use** a thing, you do something with it. Since you forgot to bring your book today, you may **use** mine. I **used** a shovel to dig a hole for the plant. ▲ **used, using.**

usual

When something is **usual,** it is expected. Hot weather is **usual** for July and August.

usually

Usually means most of the time. I **usually** walk to school in the morning.

vacation

A **vacation** is a time when people do not work or go to school. Our family went on a **vacation** to the beach last summer. ▲ **vacations.**

valentine

A **valentine** is a card that you send to someone you love on **Valentine's Day. Valentines** usually have hearts on them. **Valentine's Day** is February 14. ▲ **valentines.**

We are making **valentines** to send to our parents.

van

A **van** is a truck or a car that looks like a small bus. Large **vans** are used to move animals, furniture, or other big things. Small **vans** are used for carrying people or small things. ▲ **vans.**

The painters carry their ladder, brushes, and paint cans in a **van.**

Lynn has brought her sick cat to the **veterinarian**.

vegetable

A **vegetable** is a plant that you eat. Carrots and lettuce are **vegetables**. ▲ **vegetables**.

very

Very means a lot. I feel **very** full after I eat a big meal. We are **very** sorry you can't come with us to the circus.

veterinarian

A **veterinarian** is a doctor who takes care of animals. Eddie likes animals and wants to be a **veterinarian**. Nancy wants to be a **veterinarian** for a zoo and take care of wild animals. ▲ **veterinarians**.

vine

A **vine** is a plant with a long, thin stem. **Vines** grow on the ground or up tree trunks and walls. Grapes and pumpkins grow on **vines**. ▲ **vines**.

violin

A **violin** is a musical instrument. It is made of wood and has four strings. You play a **violin** by moving a long, thin piece of wood across the strings. ▲ **violins**.

Max plays the **violin** well.

visit

Visit means to go to see someone. Uncle Paul came to **visit** us. A **visitor** is a person who comes to **visit**. Our class is going to have **visitors** this afternoon.
▲ **visited, visiting.**

voice

Your **voice** is the sound you make through your mouth. You are using your **voice** when you speak or sing.
▲ **voices.**

Hot gases and fire from the **volcano** shoot high into the air.

volcano

A **volcano** looks like a mountain with a big hole in the top. The rocks under a **volcano** are melted by heat in the earth. Sometimes the melted rocks shoot out of the **volcano.**
▲ **volcanoes.**

volunteer

1. A **volunteer** is someone who does work without getting paid. In my town, all the firefighters are **volunteers.** ▲ **volunteers.**
2. **Volunteer** also means that you want to do something. George **volunteered** to take care of my hamster while I was away on vacation.
▲ **volunteered, volunteering.**

vote

Vote means to say that you are for or against something. Our town **voted** to build a new playground. ▲ **voted, voting.**

vowel

A **vowel** is a letter of the alphabet that is not a consonant. The vowels are **a, e, i, o, u,** and sometimes **y.** ▲ **vowels.**

Everyone is going to **vote** in the election.

Ww

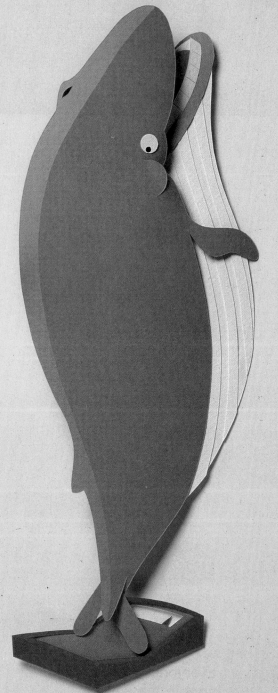

Weighing a Whale

wagon
A **wagon** is a flat box with four wheels and a handle. It is used to carry people or things. Sometimes my brother pulls me in my red **wagon.** ▲ **wagons.**

wait
Wait means to stay in a place until someone comes or something happens. Rosa had to **wait** until it stopped raining before she could go outside to play. ▲ **waited, waiting.**

wake
When you **wake,** you stop sleeping. What time do you **wake** up in the morning? We were noisy and **woke** the baby. ▲ **waked** or **woke, waking.**

walk
Walk means to move along by putting one foot in front of the other. My little sister is just learning to **walk.**
▲ **walked, walking.**

wall
A **wall** is one side of a room. Frances and I chose the color blue for the **walls** of our bedroom. ▲ **walls.**

want
When you **want** something, it means that you would like to have it. Marlene **wants** a kite for her birthday. We were all hungry and **wanted** our lunch.
▲ **wanted, wanting.**

war
A **war** is a fight between countries. Everyone was happy when the **war** ended. ▲ **wars.**

Cory and his mother and father keep **warm** under a blanket.

warm

Warm means that something is more hot than cold. The blanket kept me **warm**. Yesterday it was sunny and **warm**. Today it is **warmer**, but tomorrow is supposed to be the **warmest** day of the year.
▲ **warmer, warmest.**

was

Was comes from the word **be**. The bird **was** building a nest. Who **was** at the door? Carmen **was** sick last week.

wash

When you **wash** something, you clean it with soap and water. We **washed** our hands before dinner. We helped Dan **wash** the car. Jill and Fred take turns **washing** the dishes after dinner. ▲ **washed, washing.**

wasn't

Wasn't means "was not." Sue **wasn't** in school today. **Wasn't** that your brother we saw playing ball in the park?

Carlos wants the time on his **watch** to be right.

waste

When we **waste** something, we use more of it than we need. We **waste** water if we don't turn off the faucet. ▲ **wasted, wasting.**

watch

1. **Watch** means to look at something carefully. The baby-sitter watched the children while they played. ▲ **watched, watching.**
2. A **watch** is also a small clock that you wear on your wrist. A **watch** shows you what time it is. ▲ **watches.**

water

1. **Water** is the liquid that falls to the ground as rain. It is in oceans, lakes, rivers, and ponds. We all need **water** to live.
2. **Water** also means to give **water** to. We **watered** the plants. ▲ **watered, watering.**

wave

1. **Wave** means to move something up and down or from side to side. People often **wave** a hand when they say hello or good-bye. The flag **waved** in the wind. ▲ **waved, waving.**
2. A **wave** is also the water as it moves up and down in the ocean. The boat bounced up and down in the **waves.** ▲ **waves.**

wax

Wax is a material that is used to make things like candles and crayons. **Wax** is also used to shine furniture and cars. ▲ **waxes.**

way

1. The **way** you do something is how you do it. I know two **ways** to play this game.
2. **Way** also means a road or a path that you take to go from one place to another. Jackie knows the **way** to the store. ▲ **ways.**

This swimmer is riding a huge **wave** in the ocean.

we

1. People use **we** when they are talking about themselves. **We** are good friends.
2. We'd means "we had" or "we would." **We'd** been at the lake all day. **We'd** go with you if **we** could.
3. We'll means "we will." I think **we'll** win the game tomorrow.
4. We're means "we are." **We're** home.
5. We've means "we have." **We've** visited that city twice.

weak

1. When something is **weak,** it may break or fall. The legs of the table are **weak**.
2. Weak also means not strong. The sick pony was **weak**. ▲ **weaker, weakest.**

weapon

When people fight, they use **weapons**. Guns and knives are **weapons**. ▲ **weapons.**

wear

Wear means to have clothes or other things on your body. Kyle **wears** a raincoat and boots when it rains. Faith is **wearing** her new necklace. ▲ **wore, worn, wearing.**

weather

When we talk about rain or snow or how hot or cold it is, we are talking about the **weather**. The **weather** is sunny today.

web

A **web** is made by a spider to catch food. **Webs** are made of thin threads. An insect got caught in the spider's **web**. ▲ **webs.**

This spider **web** has a beautiful pattern.

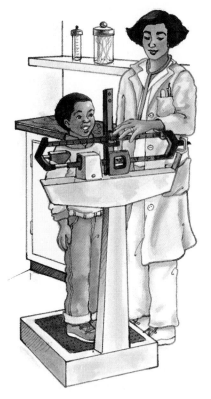

Ms. James **weighs** Marty on the scale.

Anna gets water from a **well** on her uncle's farm.

wedding

A man and woman get married at a **wedding.** There were flowers and music at my cousin's **wedding.** ▲ **weddings.**

week

There are seven days in a **week.** The days of the **week** are Sunday, Monday, Tuesday, Wednesday, Thursday, Friday, and Saturday. ▲ **weeks.**

weigh

You **weigh** something to find out how heavy it is. I **weigh** 60 pounds. We **weighed** the tomatoes on the scale. ▲ **weighed, weighing.**

weight

Your **weight** is how heavy you are. My **weight** is 60 pounds. ▲ **weights.**

well[1]

1. When you do something **well,** you do it in a good way. My uncle plays the piano **well.** Beth writes **well.**
2. **Well** also means not sick. Emily was sick last week, but she's **well** now.

well[2]

A **well** is a very deep hole in the ground. People dig **wells** to get water, oil, or other things that are in the earth. ▲ **wells.**

went

Went comes from the word **go.** My sister and I **went** to the dentist yesterday.

were

Were comes from the word **be.** We **were** having such a good time in the park that we didn't want to go home. Alex and Kim **were** at the library all afternoon.

weren't

Weren't means "were not." We got to school on time. We **weren't** late.

west

West is the direction you are facing if you watch the sun go down. **West** is the opposite of **east.**

wet

If something is **wet,** it has water or another liquid on it. Debbie's shoes got **wet** when she stepped in the puddle. ▲ **wetter, wettest.**

whale

A **whale** is a very large animal that lives in the ocean. **Whales** can swim, but they are not fish. ▲ **whales.**

what

What did you say? I want to know **what** the new baby looks like. **What** time is it?

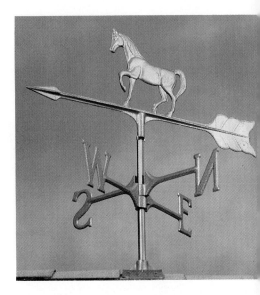

The arrow points **west,** the direction in which the wind is blowing.

The **whale** is one of the largest animals on earth.

wheat

Wheat is a kind of grass. Its seeds are used to make flour and other foods. **Wheat** is an important food for people and animals.

The big **wheels** help make the cart move more easily.

wheel

A **wheel** is a round piece of wood, metal, or rubber that helps things move easily. Cars, bicycles, wagons, and roller skates have **wheels**. ▲ **wheels**.

wheelchair

A **wheelchair** is a chair on wheels. People who cannot walk use **wheelchairs** to get from one place to another. My school has a special ramp for children and teachers who use **wheelchairs**. ▲ **wheelchairs**.

when

We use **when** to ask or tell what time something happens. **When** does the show start? Please tell me **when** I can visit you.

where

We use **where** to ask a question or tell about a place. **Where** do you live? I can't remember **where** I left my book.

which

We use **which** when we want to know what one. **Which** of the dolls do you like best? **Which** dog is yours?

while

1. While means a short time. Let's stop playing and rest for a **while**.
2. While also means during the time that something else is happening. Mom ate lunch **while** the baby took a nap.

whisper

Whisper means to speak in a very quiet voice. The teacher asked the students to stop **whispering**.
▲ **whispered, whispering.**

whistle

1. When you **whistle**, you make a sound by pushing air out through your lips or teeth. My dog always comes when I **whistle**.
The kettle **whistled** when the water boiled.
▲ **whistled, whistling.**
2. A **whistle** is also something you blow into that makes a **whistling** sound. The police officer blew a **whistle** and all the cars stopped. ▲ **whistles.**

white

White is the lightest color. **White** is the opposite of **black**. The paper in this book is **white**. New snow is very **white**.

who

We use **who** to ask which person. **Who** took my toy train? Do you know **who** left these boots here? **Who** wants an apple for dessert and **who** wants an orange?

Katie has to guess in **which** hand Robbie is holding the ball.

Rudy **whispers** a secret to Frankie.

375

These friends are sharing a **whole** pizza for lunch.

whole

When something is **whole**, it has no parts missing from it. Isaac ate the **whole** orange by himself. We got a **whole** pizza, and everyone had a piece of it. Myra read the **whole** book in just two days.

whose

We use **whose** when we talk about who the owner of something is. **Whose** coat is this? I don't know **whose** roller skates these are.

why

Why is used to ask the reason for something. I know **why** Lucy can't come to the picnic with us. **Why** are you laughing?

wide

Wide means very big from one side to the other. The chair was too **wide** to fit through the door. That bridge crosses the **widest** part of the river. ▲ **wider, widest.**

Ed can't put the box on the shelf because the box is too **wide**.

wife

A **wife** is a woman who is married. ▲ **wives.**

wild

If an animal is **wild,** it doesn't live with people. Bears and squirrels are **wild** animals. If a flower is **wild,** it means that nobody planted it. It just grew there. In the spring, the meadow is full of **wild** flowers.
▲ **wilder, wildest.**

will

We use **will** when we say that we are going to do something. We **will** go to the park tomorrow. Peter **will** be 10 years old soon.

win

Win means to be the best in a game or a contest. You will **win** the race because you can run faster than anyone else.
▲ **won, winning.**

wind

The **wind** is the air that moves over the earth. The **wind** blew the leaves on the ground all over the front yard. When it is **windy,** the **wind** is blowing a lot. We like to fly our kites on **windy** days. ▲ **winds.**

The **wind** in the sails makes the sailboat move across the water.

window

A **window** is an open place in a wall that lets in air and light. **Windows** are made of glass. If you close the **window,** the cold air won't come in. ▲ **windows.**

wing

A **wing** is a part that is used for flying. Birds and insects have **wings.** Airplanes also have **wings.** ▲ **wings.**

winter

Winter is a season of the year. **Winter** comes after fall and before spring. I like to go ice-skating in the **winter.** ▲ **winters.**

Some birds have very large **wings.**

Didi forgot to **wipe** her boots and is making dirty footprints on the rug.

wipe

Wipe means to clean or dry something by rubbing it. Please **wipe** your muddy shoes on the rug outside the door. Dad **wiped** up the milk that the baby spilled. ▲ **wiped, wiping.**

wire

A **wire** is a thin piece of metal. **Wire** can be used to make fences and cages. **Wire** can also be used to carry electricity for lights and telephones and other things. ▲ **wires.**

wish

1. **Wish** means to want something very much. I **wish** it were summer now. Jack **wished** he could paint as well as his older brother. Carole is always **wishing** for something. ▲ **wished, wishing.**
2. A **wish** is something that you want very much. Jesse made a **wish** for a new bicycle and then blew out the candles on the birthday cake. ▲ **wishes.**

witch

A **witch** is a person who is supposed to do magic things. Most people think **witches** are make-believe. In the story, the **witch** flew on a broom. My sister Judy dressed as a **witch** for Halloween. ▲ **witches.**

with

1. When you do something **with** somebody else, it means that you do it together. I went to the baseball game **with** my sister and brother.
2. **With** can be used to show that you use something. Ann dug the hole **with** a shovel.
3. **With** can also be used to show that someone has something. The boy **with** the red jacket on is my brother. The girl **with** brown hair is my sister.

Jerry and Valerie are making a **wish.**

without

Without means not having or not doing something. I love to walk on the sand **without** my shoes on. Sabrina was in such a hurry that she left **without** saying good-bye to us. Mom and Dad went to the movies **without** my brother and me.

wizard

A **wizard** is a make-believe person who can do magic things. In the story, the **wizard** could turn straw into gold. ▲ **wizards.**

woke

Woke comes from the word **wake.** I **woke** up when I heard the dog barking downstairs.

A **wolf** has short ears and a long tail.

wolf

A **wolf** is a wild animal that looks like a dog. ▲ **wolves.**

woman

A **woman** is a grown-up female person. Mothers and grandmothers are **women.** Sisters and aunts are also **women.** ▲ **women.**

Jesse is carving a piece of **wood**.

won

Won comes from the word **win**. Patty **won** the swimming race.

wonderful

1. **Wonderful** means amazing or unusual. At the circus we all stared at the **wonderful** acrobats.
2. **Wonderful** also means very good. We saw a **wonderful** football game last Sunday.

won't

Won't means "will not." Russell said he **won't** be able to play with us today.

wood

Wood is what trees are made of. **Wood** is used to build houses and other things. Mom put more **wood** on the fire. ▲ **woods.**

woods

An area with a lot of trees and other plants is called the **woods**. Animals live in the **woods**. We walked through the **woods**.

wool

Wool is a kind of cloth that is made from the hair of a sheep and some other animals. **Wool** is used to make sweaters, mittens, coats, and blankets. ▲ **wools.**

word

A **word** is sounds or letters that have a special meaning. We use **words** whenever we talk or write. ▲ **words.**

word processor

A **word processor** is a kind of computer that writes, changes, stores, and prints words. Mom uses a **word processor** when she writes stories. ▲ **word processors.**

Mercedes is learning to read some new **words**.

wore

Wore comes from the word **wear.** Sara **wore** a red ribbon in her hair.

work

1. Work is the job that someone does. People usually do **work** to earn money. My mother does **work** in a bank. A person who does **work** is called a **worker.**
2. Work also means to earn money. My father **works** in a bakery.
3. Work also means to use energy to do a job. The girls **worked** hard raking the leaves.
4. When a machine does a job, we say it **works.** The car's motor **works** well. The television is not **working.** ▲ **worked, working.**

We all **worked** together to paint the wall.

world

The **world** is where all people live. Another word for **world** is **earth.** There are many countries in the **world.** Maddie's aunt took a trip around the **world.** ▲ **worlds.**

The bird is pulling a large **worm** from the ground.

worm

A **worm** is an animal that is long and has no legs. **Worms** move by crawling on the ground. Trina and Pat dug up some **worms** to use when they go fishing. ▲ **worms**.

worn

Worn comes from the word **wear.** Have you **worn** your new hat yet?

worry

When you **worry** it means that you feel a little afraid about something. Mom and Dad start to **worry** if we come home late from school. I am **worried** about my spelling test. ▲ **worried, worrying**.

worse

Worse means less good. I am a bad skater, but my friend is **worse.**

worst

Worst means least good. This is the **worst** cold I've ever had.

would

Would comes from the word **will.** We **would** like to go with you. **Would** you please hand me that book?

wouldn't

Wouldn't means "would not." I **wouldn't** tell my friend what I made him for his birthday. **Wouldn't** it be nice if the rain stopped and we could go outside and play?

wrap

Wrap means to cover something by putting something else around it. We **wrapped** a blanket around us to keep warm. ▲ **wrapped, wrapping**.

Nikki enjoys **wrapping** presents.

wren

A **wren** is a small bird. It has brown feathers and a tail that sometimes sticks straight up. We heard the **wren** singing in the backyard. ▲ **wrens.**

wrist

Your **wrist** is the part of your body that is between your arm and your hand. You can bend your **wrist**. People wear bracelets and watches on their **wrists**. ▲ **wrists.**

In our class we **write** stories and hang them up.

write

Write means to put words on paper or some other thing. You can **write** with a pencil, a pen, a crayon, or a piece of chalk. Suzanne **wrote** a letter to her grandfather. A **writer** is someone who **writes** stories, poems, or books to earn money. Ramon's mother is a **writer** who writes about sports for our town's newspaper. ▲ **wrote, written, writing.**

wrong

Wrong means not right. The answer to the question was **wrong.**

X x Y y Z z

Xylophone for a Young Zebra

X ray

An **X ray** is a picture of the inside of something. The doctor took an **X ray** of Jesse's arm to see if the bone was broken. They took an **X ray** of our suitcase before we got on the airplane. ▲ **X rays.**

xylophone

A **xylophone** is a musical instrument. A **xylophone** has a row of pieces of wood or metal. When you hit the pieces with a special hammer, they make sounds. ▲ **xylophones.**

yard

A **yard** is an area of ground around a house or other building. We have a swing in our **yard.** ▲ **yards.**

yawn

When you **yawn,** you open your mouth wide and take a deep breath. The baby **yawned** when she was tired. ▲ **yawned, yawning.**

year

A **year** is a period of time that is 12 months long. Jerry is 4 **years** old. ▲ **years.**

yell

Yell means to say something in a very loud voice. We had to **yell** to be heard over the sound of the loud music. ▲ **yelled, yelling.**

yellow

Yellow is the color of bananas and butter and lemons. I used my **yellow** crayon to make a picture of the sun.

yes

We use **yes** when we agree with something someone says or asks. The opposite of **yes** is **no**. **Yes,** you may borrow my book.

yesterday

Yesterday is the day before today. If today is Monday, then **yesterday** was Sunday. Joan started a letter to her Grandpa **yesterday** and finished it today.

yet

Yet means now or until now. My brother is not **yet** old enough to go to school. Sara has not **yet** finished building her model airplane.

you

1. You is used to tell which person is being talked to. He asked **you** a question. Do **you** want some more soup?

2. You'd means "you had" or "you would." I came late and **you'd** already left. **You'd** have enjoyed the program on astronauts.

3. You'll means "you will." **You'll** be proud of me when **you** see my marks.

4. You're means "you are." **You're** a good swimmer.

5. You've means "you have." **You've** been a wonderful guest, and I hope you will visit us again soon.

young

Young means not old. A puppy is a **young** dog. Lynn is the **younger** of my two sisters. I am the **youngest** of all.
▲ **younger, youngest.**

The children stand in a line by age. The **youngest** is at the right.

Barry's dog wants to play with the **yo-yo,** too.

What tells you that this animal is a **zebra?**

your

Your means that something belongs to you. Let's play at **your** house. **Your** coat is blue, and mine is red.

yours

When something is **yours,** it means that it belongs to you. Is this book **yours?**

yourself

Yourself means you. Please be careful not to burn **yourself** on that hot iron. ▲ **yourselves.**

yo-yo

A **yo-yo** is a toy that rolls up and down on a string. Ruth can do many tricks with her **yo-yo.** ▲ **yo-yos.**

zebra

A **zebra** is an animal that looks like a horse. It is white with black stripes. ▲ **zebras.**

zero

Zero means nothing. If you have **zero** pennies, it means that you don't have any pennies at all. **Zero** can also be written **0.** ▲ **zeros.**

zipper

A **zipper** holds clothes together. **Zippers** can be made of metal or plastic. Does your jacket close with a **zipper** or with buttons? Clara finished packing and closed the **zipper** on her suitcase. ▲ **zippers.**

zoo

A **zoo** is a place where animals are kept so that you can look at them. Many animals in **zoos** live in cages, and some live outdoors in special areas. We saw the monkeys and the elephants at the **zoo.** ▲ **zoos.**

Words That May Confuse You

Sometimes words sound alike but have different spellings and meanings. The words are called **homophones.** It is easy to make mistakes when you try to write these words. You may mix them up and write **no** when you mean **know.** Or you may write **too** when you mean **two.** This dictionary can help you find the **right** words to **write** by showing you the meanings of words.

Look at the word **pear** and say it. Then look at the word **pair** and say that. These words sound the same when you say them. But if you look for **pear** and **pair** in the dictionary, you will find that a **pear** is a kind of fruit and that **pair** means two of something. Now look at the pictures and you will see the difference between these two words that sound alike.

pear   **pair**

Read the sentences below. In each sentence there are two homophones. If you are not sure which one to use, look up the meaning of each homophone in the dictionary.

Carol (threw, through) the ball (threw, through) the window.

Alex does (knot, not) know how to tie a (knot, not).

(Ate, Eight) mice (ate, eight) the cheese.

Player number (one, won) (one, won) the prize.

If you come (hear, here), you will be able to (hear, here) me better.

The strong wind (blue, blew) my (blue, blew) hat off.

(Hour, Our) clock rings every (hour, our).

Calendar

JANUARY

FEBRUARY

BE MINE
Happy Valentine's Day

MARCH

JULY

AUGUST

SEPTEMBER

DAYS OF THE WEEK

Monday
Tuesday
Wednesday
Thursday
Friday
Saturday
Sunday

We belong in every month!

388

APRIL

MAY

JUNE

OCTOBER

NOVEMBER

DECEMBER

September

Sunday	Monday	Tuesday	Wednesday	Thursday	Friday	Saturday
	1	2	3	4	5	6
7	8	9	10	11	12	13
14	15	16		18	19	20
21	22	23	24	25	26	27
28	29	30				

Numbers

1 one — first

2 two — second

3 three — third

10 ten — tenth

9 nine — ninth

11 eleven

12 twelve

13 thirteen

14 fourteen

15 fifteen

16 sixteen

1,000 one thousand

100 one hundred

90 ninety

80 eighty

4 four

fourth

5 five

fifth

6 six

sixth

8 eight

eighth

7 seven

seventh

| **17** seventeen | **18** eighteen | **19** nineteen | **20** twenty | **21** twenty-one | **30** thirty |

| **70** seventy | **60** sixty | **50** fifty | **40** forty |

Weights and Measures

LIQUID

8 ounces	= 1 cup	2 cups	= 1 pint
2 pints	= 1 quart	4 quarts	= 1 gallon

About 4 glasses of water or 1,000 milliliters = 1 liter

1 gallon

1 liter

1 quart

1 cup

2 cups

1 pint

DRY

16 ounces	=	1 pound
1,000 grams	=	1 kilogram

1 kilogram

1 pound

1 gram

1 ounce

Weights and Measures

CUSTOMARY
12 inches = 1 foot
3 feet = 1 yard
1 yard = 36 inches

yardstick

1 yard

1 foot

1 inch

12 inch ruler

METRIC

10 millimeters	=	1 centimeter
10 centimeters	=	1 decimeter
10 decimeters	=	1 meter
100 centimeters	=	1 meter
1 meter	=	1,000 millimeters

metric tape measure

SCHOOL FAIR

1 meter

1 decimeter

centimeter ruler

Money

SCHOOL FAIR

20¢ each

1 nickel
5 cents
5¢

penny

nickel

dime

quarter

1 dime
10 cents
10¢

GUMBALLS

dollar

1 penny
1 cent
1¢

SCHOOL FAIR

ICE CREAM

1 half dollar
50 cents
50¢

3 for 25¢
1 for 10¢

1 quarter
25 cents
25¢

15¢ a piece

1 dollar
$1.00
100 cents

5

The United States

ALASKA
ARCTIC OCEAN
Juneau ★
PACIFIC OCEAN

WASHINGTON
Olympia ★

Salem ★
OREGON

IDAHO
Boise ★

Helena ★
MONTANA

WYOMING

Carson City ★
NEVADA

Sacramento ★

CALIFORNIA

Salt Lake City ★
UTAH

Cheyenne ★

Denver ★
COLORADO

ARIZONA
Phoenix ★

Santa Fe ★
NEW MEXICO

PACIFIC OCEAN

HAWAII
Honolulu ★
PACIFIC OCEAN

MEXICO

CANADA

MAINE
★ Augusta

NORTH DAKOTA
★ Bismarck

MINNESOTA

WISCONSIN
St. Paul ★

Madison ★

Montpelier ★
VERMONT
NEW HAMPSHIRE
★ Concord

Boston

SOUTH DAKOTA
★ Pierre

MICHIGAN

Albany ★
NEW YORK
Hartford ★
MASSACHUSETTS

Providence
RHODE ISLAND
CONNECTICUT

Lansing ★

IOWA
★ Des Moines

ILLINOIS

INDIANA

OHIO
Columbus ★

PENNSYLVANIA
Harrisburg ★

Trenton ★
NEW JERSEY

NEBRASKA
Lincoln ★

Dover ★
DELAWARE
Washington, D.C. ⊛
Annapolis ★
MARYLAND

Springfield ★

Indianapolis ★

WEST VIRGINIA

Topeka ★

Jefferson City ★

★ Frankfort

Charleston ★

★ Richmond

KANSAS

MISSOURI

KENTUCKY

VIRGINIA

Oklahoma City ★

ARKANSAS

Nashville ★

NORTH CAROLINA
★ Raleigh

OKLAHOMA

TENNESSEE

SOUTH CAROLINA
★ Columbia

Little Rock ★

MISSISSIPPI

★ Atlanta

TEXAS

Montgomery ★

GEORGIA

LOUISIANA
★ Jackson

ALABAMA

ATLANTIC OCEAN

★ Tallahassee

Baton Rouge ★

★ Austin

FLORIDA

Lake Superior
Lake Michigan
Lake Huron
Lake Erie
Lake Ontario

N
W E
S

Gulf of Mexico

⊛ National capital   ★ State capital

399

The World

CONTINENTS AND OCEANS

The seven large areas of land on the earth are
called **continents**. The water that is
around all the continents is
divided into four **oceans**.

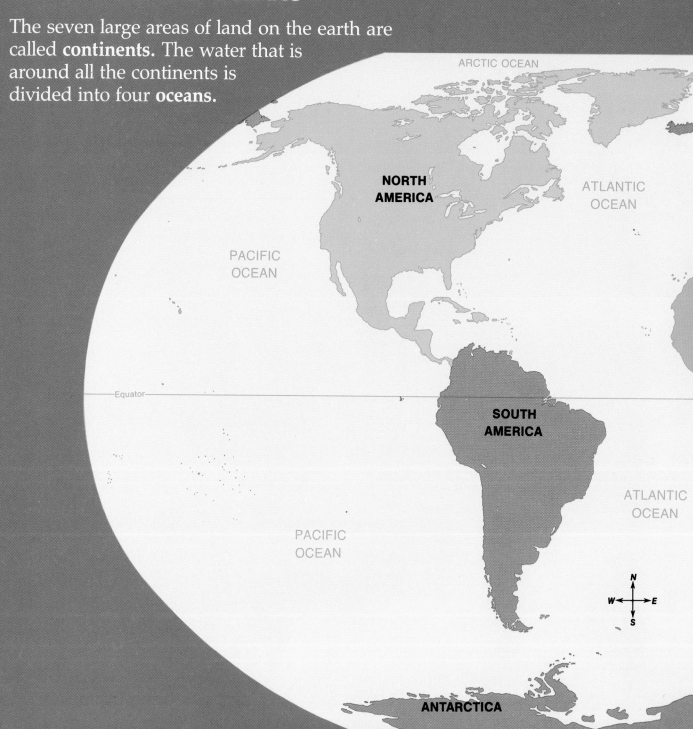

ARCTIC OCEAN

NORTH
AMERICA

ATLANTIC
OCEAN

PACIFIC
OCEAN

Equator

SOUTH
AMERICA

ATLANTIC
OCEAN

PACIFIC
OCEAN

N
W   E
S

ANTARCTICA

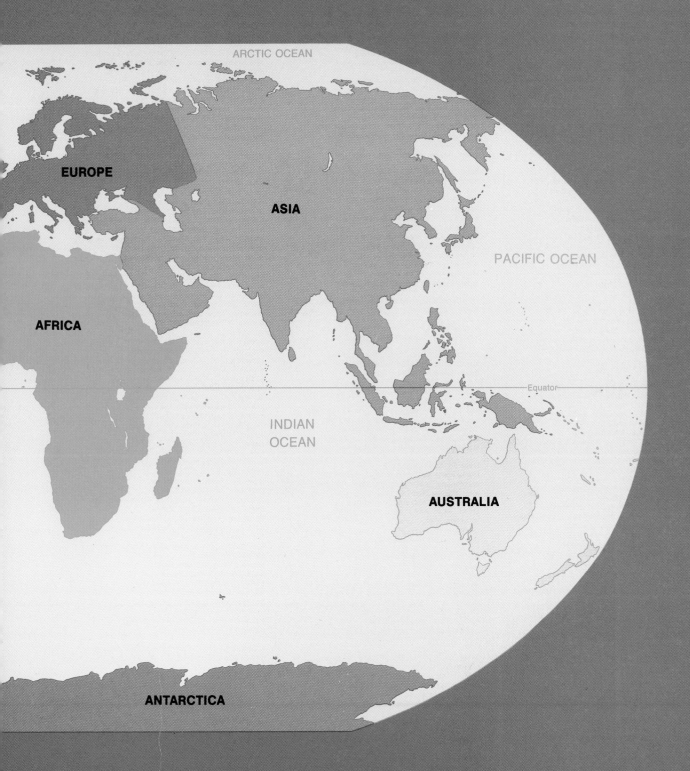

ARCTIC OCEAN

EUROPE

ASIA

PACIFIC OCEAN

AFRICA

Equator

INDIAN
OCEAN

AUSTRALIA

ANTARCTICA

Photo Credits

acrobat: Renate V. Foster/Stock Market
adventure: J. Wright/Bruce Coleman
airplane: Telegraph Colour Library/International Stock Photo
alike: Lew Long/Stock Market
alligator: Charles West/Stock Market
aloud: Michal Heron
amuse: Ann Hagen Griffiths/Omni-Photo Communications
ant: George D. Dode & Dale R. Thompson/Bruce Coleman
aquarium: Charles West/Stock Market
around: Frank Siteman/Taurus Photos
artist: Lawrence Migdale/Photo Researchers
astronaut: NASA/Omni-Photo Communications
attach: Gabe Palmer/Stock Market
autumn: Richard Steedman/Stock Market
award: Harvey Lloyd/Stock Market

balance: Gabe Palmer/Stock Market
ballet: Lowell J. Georgia/Photo Researchers
balloon: DPI
barber: Hank deLespinasse/Image Bank
barn: Carl Purcell/Photo Researchers
basket: Mike Yamashita/Woodfin Camp
beach: Gabe Palmer/Stock Market
bee: Bill Kleeman/DPI
bell: Leif Skoogfors/Woodfin Camp
below: Sebastiao Barbosa/Image Bank
beside: Richard Hutchings/Photo Researchers
between: Elyse Lewin/Image Bank
birthday: Steve Leonard/TSW-Click Chicago
bloom: DPI
both: Michal Heron/Woodfin Camp
braid: Bill Bachman/Photo Researchers
bridge: Ted Horowitz/Stock Market
bubble: Richard Hutchings/Photo Researchers
bulldozer: Edward G. Young/Stock Market
busy: DPI
butterfly: Phoebe Dunn/DPI

calf: Grant Heilman/Grant Heilman Photography
camouflage: Stan Wayman/Photo Researchers
cap: Phoebe Dunn/DPI
carriage: Serge Lemoine/Gamma-Liaison
caught: Phoebe Dunn/DPI
cave: Adam Woolfitt/Woodfin Camp
change: a) E.R. Degginger/Animals Animals b) P. Lynch/ Photo Researchers c) E.R. Degginger/Animals Animals d) F.E. Unverhau/Animals Animals
chicken: Robert Maier/Animals Animals
circle: Terry Wild/DPI
city: David R. Frazier/Photo Researchers
close: Michal Heron/Woodfin Camp
comfortable: Jeffry W. Myers/Stock Market
computer: Kenneth Karp/Omni-Photo Communications
cool: Lowell Georgia/Photo Researchers
crane: Jim Armstrong/Omni-Photo Communications
crayon: Jessica Bonder/Don Renner
cub: Leonard Rue/DPI
curve: Ulrike Welsch/Photo Researchers
cut: Gabe Palmer/Stock Market

daughter: ©Joyce Photographics/Photo Researchers
deer: Charles Krebs/Stock Market
desert: Stan Osolinski/Stock Market
doctor: Lawrence Migdale/Photo Researchers
down: Cynthia Matthews/Stock Market
drawbridge: Alese & Mort Pechter/Stock Market
drill: Richard Hutchings/Photo Researchers
duck: Alan G. Nelson/Animals Animals

earth: NASA/Omni-Photo Communications
edge: David Barnes/Stock Market
elephant: DPI
escalator: Mark Sherman/Bruce Coleman
everybody: Don Klumpp/Image Bank
except: DPI
explore: Richard Steedman/Stock Market
eye: Michal Heron/Woodfin Camp

family: Lenore Weber/Omni-Photo Communications
farm: A. Uptis/Image Bank
feed: Michael Gadamski/Photo Researchers
feel: Zabala FGA/Monkmeyer Press
ferry: Roy Morsch/Stock Market
fire engine: Fred McKinney/Stock Market
fireworks: Robert D. Rubic/DPI
flat: Michal Heron
football: Santi Visally/Image Bank
forest: DPI

fossil: Breck P. Kent/Earth Scenes
fountain: Lawrence Migdale/Photo Researchers
frog: Michael Fogden/Oxford Scientific Films/Animals Animals
fruit: Timothy Eagen/Woodfin Camp
fun: /Omni-Photo Communications

get: Philip Jon Bailey/Taurus Photos
giraffe: © IFA/Peter Arnold
glass: Gabe Palmer/Stock Market
goat: Leonard Lee Rue III/Animals Animals
gorilla: Jim Tuten/Animals Animals
grasshopper: Noble Proctor/Photo Researchers
greenhouse: Leferer/Grushow/Grant Heilman Photography
guitar: Katrina Thomas/Photo Researchers

hand: Blair Seitz/Photo Researchers
harbor: Randa Bishop/DPI
have: Jim Cartier/Science Source/Photo Researchers
helicopter: Alese & Mort Pechter/Stock Market
helmet: Gabe Palmer/Stock Market
herd: Mark N. Bauttan/Photo Researchers
high: Ken Karp/Omni-Photo Communications
hippopatamus: Gerard Lacz/Peter Arnold
hollow: Leonard Lee Rue III/DPI
horse: Clyde H. Smith/Peter Arnold
how: Robert Semeniuk/Stock Market
hug: Omni-Photo Communications
hump: Leonard Lee Rue III/Bruce Coleman

join: Danielle Hayes/Omni-Photo Communications
jump: /Stock Market

kangaroo: Mickey Gibson/Animals Animals
kite: Ed Gallucci/Stock Market

launch: NASA/Omni-Photo Communications
learn: Thomas Hoepke/Woodfin Camp
leash: James Foote/Photo Researchers
leg: Lenore Weber/Omni-Photo Communications
lesson: Brownie Harris/Stock Market
lift: Tim McCabe/Taurus Photos
lion: National Audubon Society/Photo Researchers
listen: Richard Hutchings/Photo Researchers
lobster: Zig Leszczynski/Animals Animals
log: Porterfield-Chickering/Photo Researchers
lot: Alese & Mort Pechter/Stock Market

mansion: Alex Langley/DPI
mask: Susan McCartney/Photo Researchers
microscope: Lawrence Migdale/Photo Researchers
miss: Phoebe Dunn/DPI
monkey: Patti Murray/Animals Animals
moon: NASA/Omni-Photo Communications
mountain: Keith Gunnar/Bruce Coleman
musician: P. Mezey/DPI
my: Bruce Roberts/Photo Researchers

narrow: David Sumner/Stock Market
neighborhood: Michal Heron/Woodfin Camp
nest: Phoebe Dunn/DPI
newspaper: Suzanne Szasz/Photo Researchers
noodle: Kenneth Karp/Omni-Photo Communications

off: J.T. Miller/Stock Market
on: M.P. Kahl/Photo Researchers
ostrich: Gail Rubin/Photo Researchers
owl: Roy Morsch/Stock Market

paper: Will & Deni McIntyre/Photo Researchers
parakeet: P. Winkler/Image Bank
pattern: Marma Keegan/Stock Market
penguin: Loren McIntyre/Woodfin Camp
piano: A. Glauberman/Photo Researchers
pig: Junebug Clark/Photo Researchers
pilot: DPI
pirate: Martha Swope
plaid: Linda K. Moore/DPI
point: Ed Bock/Stock Market
pole: Sonya Jacobs/Stock Market
pollution: Frank P. Rossot/Stock Market
pony: Adam Woolfitt/Woodfin Camp
porch: Michael DeCamp/Image Bank
pour: Michal Heron/Woodfin Camp
practice: John Lei/Omni-Photo Communications
protect: Richard Hutchings/Photo Researchers
pupil: Blair Seitz/Photo Researchers
puppet: Viviane Holbrooke/Stock Market

quilt: Chris Jones/Stock Market

railroad: W. Geiersperger/Stock Market
raincoat: Phoebe Dunn/DPI
rake: G. Angeline/DPI
read: Richard Hutchings/Photo Researchers
reflection: Richard Hackett/Omni-Photo Communications
relative: Michal Heron/Woodfin Camp
rhinoceros: DPI
rice: Alon Reininger/Woodfin Camp
ring: Frank Siteman/Omni-Photo Communications
ripe: Dan Hummel/Image Bank
robot: D. Goldberg/Sygma
rollerskate: Chris Springman/Stock Market
row: Richard Hutchings/Photo Researchers
run: Dan Burns/Monkmeyer Press

same: F. Bouillot/Telegraph Colour Library/International Stock Photo
scale: Tim Davis/Photo Researchers
seal: DPI
seed: P.W. Grace/Photo Researchers
shadow: Omni-Photo Communications
share: Phoebe Dunn/DPI
sheep: Porterfield/Chickering/Photo Researchers
shop: Barbara Kirk/Stock Market
short: Ann Hagen Griffiths/Omni-Photo Communications
sign: Michal Heron/Woodfin Camp
silver: Blaine Harrington III/Stock Market
skunk: Bob & Clara Calhoun/Bruce Coleman
skyscraper: Jay Dorin/Omni-Photo Communications
small: Ann Hagen Griffiths/Omni-Photo Communications
smile: Paul Barton/Stock Market
snake: Joe McDonald/Bruce Coleman
snowman: Bruce Barthel/Stock Market
soccer: Wil Blanche/DPI
soft: DPI
speak: Charles Gupton/Stock Market
spot: Joe McDonald/Bruce Coleman
statue: Joan Baron/Stock Market
stone: Richard Hutchings/Photo Researchers
straw: Jane Grushow/Grant Heilman
stretch: Tim Davis/Photo Researchers
strong: A. Boccaccio/Image Bank
study: Brownie Harris/Stock Market
submarine: John Bryson/Sygma
sung: Mark Glass/Monkmeyer Press
sunset: Marmel Studios/Stock Market
swan: IFA/Bruce Coleman

teach: Charles Gupton/Stock Market
teeth: John Warden/Superstock
tepee: Roy Morsch/Stock Market
their: Peter Miller/Image Bank
thirsty: Wil Blanche/Omni-Photo Communications
this: Charles Krebs/Stock Market
tie: Lawrence Migdale/Photo Researchers
tight: Lenore Weber/Omni-Photo Communications
tiny: Harvey Lloyd/Stock Market
together: Richard Hutchings/Photo Researchers
tongue: Kim Taylor/Bruce Coleman Inc.
tow: Joe Devenney/Image Bank
track: Blair Seitz/Photo Researchers
traffic: Larry Voigt/Photo Researchers
triangle: Joel Greenstein/Omni-Photo Communications
trophy: Charles Gupton/Stock Market
trumpet: Peter Beck/Stock Market
try: Jerry L. Ferrara/Photo Researchers
twins: Jim McHugh/Sygma

unhappy: Wil Blanche/Omni-Photo Communications
upside down: Mark Snyder/Stock Market

violin: Roy Morsch/Stock Market
volcano: Joanna McCarthy/Image Bank

wave: Max Maderos/Woodfin Camp
web: Lynn M. Stone/Bruce Davidson
west: Wil Blanche/Omni-Photo Communications
whale: Francois Gohier/Photo Researchers
wheel: Judith Levey
whisper: Susan Johns/Photo Researchers
wind: Int'l Inc./DPI
wolf: Stephen J. Krasemann/Photo Researchers
word: Gabe Palmer/Stock Market
work: R. Preuss/Taurus Photos

young: Ron Sutherland/Tony Stone Worldwide

zebra: John McKeon/Taurus Photos

Backmatter: pair; pear: Joseph Bocconi

402